OXFORD STUDIES IN POSTCOLONIAL LITERATURES

The *Oxford Studies in Postcolonial Literatures* aim to offer stimulating and accessible introductions to definitive topics and key genres and regions within the rapidly diversifying field of postcolonial literary studies in English.

Under the general editorship of Professor Elleke Boehmer, the *Studies* in each case elucidate and explicate the informing contexts of postcolonial texts, and plot the historical and cultural co-ordinates of writers and of the leading movements, institutions, and cultural debates situated within those contexts. Individual volumes reflect in particular on the shaping effect both of international theory and of local politics on postcolonial traditions often viewed as uniformly cross-cultural, and also on the influence of postcolonial writing on the protocols of international theory. Throughout the focus is on how texts formally engage with the legacies of imperial and anti-imperial history.

OXFORD STUDIES IN POSTCOLONIAL LITERATURES

Australian Literature
Graham Huggan

Pacific Islands Writing
Michelle Keown

West African Literatures
Stephanie Newell

Postcolonial Poetry in English
Rajeev S. Patke

The South Asian Novel in English
Priyamvada Gopal

OXFORD STUDIES IN POSTCOLONIAL LITERATURES

GENERAL EDITOR: ELLEKE BOEHMER

AUSTRALIAN LITERATURE

Postcolonialism, Racism, Transnationalism

Graham Huggan

OXFORD

UNIVERSITY PRESS

OXFORD

UNIVERSITY PRESS

Great Clarendon Street, Oxford OX2 6DP

Oxford University Press is a department of the University of Oxford.
It furthers the University's objective of excellence in research, scholarship,
and education by publishing worldwide in

Oxford New York

Auckland Cape Town Dar es Salaam Hong Kong Karachi
Kuala Lumpur Madrid Melbourne Mexico City Nairobi
New Delhi Shanghai Taipei Toronto

With offices in

Argentina Austria Brazil Chile Czech Republic France Greece
Guatemala Hungary Italy Japan Poland Portugal Singapore
South Korea Switzerland Thailand Turkey Ukraine Vietnam

Oxford is a registered trade mark of Oxford University Press
in the UK and in certain other countries

Published in the United States
by Oxford University Press Inc., New York

British Library Cataloguing in Publication Data
Data available

Library of Congress Cataloging in Publication Data
Data available

Typeset by Laserwords Private Limited, Chennai, India
Printed in Great Britain
on acid-free paper by
Biddles Ltd., King's Lynn, Norfolk

ISBN 978–0–19–927462–8 (Pbk.)
ISBN 978–0–19–922967–3 (Hbk.)

1 3 5 7 9 10 8 6 4 2

PREFACE

Towards the end of 2005, as this book was nearing completion, there were ugly scenes at Cronulla and other beachside suburbs in Sydney. White and Lebanese youth squared off in a series of violent inpromptu encounters which, leaving bystanders bruised and property vandalized, propelled a nation that had long prided itself on its reputation for interethnic tolerance into a state of much-publicized collective shock. Were these race riots or not? Perhaps, as Cornel West had argued of the much more serious upheavals in LA more than a decade before, easy terms such as 'race riot' and 'class rebellion' are not applicable in such cases; rather, what was being witnessed in Cronulla and elsewhere was a 'multi-racial, trans-class . . . display of justified social rage' (West 1994: 3). 'There is no escape from [the] interracial interdependence [of America]', suggested West in the wake of the 1992 turmoil in LA, 'yet enforced racial hierarchy dooms us as a nation to collective paranoia and hysteria—the unmaking of any democratic order' (West 1994: 8).

Does a similar situation apply to Australia at the turn of the twenty-first century? Most Australians would say not, and this book will fall short of saying it either. Australia and America are the products of radically dissimilar histories; and if the Cronulla incidents were not just born of local causes, their social tensions were more obviously illustrative of conditions loosely connected to the global fall-out from 9/11 than the aftershock of LA. Still, parallels exist between the two cases, despite their obvious differences of scale and context. As West argues in the American case, 'To engage in a serious discussion of race . . . we must begin not with the problems of black people but with the flaws of American society—flaws rooted in historic inequalities and longstanding cultural stereotypes' (West 1994: 6). Racism, West suggests, is deeply embedded within the foundational structures of American society. So too, it could be argued, in Australia, for all its official commitment to multiculturalism and social egalitarianism;

for all its public revulsion of the mob violence and ideological extremism which, periodically resurfacing in the nation's history, provide reminders of what some persist in seeing, melodramatically no doubt, as the dark side of the Australian Dream.

Racism, however, as this book will suggest, is not just a national phenomenon; rather, it is an effect of the complex transnational network of capitalist-inspired social relations that structures our contemporary world. It is also the effect of what might provisionally be termed a *transnational imaginary* which, shuttling continually between local and global perspectives, suggests that imaginative outlets such as literature might have as much to say about race/racism as sociological treatises, even if literary works cannot be seen any more than sociological studies as direct expressions of racial sentiments and concerns (Wilson and Dissanayake 1996; see also Quayson 2003). This book is an attempt to show the changing relationship between race/racism and the national imaginary, but it also indicates the need to go beyond the nation in assessing a history of fractured social relations in Australia—relations that the national literature has arguably played as big a part in reproducing as it has imaginatively transformed.

One argument the book makes, then, is that Australian literature has been constitutive, rather than merely reflective, of the history of social relations in Australia, and that this constitutive role is perhaps most visible in the discourse it has produced, and continues to produce, about race, both within the national context and beyond. This argument is hardly new; indeed, it is the consensus among many contemporary Australian literary critics (see, for example, Dixon 1995; Sheridan 1995; Whitlock 1999). Australian literature, so the argument runs, is both producer and product of continuing racial tensions and anxieties, born in part out of a legacy of settler colonialism, but also attributable to the changing place of a nominally postcolonial nation in an increasingly globalized world.

The extent to which Australia and its literature can be seen as postcolonial at all remains a bitterly contested issue: an issue the book, as its title suggests, tries to address even though—for reasons which I hope will eventually be understood—it cannot quite bring itself to resolve. This much can be said at the beginning: that the racisms that permeate Australian society, and for which its literature serves as a necessarily unreliable index, are not just products of colonialism; that their roots reach back further than the history of the nation itself, and extend far beyond its geographical borders; and that Australian racisms, paradoxically perhaps, do not belong to Australia proper, even though the question that continues to exercise them—to excite them—is that age-old question, forever reinvigorated, of who has the right to belong.

A recent Australian literary work to capture these unwelcome truths is Christos Tsiolkas's hallucinatory novel, *Dead Europe* (2005). The novel joins the realist narrative of its protagonist Isaac, a Greek-Australian photographer on tour in the blighted heartlands of post-communist Europe, to a Gothic fable underpinned by the atavistic curse of anti-Semitism—a curse eventually revisited, with harrowing consequences, on the photographer himself. As the two narratives merge, the past superimposes itself alarmingly onto the present (McGann 2005: 26), and the vampire Isaac is unleashed on an alien world of similarly vicious predators, twisted servants of a parasitic capitalism that has turned sexual, racial, and religious enmity into a commodity, and that feeds voraciously off the itinerant under-classes—refugees, asylum seekers, immigrants—its unchecked greed has helped create (McCann 2005: 27). None of the grand themes of *Dead Europe*—the moral depravity of global consumer capitalism, the resurgence of tribal racism and bloodlust in 'post-ideological' Europe, the return of barbarism to the so-called civilized world—are immediately suggestive of a work of Australian literature; but Tsiolkas makes it clear that Australians are complicit in upholding this nefarious world order and, by association, that the Australian readers of his novel are involved. Perhaps, as Andrew McCann suggests, *Dead Europe* is ultimately neither European nor Australian; rather, it is a 'global novel' which demonstrates, plausibly if pathologically, the 'sprawling networks of exchange, violence and desire that have been moulding the modern world for at least the past two hundred years' (McCann 2005: 28). Needless to say, however, this global novel throws off sparks for contemporary Australia, alluding both to hostilities against (illegal) migrants in the Howard-Ruddock era and to the repeatedly frustrated search for a national identity that remains haunted by the past from which it wishes to free itself, forcing the nation's younger citizens back into reliving the nightmares of another, older world.

To some extent, these are the sparks also thrown up by this book, even if it stops well short of Tsiolkas's incandescent pessimism.

Australian literature, it has been suggested often enough, offers a set of local variations on the ghost story; it is recurrently afflicted, if not by horror, then at least by some deep-seated sense of ontological dis-ease (see, for example, Gelder and Jacobs 1998; also Hodge and Mishra 1990; Kane 1998). It would be reductive, of course, to see the nation's literature—the nation itself—as being gripped by a form of recurring collective psychosis, although some cultural commentators claim to have found evidence of this. Australian literature is as likely to be celebratory of national achievement as to expose the paranoid underside of nationalist concern. In any case, Australian literature is not obliged, nor necessarily inclined, to comment on the nation; its degree of 'Australianness' is often of significantly less concern to the writer than it is to the critic, for whom autocthonous 'traditions' are always ready to be made, or unmade, if not exactly waiting to be found.

But if the 'Australianness' of Australian literature is factitious, that does not make it fatuous; nor do the increasingly global contexts in which Australian literature is read and written make it any less an Australian concern. To see Australian literature in a postcolonial context is to recognize the dialectical interplay between one, frequently mythologized location (e.g. 'Australia') and another (e.g. 'Europe', 'Asia', 'America'). To put this another way: Australian literature has helped make Australia what it is by engaging with what others have made out of Australia. In this sense, the 'postcoloniality' of national literatures such as Australia's is always effectively *transnational*, either derived from an apprehension of internal fracture (e.g. via the figure of the culturally hyphenated migrant), or from a multiplied awareness of the nation's various engagements with other nations, and with the wider world.

It goes without saying that no single cultural heritage exists for Australian literature, any more than one exists for Australia. Despite this, the battle over heritage—which is also a battle over ownership—has been keenly fought. Race, as this book will suggest, represents the often hidden face of the continuing struggle for cultural ownership in Australia. Some of the nation's writers have articulated this struggle directly enough; many more have preferred to allude to it. At its heart is a fundamental dissonance between what we might call the politics of ownership and the poetics of belonging. This dissonance takes many forms: in settler writing, in what Terry Goldie has called 'the impossible necessity of becoming indigenous' (Goldie 1989: 13), whereby belonging might somehow provide the moral grounds for illegitimate ownership; in indigenous writing, in the embattled, sometimes elegiac awareness that poiesis involves the bringing into being of an originary world that others have since granted themselves the title to own, if never the birthright to belong; in migrant writing, in the apprehension of the multiple, often conflicted genealogies through which identities are negotiated and properties transacted, so that what one owns is not necessarily where one lives, and where one lives is not necessarily how one belongs.

Taken together, these three strands of Australian writing constitute a postcolonial literature marked by evidence of the residual colonial ideologies from which it continually struggles to free itself. Not all Australian literature, of course, can be assimilated to this grand-scale cultural formula. It is quite possible to argue that the nation's literature has been more concerned (as has the nation itself) with negotiating its own, more or less localized forms of global modernity than with combating the attitudinal legacies that are the largely unwanted, if never entirely rejected, products of its colonial past. The postcolonial model, it might be said, short-circuits both the *local* dimensions of Australian literature—its high degree of regional variability as in, say, the 'western' fictions of Tim Winton—and the *global* outreach of the various modernities within which it freely circulates, and to which both its writers and its readers are inextricably bound. An opposed view would be that a postcolonial approach to Australian writing has the advantage of linking the local to the global; few approaches, after all, are more attuned to the shifting politics of location or to the intricate global circuitry within which cultural identities—regional, national, transnational—are strategically refashioned and commercially deployed.

All the same, this book is not just an apology for postcolonial criticism and its capacity to re-energize Australian literary studies; it is also an attempt to unravel what remains one of postcolonialism's least theorized aspects—the cultural politics of race. Combining recent insights derived from postcolonial and critical race theory, the book is situated at the convergence of two related critical moments. The first of these moments involves the recognition that Australian literary criticism continues to be hindered by its reliance on national(ist) tropes and mythologized binary oppositions, which often work to displace deeper or more widely dispersed sources of antagonism: Old World versus New; settlers versus land; city versus bush; (middle-class) 'pioneer' versus (working-class) 'Australian' legends; and so on. The second moment arises out of the acknowledgement that postcolonial literary and cultural criticism, despite its relatively recent provenance, has become similarly ossified, tending to fall back on standard rhetorical manoeuvres and paradigms ('othering', Orientalism, hybridization), or to seek refuge in fashionably self-conscious Anglo-American (meta)critical and theoretical routines.

There is something belated, then, about the call for a return to postcolonial approaches to Australia and Australian literature. But there is also something paradoxically revitalizing, as an independent nation is made once again to confront its own repressed history of internal colonialism, and to close the gap that separates its own closely nurtured 'victimological narratives' (Curthoys 2000) of embattlement and emergence from now-discredited supremacist, even eugenicist assumptions about white Australians as a European 'master race'.

'New' racisms have appeared, meanwhile, that require close critical attention—including the tacit racisms lodged in the supposedly emancipatory discourses of postcolonialism and multiculturalism themselves. These racisms, while they have taken on a distinct inflection in contemporary Australian society and culture, are by no means limited to Australia; on the contrary, they reflect shifting relations of power and modes of cultural perception under the current conditions of late-capitalist globalization, as the Australian national imaginary finds itself increasingly inflected by a variety of complex transnational cultural flows (Carter 1999). A return to postcolonialism, under these conditions, marks an awareness of Australia's changing position in the world, including its historical links with other former settler colonies such as Canada, South Africa, and New Zealand, while registering an ongoing need to balance 'centripetal' narratives of local, still often framed as national, community against 'centrifugal' experiences of global fragmentation and displacement (Dixson 1999; Whitlock 1999).

Such a return is likely, though, to raise several methodological problems: (1) how to move beyond the binary modes and models around which postcolonial approaches to Australia and/or Australian literature have tended until recently to be mobilized; (2) how to resurrect *race* as a viable theoretical category within postcolonial literary

and cultural criticism, while taking full account of *racism* as a practical component of many indigenous and ethnic-minority Australians'
daily lives; (3) how to build an account of Australian literature,
and Australian literary criticism, that avoids the pitfalls of essentialized 'political' readings: the mistaken assumption, for example,
that there is an unmediated relationship between literary texts and
sociopolitical realities; or that fiction can be treated unproblematically as evidence; or that a directly proportional relationship exists
between literary/cultural production, the workings of ideology, and
the 'governmentality' of the modern (post)colonial state (Dixon 2001).

Alert to these dilemmas, the book—perhaps appropriately at this
current conjuncture in postcolonial critical history—is framed by a
series of partial disclaimers. It is *not* an alternative literary history of
Australia, although it is certainly aware of the problems of writing
literary history. It is *not* an account of changing perceptions of the
Australian cultural other, although it certainly acknowledges that discursive constructions of Australian identity, including those mediated
by literature, continue to depend on the dialectical negotiation of
self-other images and representations. It is *not* an attempt to lock
Australian literature into a perpetual feedback loop of white racism,
although it certainly aims to explore articulations of racial anxiety
across a wide range of Australian literary and cultural production:
the revived debate on the function of 'whiteness' in Australian society
and culture; the recrudescence of paranoid languages of 'white panic'
(Morris 1998) and economically recoded racial threat; the perhaps
necessarily ironic reimagining of a nation of self-mythologized 'unsettled settlers', untiring in their efforts to reinvent the meaning of home
(Gelder and Jacobs 1998; Stasiulis and Yuval-Davis 1995). What the
book attempts, in this last sense, is to track a variety of either explicitly
or implicitly racial themes, and the racialized discourses that underpin
them, across a broad swathe of geographical and historical territory,
with a distinct bias towards twentieth-century material, and with
a view towards establishing an 'Australian literary imaginary' (Nile
2002) that is seen, beyond the immediate parameters of the nation, in
the light of contemporary global social transformations and cultural
trends.

The book begins by considering how Australian literature might
be defined or, more particularly, where it might be culturally and
politically *located*. At its most basic, Australian literature can be

defined as a medium-sized national English-language literature, in competition with larger national literatures such as America's and, particularly, Britain's, on whose economically stronger, residually colonialist culture-industrial base it still continues to some extent to depend (Carter 1999; see also Nile 2002). However, the status of national literatures such as Australia's has undergone significant shifts under the conditions of globalization. One effect of globalization has been a shift to cosmopolitanism, reflected in changing patterns of both cultural production and consumption (Cheah and Robbins 1998); another has been the emergence of the global celebrity writer (Nile 2002). Australian literature is flaunting its mobility like never before, although it continues to be influenced heavily by what is seen abroad as 'Australian' in markedly—marketably—stereotypical terms (Nile 2002; see also Huggan 2001).

The constant reshuffling of cultural repertoires under the aegis of globalization, while opening up potentially parochial definitions of the nation and the national literature, has also brought with it a number of less desirable side-effects. One of these effects has been the emergence of 'new', culturally determined *racisms*. These racisms can be seen in the context of the ongoing 'culture wars' in Australia, through which well-established debates surrounding the white-male dominance of the Australian literary canon, the appropriation of Aboriginal cultural material, and the burgeoning multiculturalism industry have all been updated and significantly reassessed. These debates benefit from being seen from a postcolonial perspective: one alert to the surveillance and management of cultural difference; to the resurgence of virulent forms of racist populism; and to the contradictions of an often half-hearted reconciliation policy seemingly designed not so much to confront the past as performatively to 'lay it to rest' (Markus 2001). The first chapter of the book ends by reconsidering the history of postcolonial literary criticism in Australia. Its main argument is that the strength of a postcolonial approach lies in its capacity to effect transnational understandings of social, cultural, and political processes which, while relocalized within the context of the nation, supersede the national frameworks within which they are usually explained.

The second chapter of the book focuses on one particular aspect of the 'culture wars' in Australia: contending interpretations of history. It begins by offering reflections on the practice of *literary* history in Australia. Australian literary history, it suggests, has been consistently troubled, even haunted, by the problem of cultural origins, a problem it has sometimes sought to deflect by anchoring the literary past in a series of 'originary' or 'foundational' texts. The chapter opens up this debate by looking both at a number of reputedly foundational works in Australian literature and at the often divisive politics of recognition and reputation that underlies the concept of the foundational work itself. In terms of *indigenous* writing, it enquires into the tensions that arise between the individualist ethos of Western literary history and collective Aboriginal custodianship; in terms of (white) *colonial* writing, it looks critically at the work of several Australian classic authors—Gordon, Clarke, Lawson, Franklin, etc.—who have been propelled, sometimes unwillingly, into fulfilling a cultural gatekeeping role. Shifting its sights to the late-twentieth-century boom in 'neo-historical fiction' (Pierce 1992), the chapter ends by gauging the status of the global memory industry and its current impact on the postcolonial renarrativization of the nation's historical past.

The third chapter of the book goes on to look at a selection of twentieth-century Australian writing in the light of recent debates on the social construction of 'whiteness' and the putatively jeopardized status of the majority 'White Nation' (Hage 1998). Discourses of whiteness arguably betray both the privileges and the preoccupations of a majority of Australians. Although these privileges are often masked, not least in literature, the anxieties surrounding a racially unmarked whiteness continually threaten to resurface in a return of the repressed. The chapter considers some landmark works of Australian literature like Katharine Susannah Prichard's *Coonardoo* and Xavier Herbert's *Capricornia* in terms of what they reveal, and conceal, about whiteness; it also looks at more recent indigenous narratives like Sally Morgan's *My Place* and Kim Scott's *Benang*, which take place within the context of genocidal attempts to fade out Aboriginal bloodlines and to promote the superiority of the 'white race'. Finally, the chapter considers various attempts to explore self-privileging 'white mythologies' (Young 1990) in Australia, including some of the covert means (reverse passing, going native, etc.) by which these privileges are safeguarded, even as the desire to reach out to the non-white other is apparently expressed.

The fourth and last chapter of the book builds to some extent on the debates already initiated in previous chapters. Its focus is on multiculturalism, alternately seen as a 'workable model for civic tolerance' (Hutcheon, qtd in Huggan 2001: 126) in a postcolonial society, and as a mechanism for the management of cultural difference in a country where white people have been given historical licence to 'reign supreme' (Hage 1998: 232). These two alternatives are weighed in a critical consideration of multicultural writing, which is seen as labouring under the burden of the classificatory models—often manipulated for their commercial viability—it implicitly contests. If one problem is the term 'multicultural' itself, alternative terms such as 'intercultural' and 'transcultural' prove to be equally problematic. The chapter suggests that the strategic deployment of these terms, e.g. in the context of contemporary ethnic-minority writing, is less revealing of a dialogue between different cultures than of a semiotic network of cultural difference through which cultural identities are exchanged, not always voluntarily, rather than openly performed.

The book concludes by making a plea for a transnational, comparative approach to Australian literary studies that counteracts the critical tendency to consider Australia as 'a nation apart' (Whitlock 1999: 154). Postcolonialism, it suggests, is less the name for a set of given historical conditions and circumstances than the codeword for a continuing critical sensitivity to the global dissemination of local cultural issues and debates. The book ends, as it began, by arguing the need for an Australian-centred postcolonialism capable of generating new ways of thinking about the nation and the national, *and* the need for a comparative postcolonialism in which Australian literary/cultural trends and movements are understood within the larger context of transnational cultural traffic and global economic flows. This combined approach is well equipped, both to address the specificities of Australia's national literature, and to gauge the larger discursive structures within which Australia has renegotiated its relationship to itself and to the wider world.

ACKNOWLEDGEMENTS

Short sections of this book have been published before: thanks to the publishers for agreeing to release material that previously appeared, in modified form, in *The Making of Pluralist Australia* (Peter Lang, 1992), *The Postcolonial Exotic* (Routledge, 2001), *Australian Literary Studies* (2002), *Perspectives on Endangerment* (Olms Verlag, 2005), *Europe and America: Cultures in Translation* (Winter Verlag, 2006), and *Southerly* (2006). Thanks also to the many people, including the series editor, Elleke Boehmer, who contributed towards the making of the book.

CONTENTS

Preface   *v*
Acknowledgements   *xv*
Australian Timeline   *xviii*

1 Australian Literature, Race, and the Politics of Location   1

   1.1 Locating Australian literature   1
   1.2 New racisms and culture wars   14
   1.3 Postcolonial approaches   27

2 Beginning Again   35

   2.1 Some reflections on literary history   35
   2.2 Founding fictions   44

3 Interrogating Whiteness   71

   3.1 Whiteness and core culture   71
   3.2 Extra/ordinary whiteness   78
   3.3 Shades of white   89

4 Multiculturalism and its Discontents   108

   4.1 Demidenko, before and after   108
   4.2 Discrepant multiculturalisms   116
   4.3 Demystifying 'Asia'   131

Afterword   *145*
Notes   *152*
References   *157*
Index   *179*

AUSTRALIAN TIMELINE

The following, highly selective chronology should be read in tandem with the critical reservations about canonicity and historical sequence that are expressed at various stages of this book. The chronology is an attempt, deeply indebted to such reliable sources as the *Oxford Literary History of Australia* (1998) and the *Cambridge Companion to Australian Literature* (2000), to provide what the latter calls, and I can only repeat here, 'a basic framework of dates in Australian history, together with major literary and cultural events, and selected publications of particular historical or literary significance' (Webby 2000: xi).

40,000 BC	Earliest evidence to date of Aboriginal peoples living in Australia
20,000 BC	Earliest evidence to date of Aboriginal rock art
1616	First recorded European landing (Dirk Hartog)
1642	Landing of Abel Tasman (Blackman's Bay, Van Diemen's Land)
1703	William Dampier, *A Voyage to New Holland in the Year 1699*
1770	Landing of James Cook (Botany Bay); New South Wales claimed for Britain
1788	Arrival of First Fleet; establishment of penal settlement at Sydney
1789	Watkin Tench, *A Narrative of the Expedition to Botany Bay*
1819	Barron Field, *First Fruits of Australian Poetry*
1833	Charles Sturt, *Two Expeditions into the Interior of Southern Australia*
1845	Charles Harpur, *Thoughts: A Series of Sonnets*; James Tucker, *The Adventures of Ralph Rashleigh*
1851	Gold discovered in New South Wales and Victoria
1854	Unsuccessful miners' revolt at Eureka Stockade (Ballarat, Victoria); Catherine Helen Spence, *Clara Morison*
1859	Henry Kingsley, *The Recollections of Geoffry Hamlyn*
1869	Henry Kendall, *Leaves from Australian Forests*

1870	Adam Lindsay Gordon, *Bush Ballads and Galloping Rhymes*
1874	Marcus Clarke, *His Natural Life*
1880	Ned Kelly captured and hanged; *The Bulletin* established (still running)
1887	Ada Cambridge, *Unspoken Thoughts*
1888	Rolf Boldrewood, *Robbery Under Arms*
1893	Rosa Praed, *Outlaw and Lawmaker*
1894	Henry Lawson, *Short Stories in Prose and Verse*
1895	A.B. Paterson, *The Man From Snowy River*
1901	Australia becomes a Federation; Miles Franklin, *My Brilliant Career*
1902	Barbara Baynton, *Bush Studies*
1913	Christopher Brennan, *Poems*
1915	Allied forces land at Gallipoli (Turkey) on 25 April, now Anzac Day
1929	Katharine Susannah Prichard, *Coonardoo*; David Unaipon, *Native Legends*
1930	Henry Handel Richardson, *The Fortunes of Richard Mahony*
1938	Xavier Herbert, *Capricornia*
1939	Kenneth Slessor, *Five Bells*
1940	Christina Stead, *The Man Who Loved Children*
1941	Eleanor Dark, *The Timeless Land*
1944	Ern Malley hoax
1945	Australian Book Council established in Sydney
1946	Judith Wright, *The Moving Image*
1947	European migration programme begins
1954	Vance Palmer, *The Legend of the Nineties*

(*Contd.*)

AUSTRALIAN TIMELINE (*Contd.*)

1955	First full-year course in Australian Literature (Canberra); A.D. Hope, *The Wandering Islands*; Ray Lawler, *Summer of the Seventeenth Doll*
1957	Patrick White, *Voss*
1962	First Chair of Australian Literature (University of Sydney)
1964	Oodgeroo Noonuccal (Kath Walker), *We Are Going*
1967	Aboriginal Australians recognized as Australian citizens
1969	Bruce Dawe, *Beyond the Subdivisions*
1970	Multiculturalism on the political agenda
1971	James McAuley, *Collected Poems*
1972	Withdrawal of Australian troops from Vietnam
1973	Patrick White wins Nobel Prize for Literature; end of White Australia policy
1975	John Romeril, *The Floating World*
1977	Association for the Study of Australian Literature founded
1978	Christopher Koch, *The Year of Living Dangerously*
1979	Brian Elliott, *The Jindyworobaks*
1982	Les Murray, *The Vernacular Republic*
1983	Brian Castro, *Birds of Passage*; Mudrooroo, *Doctor Wooreddy's Prescription for Enduring the Ending of the World*
1985	Jack Davis, *No Sugar*
1987	Sally Morgan, *My Place*
1988	Bicentenary celebrations (accompanied by Aboriginal protests); Kate Grenville, *Joan Makes History*
1991	Tim Winton, *Cloudstreet*

1992	Mabo land rights ruling
1993	David Malouf, *Remembering Babylon*
1994	Helen Demidenko, *The Hand that Signed the Paper*
1995	David Williamson, *Dead White Males*
1997	*Bringing Them Home Report* (on the Stolen Generations)
1998	*Oxford Literary History of Australia*
1999	Republic referendum; Kim Scott, *Benang*
2000	Peter Carey, *True History of the Kelly Gang*
2001	Tampa crisis; Richard Flanagan, *Gould's Book of Fish*
2005	Cronulla riots; Christos Tsiolkas, *Dead Europe*

1

Australian Literature, Race, and the Politics of Location

1.1 Locating Australian literature

1.1.1 Why study Australian literature?

One of the most popular Australian writers, both within and outside the country, is the turn-of-the-century bush poet, A. B. ('Banjo') Paterson. It's worth comparing the endings of two of Paterson's most famous ballads, 'The Man from Snowy River' and 'Saltbush Bill', for what they imply about the continuing history of Australian literature. In the first ballad, the legendary exploits of the eponymous horseman are passed down from generation to generation: 'And where around the Overflow the reed-beds sweep and sway / To the breezes, and the rolling plains are wide, / The Man from Snowy River is a household word today, / And the stockmen tell the story of his ride' (Paterson, in Heseltine 1972: 82). In the second, the drover Saltbush Bill, self-appointed King of the Overland, gets into a fight with his new chum rival, the English Jackaroo, and loses. Yet the story of his loss is as legendary as that of the triumph of the Man from Snowy River, and he himself is not averse to taking pride in it: 'And Saltbush Bill, on the Overland, will many a time recite / How the best day's work that he ever did was the day that he lost the fight' (Paterson, in Heseltine 1972: 85). Victory and defeat turn out to be equally newsworthy; what matters is not the outcome of the battle but the battle itself. And what matters even more is, precisely, its degree of 'recitability'—a quality characteristic of the shift from popular orature to literature, and a measure of the compulsive, collectively self-mythologizing storytelling that has remained a feature of Australian literature, from the mock-demotic yarns and bush ballads of the 1890s to their more self-consciously sophisticated counterparts in the present day.

A good example of this more recent kind of writing is the work of the multiple prize-winning author Peter Carey, some of whose novels—*True History of the Kelly Gang* (2000), for instance—practise a mock-demotic of their own. In Carey's work, as in Paterson's, demotic speech is a sign of the local, often though not necessarily the national. At the same time, it is made clear—increasingly clear—that both 'the local' and 'the national' are signs circulating within a global symbolic economy; thus, even such catch-phrases as the 'spirit of Australia' operate as reminders of the malleability and, for that matter, marketability of nationality, a combination also apparent in the fact that the New York-based Carey continues profitably, if not always with impunity, to spin his 'Australian' yarns from the other side of the world. To invoke the national specificity of Australia and/or Australian literature is thus often a conspicuously *trans*national activity; also frequently a confusing one, as in spatially indeterminate stories like Carey's 'A Windmill in the West' (1980).

In the story, an American soldier, instructed to guard the border between two indefinite zones, is so perplexed by his mission that he is 'no longer sure as to what he has misunderstood' (Carey 1980: 64):

Perhaps the area to the geographical east is to be considered as part of the United States, and the area to the west as Australian. Or perhaps it is as he remembered: the west is the United States and the east Australian; perhaps it is this and he has simply misunderstood which was east and which west.

(Carey 1980: 64)

Such geographical—and not only geographical—misunderstandings are common in the history of Australian literature in so far as the images of 'Australianness' it is repeatedly called upon to demonstrate are either internally riven or internationally realized: a reminder that even the most nationalistic of national literatures is always the product, at least in part, of a 'transnational imaginary' that is persistently if inconsistently regulated by a wide variety of rapidly changing global cultural and economic flows (Wilson and Dissanayake 1996).

So why study Australian literature? The question is nothing if not direct, and it deserves a direct answer. Australia has a large, diverse, and exciting body of creative writing that is at least the equal, possibly the envy, of many other national literatures. Its compelling themes—the quest for belonging and identity, the pull between land and language

(Goodwin 1986), the continuing attempt to recover and come to terms with an often violent past—reveal links with other nation-oriented settler literatures: American, Canadian, New Zealand, South African. But they also resonate with the concerns of an international, increasingly a globalized, modernity. Australia's literature is a distinctively, even a defiantly national achievement; but its writers just as unmistakably belong to the wider world. While Australian literature stands on its own, it also represents a genuine 'Anglophone alternative' (Birns 2002): a refreshing challenge to the imagined supremacy of British and American literatures, and to the high-handedness and parochialism that continue to underlie the teaching and study of English literature at many schools and universities, both in Australia and elsewhere.

However, none of this has been enough to dispel a deep-seated anxiety over the future of Australian literary studies. This anxiety exists at several levels, not least the institutional level. At Australian universities, recent trends suggest a possibly irreversible shift away from a specialized, residually elitist Australian *literary* studies towards a more expansively conceived, socially representative *cultural* studies, even though this mediated battle of the disciplines has been frequently mythologized and strategically misunderstood. Meanwhile, literary studies itself, subjected to the pressures of the corporate university and the global market economy, increasingly comes to be perceived as a conservative enclave or an unaffordable luxury, prompting playfully apocalyptic treatises on the death of literature-as-we-know-it and the imminent end of the printed book.

The Australian cultural critic McKenzie Wark, for instance, breezily enjoins us to read less, arguing that '[w]e all have a touch of *arboreophilia* in us. In a world of electronic networks and archives, we love the old dead trees of knowledge and culture, those broad arbours that shelter and nurture the traditional intellectual' (Wark 1992: 683; his italics). Wark's main aim is presumably to jolt his old-fashioned academic colleagues into becoming more media-literate. (A secondary objective, it appears, is to flaunt his own unsurpassing media knowledge.) But Wark's fashionable views, irritating though they are, have wider implications for academic culture, and not only in Australia. One implication is contained within the catch-phrase: the contemporary 'crisis of literacy'. This phrase admittedly has something of a conservative ring to it. The scope of reading has expanded with the advent of the Internet; it is not that academics, or their students, are regressing into a secondary illiteracy, but rather that their reading is now more likely to extend to a wider range of cultural and media forms. Still, the perceived lack of time for in-depth reading is one of the problems of accelerated Western consumer societies. As Ruth Brown wryly observes in the Australian context: 'Not reading the books is gradually shaping the whole process of debate about the status of Australian literature' (Brown 2002: 26). The main culprit here, for Brown, is 'not readers who are too lazy to read but a market-dominated higher education system whereby attentive reading of all the relevant texts cannot be the first priority' (Brown 2002: 27).

Similarly wry is the American literary theorist J. Hillis Miller, who begins his defence of literary studies by teasingly announcing that '[t]he end of literature is at hand. Literature's time is almost up' (Miller 2002: 1). This mock-obituary notice is immediately parried by the claim that 'in spite of its approaching end, [literature] is . . . perennial and universal' (Miller 2002: 1). Maybe so, but Miller is still canny enough to acknowledge that

technological changes and the concomitant development of new media are bringing about the death of literature in the modern sense of the word . . . Printed literature used to be a primary way in which citizens of a given nation state were inculcated with the ideals, ideologies, ways of behavior, and judgment that made them good citizens. Now that role is being increasingly played, all over the world, for better or worse, by radio, cinema, television, VCRs, DVDs, and the Internet. This is one reason for the difficulties literature departments have these days in getting funding. Society no longer needs the university as the primary place where the national ethos is inculcated in citizens. That work used to be done by the humanities departments in colleges and universities, primarily through literary study. Now it is increasingly done by television, radio talk shows, and by cinema.

(Miller 2002: 9)

Miller's counter-argument to this is that 'we [still] see the world through the literature we read, [and] then act in the real world on the basis of that seeing' (Miller 2002: 20); Wark is less convinced. But despite their different views, both endorse the important role cultural production (if not exclusively or even principally *literary* production) plays in inculcating the national ethos. Two questions come immediately to mind here: what is the function, however marginally conceived, of a national literature? And what are the implications of seeing Australian literature as a national cultural form?

1.1.2 What is Australian literature?

A common view of Australian literature is that it represents a collective national project. According to this view, Australian literature is an index of the national consciousness if, at the same time, a necessarily unreliable descriptor of the rapidly transforming realities of national social and cultural life. The idea of a national project risks reducing Australian literature to an instrumental form of medium-impact patriotism. But to jump to this conclusion would be to confuse the national with the nationalistic, and the writing itself with the uses to which it is put. The history of Australian literature, to be sure, reveals more than its fair share of egalitarian patriots. (It also has its fair share of rabid anti-nationalists and insufferable cultural snobs.) It would probably be fair to say, though, that many of the most fervent patriots have been not creative writers but literary and cultural critics. The nationalism allegedly enshrined in Australian literature is less a product of the literature itself than of the material circumstances in which it has been produced and evaluated, and the by no means consistent ideological ends towards which that literature has been deployed.

A case in point is the production of the radical-nationalist Australian Legend—to which I will return later. More recently, ideological constructs such as the Legend have been rightly criticized for the selectivity of their nationalism. The fact remains that Australian literature, and the critical industry to which it gave rise, emerged out of—and in part-response to—a colonial context in which British literary and cultural models were enduringly aspired to, and in which the small number of local universities where it was taught and studied were remarkably successful in 'perpetuating English cultural hegemony...while appropriat[ing] the national as a discourse of affiliation rather than dissent' (Dale 1992: 405).

Against such a background, the patronizing view of Australian literature as merely a branch of English literature is clearly to be avoided. However, the opposing view of Australian literature as an anti-colonialist literature of national self-affirmation cannot be unequivocally accepted either. Rather, Australian literature has steered a not always careful path between metropolitan accommodationism and postcolonial resistance. This ambivalent context allows for the provisional definition of Australian literature as—adapting Tom O'Regan's formulation for Australian film—a medium-sized English-language national literature that exists in semi-permanent tension with its larger British and American counterparts (O'Regan 1996; see also Carter 1999). This tension is the accumulated product, as suggested above, of Australia's residually colonial education system; it is is also a composite effect of the persistently uneven development of the international book trade on the marketing and market-driven perception of Australian literary works. These twin sources can be linked, in turn, to the double-edged status of English as a world language. Richard Nile, in his book *The Making of the Australian Literary Imagination* (2002), describes the nature of the problem facing Australian writers and publishers. As the consciousness of an Australian national literature began to develop, says Nile, arguments about language tended to revolve around two central, essentially economic issues:

The first was that Australian literature had to compete in a small domestic market with offshore titles which made up the bulk of book sellers' lists in Australia. The second was that the status of English as a global language . . . presented possibilities of a market that spanned the world, from those who spoke English as a second or other language, or more lucratively, in the massive first-language market of North America and the United Kingdom. On the one hand, Australian writing struggled for positive notices and space in a market of less than twenty million people[;] on the other, perhaps as many as one billion people awaited the best creative literatures the nation could produce.

(Nile 2002: 11)

What this meant, and still means, is that Australian literature has always been shaped as much by external market forces as by internal producers and commentators. The national literature has been subject to international arbitration, not infrequently in limited or even stereotypical ways that are antithetical to Australian writers' immediate concerns. The publishing history of Australian literature reveals a protracted struggle to provide alternatives to the all-powerful British book market: a 'colonized market' (Lyons and Arnold 2001) in which Australian literary works were often simultaneously patronized as quaint colonial curios and readjusted to the sensibilities of a metropolitan readership secure in the knowledge of superior English cultural taste (Lyons and Arnold 2001; see also Nile 2002).

The demands of the contemporary global market are more varied, but not entirely dissimilar. The expectation remains, broadly speaking, that Australian literature should be identifiably Australian, but not necessarily in ways that the writers themselves, even those with conspicuously cultural-nationalist sentiments, would be likely to recognize or endorse. Exceptions might be made for those considered to have transcended their place of origin—for what Nile calls Australia's 'global celebrity writers' (Nile 2002: 12)—but many of the rest are seen and sold on the basis of an imaginary 'Australianness' that often smacks of colonialist cultural stereotyping, a disempowering process that the reviewing and, sometimes, the teaching of representative Australian literary works in countries other than Australia may inadvertently reproduce (Callahan 2002: 13). (This is not to say that local reviewers, teachers or, for that matter, creative writers are immune from stereotyping, or that stereotypes themselves are always disempowering; indeed, strategic self-stereotyping is highly evident in many spheres of contemporary Australian cultural production, especially audio-visual culture, as the huge international success of such self-styled export products as Peter Faiman's Crocodile Dundee films or their more recent spin-off, Steve Irwin's Crocodile Hunter series, attests.)

The definition of Australian literature as an English-language national literature might well seem self-evident, but each component within this definition can be challenged, up to a point. Is Australian literature, for instance, *only* an English-language literature; what about the increasing number of other languages in which it is written, and what about the status of Aboriginal writing, which in both linguistic and other cultural respects can be considered as a hybrid literary form? How inclusive is a nation's literature anyway, and what are the definitional boundaries of the literary? Most literary histories of Australia concentrate on works with some claim or other to the canonical; popular works remain significantly underrepresented in these histories, as they still do in the majority of university Australian literature courses (and, for that matter, in this book). Institutional definitions of Australian literature—literature itself—tend to exclude the casual reader, and to ignore the obvious truth that most Australian best sellers are unlikely to be accommodated within university curricula and examination structures. Such best sellers—books on sport or pets or gardens, harlequin romances and detective potboilers—continue to be seen as unworthy of serious study or, even if given the benefit of the doubt, are much more likely to surface in a cultural studies than a literary studies course.

This raises the question again of the elitism of Australian literary studies, a charge that is perhaps too easy to make but far less easy to fend off. Regal Arnoldian definitions centring on the 'best that is thought and said' have long since fallen out of fashion, but more democratic understandings of literature have obvious problems of their own. Is literature to be understood as *everything* that is written? And if not, then where is the line to be drawn, and who has the authority to draw it? Clearly, the most pragmatic definition of literature—whatever is *designated* as literature—is a highly political one. Literature is a more or less complex form of cultural production; but it also has a stake, like other such forms, in the politics of cultural representation—a politics in which not only creative writers participate, but also critics and reviewers, publishers and editors, teachers and students, and many more. Literature, in this sense, is a useful entry point into wide-ranging cultural debates and issues, although the caveat should be added that literary works, which have a rich aesthetic life of their own, are irreducible to symptoms of broader social and cultural trends (Culler 1997).

Finally, the self-evident status of a national literature should be interrrogated. The claim of a national literature, as suggested above, is at least implicitly a political one, although this doesn't mean of course that the writers themselves are all nationalists or that they are automatically co-opted into the greater national cause. A national literature, however, does beg the question of cultural representativeness, and of the perceived 'Australianness' of the nation's touchstone literary works. The representativeness of Australian writers is largely a function of their instrumental value: as voices of the nation, as national commentators, or perhaps indeed as champions of whatever is perceived at any historical moment to be the national cause. Needless to say, it is asking a great deal for writers to carry the baggage of these ideological ambitions; it may also be asking too much for Australian literature to be recognizably Australian, or conversely asking too little in so far as ' "Australianness"... at best introduces extra-literary considerations into criticism, [and] at worst proposes a severely limited view of the possibilities of Australian literature' (Kramer 1981: 231).

1.1.3   Where is Australian literature?

The history of Australian literary criticism reveals an unresolved tension between the desire to praise the use of local idiom and other outward signs of a non-derivative national literature (Kramer 1981) and the justifiable suspicion towards such inchoate terms as 'Australianness' and its equally intractable correlate, 'Australian national identity'. The quest for identity, while undoubtedly a major theme of Australian and other so-called settler literatures, has long since become a critical commonplace; references to it now are perhaps most likely to produce a politely stifled yawn. There are at least two reasons for this. The first is that identity itself has been made subject to exhaustive theoretical enquiry. Quite apart from the problems involved in using literary works to psychologize national or any other kind of identity, few critics now believe in the notion of a stable or, for that matter, a singular identity—a notion carried over into debates on the nation, which, as Graeme Turner argues, is neither a unified socio-political entity nor the transparent vehicle for a common communitarian cause (Turner 1994; see also Carter 1999).

As Turner convincingly suggests, the conflict-ridden Australian Bicentenary of 1988 acted as something of a critical watershed in discussions of Australian national identity:

[The Bicentenary] demonstrated the inadequacy of earlier, traditional definitions of Australian national identity and the futility of offering a singular, consensual explanation of that identity to the Australian people. . . . The task before alternative formations of collective identity is much more complex. Among other things, they must be plural: identities rather than identity. They must be built on the recognition rather than the overriding of cultural difference, and they must accept Australia's dual role as colonised and coloniser. This does not have to be impossible just because it is contradictory. Indeed, new ways of thinking about the nation would necessarily involve the acceptance of a degree of internal contradictoriness: for instance, the need to acknowledge cultural differences at home while presenting a more cohesive political identity in our relations with other nation-states.

(Turner 1994: 123)

Turner proposes a thoroughgoing revision rather than a wholesale rejection of the concept of national identity, in keeping with his conviction that 'even tired or irrelevant definitions of the nation maintain the capacity to revive and resituate themselves within a changing

Australian identity' (Turner 1994: 9). Turner's shrewd analyses of changing national discourses, and their role in shaping a collective Australian identity, have been influential. At the same time, the idea of a collective identity, however multiple and contingent, enshrined in the nation's *literature* is now increasingly challenged, not least by Turner himself.

A second reason emerges here for the widespread feeling that, even if the paradigm of identity itself is not completely exhausted, the corresponding view of Australian literature as a container for *national* identity is increasingly under threat. This has to do with changing conceptions, both of the nation and, by corollary, national literatures under the transformed conditions of contemporary global modernity. The effects of globalization on the nation-state have been greatly exaggerated, while it is folly to think, as some globalization theorists do, that we now all live in each other's back yard (see, for example, Featherstone 1996). Globalization, in fact, is much less global than many of these theorists want to imagine. Many of the world's poorest countries are conspicuously excluded from processes of economic globalization; globalization, however generously defined, has neither succeeded in producing the ideal of economic uniformity that neo-liberalism aspires to, nor has it led to what neo-liberalism's critics like to see as an inexorable homogenization of (trans)cultural processes and effects. In fact, there is evidence in the cultural sphere that globalization has stimulated a revived interest in local, regional, and, not least, national issues, while it is also possible to argue that 'globalisation, far from eradicating nationalism, [has] actually served to produce it' (Turner 1994: 121; see also During 1998).

As Ellen Meiksins Wood has observed, much of what passes for globalization talk (e.g. the breathless assertion of a new post-national order) is 'globaloney' (Wood 1986). All the same, it would be equally wrong-headed to claim that globalization has not had profound effects on the 'national imaginary' (Dixson 1999), or that economic processes of globalization have not produced a number of discernible cultural effects. One of these effects, Ulf Hannerz argues, has been the creation and consolidation of transnational affiliations and alliances (Hannerz 1996). Another has been the questioning of a discrete national culture, and the accompanying awareness that the national imaginary is increasingly inflected by a series of transnational/global cultural flows (Appadurai 1996).

In the field of literary production, globalization has also had a noticeable impact. It is now generally recognized, for instance, that national literatures are globally produced, often by expatriate or diasporic writers who have spent little time in the home country, but who may still choose to market their 'Australianness' (or 'Indianness' or 'Africanness'), both for a domestic audience and a larger audience elsewhere. It is not necessary for a writer to *live* in Australia to be an Australian writer. And certainly, it is not necessary for a writer to *like* Australia: some of the best-known Australian writers have conducted well-documented love–hate affairs with Australia (Patrick White), while others have been persuaded into exile (Henry Handel Richardson) or driven to despair (Henry Lawson). (Hating Australia is a popular trope in Australian literature, an extreme version of what the critic John Docker memorably calls the 'gloom thesis';[1] leaving Australia is another frequent trope, and a material reality for several Australian writers.)

A more intriguing question is whether it is necessary for a writer to *be* Australian. Here, it seems reasonable to expect that an Australian passport should be the minimum requirement for eligibility as an Australian writer. However, there are some exceptions to the general rule, and numerous contested instances of dual or changing citizenship—raising the further intriguing question of whether it is possible, say, to be an Australian *and* a British writer, or an Australian *then* an American writer, or perhaps all of these at once. My examples are flippant, no doubt, but they do address the important issue of what it takes to be an Australian writer; and why it is that certain writers are considered more Australian than others, and are thus more likely to be accepted into the 'Australian literature' fold.

What I am trying to suggest here is that the 'Australian writer' is a social category that needs to be understood historically. Not all writers who happen to be Australian are constructed as 'Australian writers'; whether they are or not depends on their usefulness to particular readerships at particular historical moments. Whether they are or not may also fluctuate according to the prevailing ideological climate. Cultural nationalisms, for instance, tend to construct a view of national writers in terms of their ability to 'image collectivity' (Thomas 1997: 256). This collectivity, however, doesn't hold good for all times or apply equally in all places; rather, it is made to cater to the ideological needs of a specific group of people at a specific time and place. (An obvious distinction should be made here between national imagining and nationalist image-making; but it is precisely this distinction that cultural-nationalist discourses tend to obscure or collapse.)

Critical debates surrounding the construction of the 'Australian writer' have been contentious, sometimes openly contradictory. Frequently, they have been conducted around the fraught politics of cultural location. Consider the case of C. J. Koch, the contemporary German-English-Irish Australian writer. Koch begins his essay 'The Lost Hemisphere' (1987) with a series of apparently disconcerting questions: 'Where does an Australian writer belong? Is he or she actually the product of a distinct culture? Is ours, in other words, a society that's different in any way from the European source?' (Koch 1987: 91). Koch spends roughly the first half of the essay answering no to this last question, the second half answering yes. He attributes this equivocation to a gradual sea-change in Australian cultural consciousness; a sense shared by many Australians, and articulated by several Australian writers, that while the nation is still shadowed by the colonial past,

[the Australian] is no longer a little duplicate Englishman—he [*sic*] hasn't been that for a long time; it was almost over by Henry Lawson's day. And he is now (if he is not Chinese, or an immigrant from South-East Asia) a European of mixed origins, dealing with a new hemisphere he has made his home (and in which he *is* at home), but which he still has to absorb fully into his unconscious. This continuing drama of creating a new society here—a variant of the European model—is what much of Australian literature is about.

(Koch 1987: 96–7)

Koch is less interested, however, in *what* Australian literature is than *where* it is—the geopolitics of culture. The writer plays an important role in reorienting the national imaginary; for Koch, this will almost certainly entail a greater recognition of Australia's place within the wider Asia-Pacific region: '[A]s young writers undergo formative experiences in Asia, they will set their work there. We will then have to become less narrow in deciding what constitutes a work of "Australian literature". There are still those who hold the curious view that it must be set within our boundaries to qualify' (Koch 1987: 103). Koch's customary cocktail of geographical determinism, racial essentialism, and gender-specific language makes for highly questionable cultural politics. Still, his argument in favour of an expanded Australian literature/literary studies is salutary. Australian literature need not be set in, or even make reference to, Australia; nor should Australian literary studies be regarded as the private playground of Australian readers and critics (Callahan 2002).

Similarly, the notion of an Australian literature written by Australians for Australians—if this ever applied—is woefully outdated, despite Koch's defensive assertion that it isn't possible 'for a writer to portray at any great depth a people other than his own' (Koch 1987: 103). Koch's internationalism thus always risks being undercut by a reactionary form of cultural insiderism, as in his firm belief that Australian literature is 'usually...best understood by Australian readers and critics' (102); his clear sense of himself as writing first and foremost for an Australian audience; and his default view that '[a] writer can't finally escape his own country' (103).

I am not trying to claim here that Koch's views are representative, rather that they indicate a recurring anxiety about the location and associative reach of Australian literature that arguably runs through the entire history of Australian literary studies, persisting up to the present day. This anxiety previously focused on the local, contemplating the uncertain notion that 'there is a definable community whose character a properly national literature would express' (Kramer 1981: 9); there is now considerable evidence that it revolves around the *global*, taking in the idea that the national literature, in dramatically expanding its geographical and cultural horizons, is rendered accountable to the wider world. This local/global dialectic is hardly new, and is probably a shared feature of all national literatures. Still, it is unquestionably the case that critical discussions surrounding the past, present, and future of Australian literature/literary studies have become increasingly international in the last decades, even if many of these discussions have simultaneously insisted on the enduring usefulness of the nation as a 'political and cultural formation around which value and meaning are accrued' (Carter 1999: 138; see also Turner 1994). This internationalization is to be welcomed, enabling a reassessment both of the shifting state of Australia's national literature and of the changing place of Australian nationhood in a rapidly globalizing world.

1.2 New racisms and culture wars

1.2.1 *Race, racism, and the new racism*

While globalization has led to the restructuring of social relations across geographical and cultural borders, it has not led to a diminishment of racism, which has frequently needed such physical and ideational borders to justify its own existence and to explain its practitioners' acts (Anthias and Yuval-Davis 1992). On the contrary, globalization has thrown up new and often virulent forms of racism that arguably reflect the increasing 'division of humanity within a single political space' (Balibar 1991: 21). These new racisms are not as new as some social theorists imagine, nor—like any other kind of racism—are they either uniform in their deployment or consistent in their effects. But before looking critically at various manifestations of the new racism, it seems worth turning back to the core ideas of race and racism, both of which have benefited from an explosion of scholarship in the humanities and social sciences in recent years (see, for example, Back and Solomos 2000; Bulmer and Solomos 1999; Fredrickson 2002; Gilroy 2000).

Race and racism are semantically slippery and historically shifting; no single definition holds for either, since both are ideological constructs whose meanings are continually contested, and whose social function and effect may vary considerably across time and space (Bulmer and Solomos 1999: 15; see also Goldberg in Back and Solomos 2000: 362–3). One way of distinguishing between race and racism is as follows: race is a phantom *theory*, founded on the imagined existence of genetically 'deficient' human descent groupings; racism, by contrast, is an empirically verifiable *practice*, based on an attribution of ineradicable differences that justifies the exploitation, exclusion, or elimination of the people assigned to these 'inferior' groups (Fredrickson 2002). Distinctions apart, the relationship between race (which doesn't exist) and racism (which does) is perhaps best seen as dialectical. As Kenan Malik argues in *The Meaning of Race: Race, History and Culture in Western Society* (1996), racist practices have always been dependent on an understanding, however rudimentary or perverse, of some form or other of racial theory. Meanwhile, the discrediting of race as an ideological tool hasn't necessarily entailed its disappearance; indeed, it has enjoyed something of a return to favour after the post Second World War taboo (Malik 1996: 2).

Why the renewed focus on race? One reason is the need to account for the enduring seductiveness of race as a pseudo-explanatory category, whose imagined capacity to shore up threatened identities or, just as important, to create the *illusion* of threatened identity, is significantly enhanced at a time of rapid global change and social fragmentation. (As the sociologist George Fredrickson points out, the explanations served up by race are not just psychologically reassuring, but often materially rewarding for individuals and groups who define other individuals and groups as 'inherently different from [themselves] in ways justifying the treatment [they] receive' (Fredrickson 2002: 148).)

Another, related reason is the availability of race as a self-empowering construct. While race has clearly played a major part in 'structuring the social and political marginalization of minority communities' in many modern Western societies, it has also played a role in challenging that marginalization, providing a form of collective agency for the socially oppressed (Back and Solomos 2000: 10). Hence the practice of *self-racialization*, both as an oppositional gesture and as a flexible means towards the fashioning of new, non-essentialized racial/ethnic subjectivities in the nominally postmodern era (Hall 2000b; hooks 1993). The (post)modern practice of self-racialization goes explicitly against the conventional designation of races as fixed biological entities, chillingly distilled in Zygmunt Bauman's definition of racism in his book *Modernity and the Holocaust* (1989): 'Man is before he acts; nothing he does may change what he is. This is roughly the philosophical essence of racism' (Bauman 1989: 60; also qtd in Fredrickson 2002: 157).

Self-racialization depends on the recognition of race as a political and ideological construct, linked to the exercise of social authority and differential relations of power (Back and Solomos 2000: 6). Self-racialization is not necessarily exempt from what the sociologist Paul Gilroy calls 'ethnic absolutism'—the tendency of self-identifying racial/ethnic groups to seal themselves into separate compartments, often for the explicit purpose of exerting dominance over other, similarly designated groups (Gilroy 1993). But it would be going too far to see it as just another form of racism; much more usually, it involves a strategic assertion of the value of specific cultural differences, without these differences being seen as in any way permanent or unnegotiable, and without them being used to dominate or denigrate other culturally defined individuals and groups (Fredrickson 2002: 169–70). All the same, the double movement described by a blurring of race and *ethnicity*, on the one hand, and a transposition of race onto *culture*, on the other, raises several unsettling questions. Is ethnicity, as Malcolm Chapman provocatively suggests, merely ' "race" after an attempt to take the biology out'? (qtd in Malik 1996: 176). And to what extent is cultural essentialism merely a refined, euphemistic form of biological racism, in which cultural differences have become the primary vehicle for racial ideology and culture is now made to 'do the work of race'? (Fredrickson 2002: 141; see also Malik 1996: 7–8).

These two questions can be bracketed under the heading of the 'new racism'. The new racism, in the words of Étienne Balibar, 'fits into a framework of "racism without races" . . . It is a racism whose dominant theme is not biological heredity but the insurmountability of cultural differences, a racism which, at first sight, does not postulate the superiority of certain groups in relation to others but "only" the harmfulness of abolishing frontiers, the incompatibility of life-styles and traditions' (Balibar 1991: 21; see also Castles 1996). This racism is hardly new, with roots going back at least as far as the Enlightenment (Todorov 1993). Nor, strictly speaking, is it singular; like other racisms, it takes on a number of contingent, not necessarily compatible forms.

What these racisms have in common is their 'displacement of biological onto linguistic, historical and psychological differences' (Malik 1996: 176), with the codeword 'culture' being used as a marker for this aggregate of differences, and with the modern sociological category 'ethnicity'—wryly described by Malik as 'an acceptable container for cultural differences' (176)—supplanting the ideologically contaminated 'race'. In the euphemistic vocabulary of the new racism, the principle of cultural incommensurability stands in for that of biological inviolability. The disguise soon wears remarkably thin. Historically vouchsafed, cultures become territories to protect against the invasion of unwanted foreign bodies; social fragmentation is recast in the language of moral degeneracy; the nation becomes a privileged site for the consolidation of an historically authenticated core culture, by no means *superior* to other cultures but fundamentally *different* from them. The new racism, in this last sense, claims to support a broad vision of intercultural tolerance and harmony even as it provides the ideological pretext for a sequence of bitter internecine conflicts: the so-called 'culture wars'.

1.2.2 Racism, the culture wars, and Australia

While the culture wars are linked to the global problems invoked by the new racism, they are initially more likely to be seen within a specific cultural context: the perceived crisis in American humanities education during the last two decades of the twentieth century. On the surface, this crisis was expressed in the flaring up, particularly in the late 1980s and early 1990s, of well-established debates about the function of critical theory, the expansion of the literary canon, and the relative merits and demerits of that baleful spectre of American liberal pluralism, 'P.C.'. Underneath, it was the result of a highly mediated conflict, both *within* the academic humanities and *between* them and the designated 'outside world' (Graff 1992). Many of the exchanges now come across as highly petulant and childish, producing a wash of inflationary rhetoric in which the conflict between traditionalists and revisionists was elevated into an epic struggle between (Western) culture and barbarism, and conservatives were portrayed as 'last-ditch defenders of civilization against the invasion of barbarian relativists and terrorists', bent on destroying the noble edifice of the humanities from within (Graff 1992: 5; see also D'Souza 1992).

The university was duly recast as a hotbed of fiercely clashing ideologies, allowing the humanities to feature as a major political battleground in the wake of the so-called 'cultural turn' (Graff 1992: 195). Behind all the posturing, however, was a real material struggle. For in large part, the US culture wars reflected the frustrations of educational reform under economic pressure or, as Malik puts it, they were the effect of 'institutionalised pluralism and its championing of cultural diversity meeting a scarcity of economic resources' (Malik 1996: 180). This economic struggle was recoded in cultural terms, as embattled conservatives sought to shore up what they saw as core Western civilizational values while seizing an opportunity to cast multiculturalists as a convenient new scapegoat for the post Cold War era (Malik 1996: 180).

More recently, the culture wars have been recognized as neither a specifically academic nor a uniquely American phenomenon. Rather, they were and are reflective of a general conflict between 'entrenched pluralism and assertive nationalism' (Malik 1996: 180) in several late twentieth-century/early twenty-first-century Western societies, expressed in heated debates over the impact of immigration on relatively homogeneous Western cultures; over the compatibility of different religious traditions inhabiting the same social space; and over changing configurations and conflicting interpretations of the national culture. These debates have often borne a distinctly racial tenor. Malik is not alone in making a connection between the new racism and the culture wars; as Gilroy puts it in the context of resurrected European cultural nationalisms:

[W]e increasingly face a racism which avoids being recognised as such because it is able to link 'race' with nationhood, patriotism and nationalism, a racism which has taken a necessary distance from the crude ideas of biological inferiority and superiority and now seeks to present an imaginary definition of the nation as a unified *cultural* continuity.

(Gilroy 1990: 187; his italics)

In what follows, let me briefly consider the more specific link between the new racism and *Australian* contributions to the culture wars, focusing on recent patterns of cultural racism in Australia, their historical antecedents, and the impact of race thinking on current national debates.

Racism in Australia has a long and undistinguished history. Early relations between Aborigines and white settlers were characterized by the often extreme racial antagonism that is a staple of violent frontier societies, occasionally leavened by the type of moralizing Christian sentiment that permitted itself to express sympathy for the unfortunate natives without doubting for a moment that they belonged to an inferior, quite possibly a dying, race. By convicts, Aborigines were seen as targets for retributive anger at the system that constrained them; by pastoralists, as a direct threat to the land they considered rightfully their own; by missionaries, as an opportunity for the religious conversion that would no doubt assist in civilizing them; by philanthropists, as a test-case for the humanistic ideals of Enlightenment thought. Colonial racial attitudes were by no means uniform or historically consistent. But they often set into readily identifiable patterns shaped by the primitivist myths and stereotypes derived from European philosophy and literature, especially travel writing; by anxious debates about slavery and post-Civil War US society; by alarmed reactions to the Indian Mutiny of 1857; and, perhaps above all, by arguments taken from social Darwinism about unequal competitors in the struggle for existence and the deadly threat that mixed bloodlines posed to racial purity and national health (Yarwood and Knowling 1982: 188).

Colonial racisms were generally of the standard biological variety. Aborigines and, later, Chinese and other Asians were obsessively identified with their innate (i.e. bad) habits and gradations of skin colour, both of which features indelibly marked them as members of an irremediably inferior race. While there was little direct transference of racial attitudes from Aborigines to Asians, there were some important structural parallels, including the 'natural' homology between physical make-up and moral and mental state (Curthoys 1979; Yarwood and Knowling 1982). Asians were constructed as the racial competitor, Aborigines as the racial stranger. In both cases, racial prejudices were exacerbated by widespread linguistic and cultural ignorance, the often exaggerated fear for physical safety, and fierce competition over limited economic resources in the unruly frontier state (Markus 2001; Yarwood and Knowling 1982).

After Federation, anti-Asian sentiment, in particular, was to harden into the notorious White Australia policy, explicitly designed to prevent non-European migrants from entering the country. Anti-Asianism was further stoked by invasion fears (the so-called 'Yellow Peril') and war-fuelled perceptions of Australia as a continent under threat (Walker 1999). Overt racial discrimination continued well into the post-Second World War period: the White Australia policy, instituted with the Immigration Restriction Act of 1901, was to continue until at least mid-century, while Aborigines were only recognized in the national census in 1971. The move from protectionist to assimilationist policies arguably exchanged one set of paternalistic pieties for another. In many Aboriginal communities, mortality and imprisonment rates were high, educational and employment opportunities low, and poverty endemic. Grave human rights abuses—deaths in custody, serial rape, the forced removal of Aboriginal children—were systematically suppressed, Aboriginal workers were routinely mistreated, and the road to indigenous self-determination remained, for the most part of the century, firmly blocked.

The picture gradually brightened during the latter part of the century. The 1970s, in particular, saw the institution of multicultural policies, some recognition of indigenous land rights, and the relaxation of restrictions on non-European migration. A. T. Yarwood and M. J. Knowling optimistically see this as evidence of 'racism in retreat', and of the government-sponsored attempt to liberalize thinking towards Aborigines and other non-European peoples (Yarwood and Knowling 1982). More recent commentators such as Andrew Markus tend to see it differently. Markus acknowledges the distinct gains of the 1970s and 1980s: the recognition of previous abuses and the gradual move towards self-determination and multiculturalism; the establishment of anti-discrimination laws; the increased success of Aboriginal land claims, culminating in the historic Mabo ruling of 1992.[2] But he sees these gains as having been undermined, if not overturned, by mid-1990s policies connected back to earlier, unashamedly race-based, nationalisms and brought into alignment with the contradictory ideals of modern economic-rationalist thought.

One contradiction centres on the unexamined assertion of 'race-blindness' in universal equal-rights doctrine. As Markus points out, equal rights are the redress of a residually unequal society. In Australia, as in other Western societies, it is obvious that while all citizens are theoretically equal, some in practice are more equal than others; in this context, the appeal to equal rights can serve either as a pretext for national conformism or as a pseudo-philanthropic alibi for continuing social neglect (Markus 2001).

The policies of the 1990s were an indication of a resurgence of racism in Australia; but not of the 'older', biological variety, rather of the 'new', culturally oriented type (Markus 2001; Stratton 1998). Cultural racism, for Markus, is a racism in denial. Its practitioners vehemently disclaim all pretensions to superiority and bigotry; but by appealing instead to a 'common-sense' appreciation of cultural difference that masks ignorance and intolerance, they end up legitimizing bigotry in their own right (Markus 2001: 5). One form cultural racism takes is the 'reasonable' view that no racial/ethnic group is entitled to special privileges. Ken Gelder and Jane Jacobs call this 'postcolonial racism', linking it to the perception that in postcolonial Australian society, 'the interests of minorities have been increasingly recognized, [but] credited with a significance that some may feel is more than their "minority" status deserves' (Gelder and Jacobs 1998: 17). Postcolonial racism, like other kinds of cultural racism, is deeply split in its attitudes; it can acknowledge that Aboriginal people—say—have been given far too little, while simultaneously hoarding resentment at the idea that they are now being given far too much (Gelder and Jacobs 1998: 65).

Another form cultural racism takes is the equally 'reasonable' attempt to subordinate specific differences to the unifying cause of the nation (Gilroy 1990). The assertion of a common culture may override, even ignore specific cultural differences. In some cases, it may also attempt to turn the clock back to an earlier, ethnically homogeneous nation in which people co-existed peacefully within a social system largely free from serious conflict, and exemplary in its respect for the egalitarian principles of democracy and human rights. Needless to say, such a place has never existed; Australia is no exception. The self-congratulatory fantasy of a Happy White Australia is as oblivious to the complexities of modern social inter-action as it is amnesiac towards the nation's violent colonial past (Hage 1998). Its popular appeal has been registered, nonetheless, in the short-lived but politically significant successes of Pauline Han-son's unashamedly xenophobic One Nation Party;[3] while, in more diluted form, it has also been apparent in the tub-thumping cultural-nationalist rhetoric of the current Prime Minister John Howard, whose beloved Australia is shouted from the rooftops as 'one of the fairest, most egalitarian and tolerant societies in the world' (qtd in Markus 2001: 107).

Many of Australia's current culture wars coalesce around these potent, racially inflected national issues: the function of the nation in a global age; the pull between diversity and coherence; the still-troubled relation of an independent modern nation to its chequered colonial past. It would be a mistake, however, to see these as uniquely *Australian* issues. As Markus suggests, the race politics that has emerged over the last decade in Australia is part of a complex series of global developments linked to new forms of cultural chauvinism, the end of Cold War adversarialism, increasing disillusionment with centralized political systems, and the raft of significant socio-economic changes brought about by globalization itself (Markus 2001: 200; see also Castles 1996). These developments, as will be emphasized in later chapters of this book, have also had a profound impact on the representation of race in Australian literature. The connections between race, writing, and difference now need to be examined more carefully, and placed within the history of racial representation or, perhaps better, the history of racialized discourses in Australian literary texts.

1.2.3 Race and Australian literature

A good place to start is with Henry Louis Gates's influential 1986 collection 'Race', Writing, and Difference, which is designed to counteract its editor's assertion that race has had little direct impact on twentieth-century literary studies, despite its unacknowledged existence beneath the surface of literary criticism as 'an invisible quantity, a persistent yet implicit presence' (Gates 1986: 2). Race certainly loomed large in nineteenth-century constructions of canonical national literatures, often to the extent that it assumed an almost tangible presence, 'an ineffaceable quantity which irresistibly determined the shape and contour of thought and feeling as surely as it did the shape and contour of human anatomy' (Gates 1986: 3; see also Todorov 1993). Gates suggests, however, that twentieth-century preoccupations with language and the intricacies of textuality have had the common effect of bracketing or suspending considerations of race (Gates 1986: 3–4). This latter generalization, already questionable in 1986, is almost certainly invalid today. Race has made a decisive comeback, not only into general political discussion, but also into the specific fields of literary and cultural studies, both of which are increasingly unlikely to separate themselves from current social and ideological debates (Malik 1996).

The return of race to literary studies can be read as a sign that racism is being taken very seriously, and that it is recognized as having the potential to lurk beneath even the most ideologically 'neutral' forms of literary criticism, the most apparently 'even-handed' of critical debates. Attitudes towards racial difference are now generally acknowledged as structuring both literary texts and literary criticism, even if these attitudes and the underlying ideologies that inform them often remain unannounced or strategically hidden from view

(Gates 1986: 5). The task of the critic, then, is to uncover hidden ideological traces, both in the literary texts he or she studies and in the critical approach that he or she brings to bear upon them. Nor is it enough to be conscious of the workings of race or the effects of racism on literature and literary criticism; it is also vitally necessary to 'deconstruct the ideas of difference inscribed in the trope of race, to explicate discourse itself in order to reveal the hidden relations of power and knowledge inherent in popular and academic usages of "race"' (Gates 1986: 6).

Gates's terms—'difference', 'discourse', 'hidden relations of power', etc.—are instantly recognizable items in the strongly politicized critical vocabulary of the last three decades. The term 'discourse' in particular, often associated with the work of the French historian Michel Foucault, has assumed great importance in addressing the methodological problem of how to analyse the racial ideologies that circulate within and across very different kinds of literary and other cultural texts. To examine the discursive effects of race in a literary text is not the same thing as to accuse its author of being racist. Rather, as Gates suggests, race operates as a shifting trope to which different meanings—different meanings of *difference*—are often arbitrarily attached; while the trope of race belongs, in turn, to certain orders of discourse (e.g. the self-privileging discourse of whiteness or the eroticized/pathologized discourse of the black body), in which the differences attributed to race are inscribed in conspicuously uneven relations of power (Gates 1986: 5).

This may sound baffling—and it often is. Discourse is no easier to define than race, and has almost the same potential for ideological leverage. A good general definition of discourse, by the Australian literary critic Susan Sheridan, is the sum of 'available ways of speaking [and] writing in which social power operates to produce certain objects and effects' (Sheridan 1995: ix). Discourse, in this sense, alerts attention to institutional authority, and to the position and ideological stance of the speaking/writing subject. The discursive effects of race, as might be expected, are highly variable, but they usually work to reinforce the authority and privilege of dominant groups within any given society. For example, Sheridan has shown how discourses of race operated in tandem with discourses of sex within the context of the emergent Australian nation, which could itself be understood as a discursive construct (Sheridan 1995). 'Race' and 'sex' are powerful signs with the potential not only to mark but also to produce social differences, thus reinforcing dominant ideological formations in society: patriarchal preference; the perceived if not necessarily proclaimed superiority of the 'white race'.

Literature is one instrument among others for the deployment of these often complex discursive strategies. Four strategies can be picked out briefly here for closer consideration: the representation of otherness and the racial/sexual other; the production of racial stereotypes; the use of race as a signifier of exclusion; and the appropriation of race as a self-affirming marker, in which the previously marginalized racial other re-emerges as a self-validating writing subject (Todorov 1986: 378).

Otherness is a constitutive feature of identity construction. In an obvious sense, we are who we are because we are not other; and yet, paradoxically, otherness is always a part of us—it is crucial to our sense of self (Giddens 1991). The relation between self and other is therefore best seen as reciprocal, although there are plentiful examples throughout human history of attempts to set otherness apart, to fix the other in place. The construction of a fixed other is a standard feature of racial discourse, especially under the conditions of colonialism (Loomba 1998). (One example is the attempt in European colonialist literature to create an antithetical African other, whose benighted existence serves to reaffirm the self-worth of a collective European subject: see, for example, JanMohamed 1983; Mudimbe 1988.) Otherness tends to be presented in such formations as essential and unchanging, although these supposedly eternal characteristics are ironically the product of historically contingent processes of identity construction. 'Other', in this sense, is less a descriptive *noun* than a transitive *verb*: the colonial other is a product of 'othering'; he or she is an 'othered' subject (Loomba 1998; Spivak 1987).

A typical example of colonial othering is the racial stereotype. As the postcolonial theorist Homi Bhabha argues, stereotypes are products of the desire for fixity in ideological constructions of otherness; they are not so much crude simplifications as 'arrested, fixed form[s] of representation' (Bhabha 1994: 45). The force of the stereotype is that of cumulative representation: it depends for its effectiveness on secure patterns of reproduction and repetition over time. But as Bhabha suggests, these patterns are not secure at all; they are fraught with anxiety and ambivalence. Colonial stereotypes, for instance, are often split between alternative, apparently contradictory significations: the racial other can be an object of fear, but also desire; can be a murderous savage, but also an innocent child; and so on (Bhabha 1994: 45). Thus, while such stereotypes are designed to forestall what Bhabha calls the 'play of difference', they clearly remain subject to it: 'The colonial stereotype is a complex, ambivalent, contradictory mode of representation, as anxious as it is assertive' (Bhabha 1994: 40).

An alternative way of limiting the play of racial differences is to see race as a marker of marginalization or exclusion. Yet this strategy, too, can prove to be anxiety-inducing. Some absences in literary texts are a good deal more noticeable than others; tactical exclusion can end up drawing attention to itself, reinstalling the excluded other as an unsettling absent presence (Gelder and Jacobs 1998). Finally, the trope of race can be appropriated by, say, indigenous or ethnic-minority writers as a means towards collective self-affirmation. This rhetorical manoeuvre can be seen to some extent as a form of 'strategic essentialism' (Spivak 1987). It risks the double charge of separatism and simplification in the pursuit of racialized authenticity; in announcing a common racial heritage, it also asserts the solidarity of the oppressed.

As subsequent chapters of this book will show, the history of Australian literature reveals numerous examples of all of these discursive strategies, which frequently collide and intersect with one another. White Australian literature abounds in examples of self-definition through the Aboriginal other, but also in examples of the excluded other where the figure of the 'absent Aborigine' establishes itself as a negative, sometimes a troubling or haunting, presence (Goldie 1989: 14; see also Gelder and Jacobs 1998).

Meanwhile, racial stereotypes have been extremely common in Australian literary representations of Aborigines and Asians, in particular. Terry Goldie's analysis of images of the indigene in Canadian, Australian and New Zealand literatures sets up a symbolic economy of more or less stereotypical representations of indigenous peoples—including Australian Aborigines—in which the 'standard commodities' of sex and violence, nature, orality, mysticism, and the prehistoric freely circulate and are routinely collected and exchanged (Goldie 1989). Alison Broinowski sees a similar mechanism at work in the representation of Asians in (white) Australian literature, in which collections of mostly phobic racial stereotypes serve to reinforce prevailing ideologies of the collective 'Asian threat' (Broinowski 1992).

Despite the structural patterns both authors detect, these representational histories are no more uniform or homogeneous than are Aborigines or Asians themselves. In any case, as Goldie argues, such representations belong to a general signifying chain in which the signified for each individual signifier is 'the Image'; the referent—real-life Aborigines, Asians, etc.—'thus has little purpose in the equation' (Goldie 1989: 4).

For all the ideological force of White Australia, Australian literature has no more been a relentless propaganda-machine for the production of racial and cultural stereotypes than has any other national literature. Many Australian authors/texts have been deeply critical of enduring cultural prejudices, and sceptical towards what the American anthropologist Renato Rosaldo calls 'the fiction of a uniformly shared [national] culture' (qtd in Dixon 1995: 133). Even those genres which might be expected to lend themselves to nationalist cheerleading and cultural chauvinism have been internally conflicted, as Robert Dixon shows in *Writing the Colonial Adventure* (1995), his excellent study of late nineteenth- and early twentieth-century Australian adventure romance.

As Dixon suggests, following the Marxist theorist Louis Althusser, Australian adventure romances were 'internally distanciated' from the ideologies that drove them: ideologies of imperialism, masculinity, Englishness, Australian nationhood, and, of course, ideologies of race (Dixon 1995: 200). These ideologies were often consciously reproduced but inadvertently questioned, so that the texts themselves ended up displaying the very anxieties, not least over race, they claimed to disavow (Dixon 1995: 5). Dixon's more general point is that literature is rarely if ever a simple carrier of ideology; much more often it is a complex site for contending ideologies, allowing for an exploration of the internal contradictions inherent within the concept of ideology itself (Macherey 1978). A valuable instrument for the analysis of ideological contradiction, particularly within the varying contexts of imperialism, has been postcolonial criticism; and it is to the 'postcoloniality'—or not—of Australia and Australian literature that the chapter brings me next.

1.3 Postcolonial approaches

1.3.1 Is Australia postcolonial?

In the epilogue to her previously mentioned book, *Along the Faultlines*, Susan Sheridan asks the challenging question: 'is Australia post-colonial yet?'(Sheridan 1995: 166). The question might just as easily be rephrased: is Australia still postcolonial? Australia, after all, has been an independent nation for over a century and, while still officially a British dominion, seems well set on the path towards becoming a republic in the not too distant future. The much agonized-over 'cultural cringe' is now considered by most Australians to be an irrelevant issue, although it still resurfaces from time to time in local debates over national core culture or, more obliquely, in contemporary global geopolitics, as in the opportunistic 'coalition of the willing' against Saddam's Iraq.

Australia's cultural, political, and economic ties with Britain remain strong, to be sure, but these are hardly proof in themselves of con-tinuing colonial dependency or of a residual colonial connection. The question might then legitimately be asked: when does an ex-colonial society *stop* being seen as postcolonial? Must such a society be eter-nally defined by its relationship with its colonial past? And if Australia continues to be seen as postcolonial, then for *whom* is it postcolonial; and with respect to *what*? This, like other debates surrounding post-colonialism, has sometimes been turned into an academic issue, con-fined to university circles and conducted in a rarefied language that makes few concessions to the uninitiated (Jacoby 1995). An acces-sible version of the debate is that while Australia is postcolonial with respect to its former British colonizers, it remains very much colonial or, perhaps more accurately, *neo*-colonial in its treatment of its own indigenous peoples (Brewster 1995; Hodge and Mishra 1990; Sheridan 1995). This compromise position has found favour among some left-leaning Australian intellectuals otherwise justifiably scepti-cal towards the general emancipatory claims of postcolonial thought. Aboriginal people themselves, however, have been much more likely to dismiss the term 'postcolonial' altogether, seeing it as a self-serving academic construct or a smokescreen obscuring the continuing injus-tices of the present, as well as the combined atrocities of the past (Lucashenko 2000).

Postcolonialism in Australia—particularly literary postcolonial-ism—is also embattled for institutional reasons. One result of the institutional squeezing of literary studies at Australian universities is that the study of the national literature has been given renewed priority. In a kind of pincer movement, postcolonial literary studies has been threatened on two sides, both by an emergent transnational/global cultural studies and by a reconsolidated Australian studies. Under the new dispensation, the traditionally internationalist concerns of postcolonial literary studies have given way to an analysis of the (trans)cultural effects of emergent globalist paradigms and, more specifically, to an examination of these effects on the transforming national culture. What this has meant is, first, the *renationalization*, rather than the disappearance, of the postcolonial; and, second, a shifting of the axis of postcolonial research from narrowly literary to broad-based cultural concerns. At one level, it is difficult not to see these moves as evidence of a new Australian parochialism masquerading as globalist progressivism; at another, they have lent a new urgency to the question of Australia's postcoloniality that may yet end up regenerating an apparently endangered field.

Before turning to some of the most recent interventions in Australian postcolonial studies, however, it may be useful to look back at some of the exchanges that have helped define postcolonialism in Australia, and which have contributed to continuing debates on the legacies of colonialism and, particularly, colonial racism as these have filtered into the mainstream of contemporary Australian social and cultural life.

1.3.2 Is Australian literature postcolonial?

It is sometimes forgotten that one of the foundational critical texts for postcolonial literary studies, *The Empire Writes Back: Theory and Practice in Post-Colonial Literatures* (1989), was written by three Australians. The definition these authors—Bill Ashcroft, Gareth Griffiths, and Helen Tiffin—offer for 'post-colonial' (hyphen retained) has been widely controversial, not least because of its vast historical compass: 'We use the term "post-colonial" . . . to cover all the culture affected by the imperial process from the moment of colonization to the present day' (Ashcroft, Griffiths, and Tiffin 1989: 2). This catch-all definition has the benefit, however, of including the former settler colonies within the parameters of the postcolonial. For Ashcroft, Griffiths, and

Tiffin, the postcoloniality of these ex-colonies consists in their assertion of difference from the inherited traditions of the metropole, and in the attempt to create a language appropriate to local conditions and experience.

Three issues come to the fore here: '[T]he relationship between social and literary practices in the old world and the new; the relationship between the indigenous populations in settled areas and the invading settlers; and the relationship between the imported language and the new place' (Ashcroft, Griffiths, and Tiffin 1989: 135). In each case, a local settler literature emerges that continues to be marked by the European traditions from which it wishes increasingly to dissociate itself, and that is characterized by the sustained effort to move beyond a merely 'filiative relationship with [the] dominating culture' towards new definitions of the meaning of 'home' (Ashcroft, Griffiths, and Tiffin 1989: 26). This pattern, claimed in common for the 'countries of the white diaspora' (Ashcroft, Griffiths, and Tiffin 1989: 19), reconfirms the dis-ease—the epistemological, even metaphysical uncertainty—which accompanied historical processes of white settlement; and which is reflected, in turn, in literatures that register a profoundly ambivalent attitude towards their native environment, and a recurring fear that 'language [is] drenched with . . . non-belonging' for writers obsessively driven to 'recreate, again and again, the experience of writing in a colonial space' (Lee 1974: 163, qtd in Ashcroft, Griffiths, and Tiffin 1989: 142).

The view of settler writing—settler culture at large—as being riven by ambivalence has been influential in Australia, suggesting a shared awareness that colonizer/colonized distinctions are inherently problematic in former settler colonies, like Australia, which can be considered as both European and not, colonizer and colonized at once (Lawson 1995; Turner 1994). This 'ambivalence model' has been used to argue for the centrality of settler colonies and their literatures to postcolonial analysis, in so far as the specific problems these literatures pose point to the constitutive insecurity of postcolonialism's foundational categories: self and other; colonizer and colonized; colonialism itself (Slemon 1991; Tiffin and Lawson 1994).

As might be expected, the model has been a goldmine for a variety of poststructuralist critics, who have used it to posit a flexible cross-cultural alternative to the nationalist/anti-nationalist dichotomies that had so often structured critical discussions of Australian and other settler literatures in the past (Arthur 1988; Huggan 1994). However, more specifically materialist and/or historicist critics have also tended to be suspicious of the self-heroicizing view of an Australian 'resistance literature' (Slemon 1991) struggling to free itself from its European conceptual legacy, and locked in a permanently combative relationship with the nation's colonial past. For such critics, the ambivalence of settler writing functions as the sign less of *resistance* than of *complicity*, a view articulated forcefully in a book written in part-response to Ashcroft, Griffiths, and Tiffin's, Bob Hodge and Vijay Mishra's *Dark Side of the Dream: Australian Literature and the Postcolonial Mind* (1990).

Hodge and Mishra see Australian culture in general and its litera-ture, more specifically, as 'still [being] determined massively by [their] complicity with an imperialist enterprise' (Hodge and Mishra 1990: x). This is not to say that the term 'postcolonial' cannot be applied to Australian literature and culture, but rather to suggest that Aus-tralia's postcoloniality doesn't necessarily involve uniform resistance to metropolitan/imperial norms. Hodge and Mishra's key distinction here is between what they call 'oppositional' and 'complicit' modes of postcolonialism (Hodge and Mishra 1990; see also Hodge and Mishra 1994, Hutcheon 1990). The former is largely attached to Aboriginal and other marginal forms of literary/cultural production; the latter to the neo-colonialist literature of the white majority, which is encapsulated in the contradictory figure of the (male) explorer/convict/bushranger, forever battling to assert presence in a country not his own.

White Australian literature, for Hodge and Mishra, demonstrates the schizoid consciousness of a settler society. It is the literature, they suggest, of

a cultural fragment of the metropolitan centre, ossified at the moment of contact with the land under the weight of its own colonial mission, and largely reactionary as a consequence. It is precisely this paradoxical relationship with the centre, an urge towards radicalism grafted upon an inescapable conservatism (the paradox of all fragment societies) which makes theories of postcolonialism such an awkward hermeneutic for the study of Australian literature.

(Hodge and Mishra 1990: 196)

For Hodge and Mishra, the much-vaunted radicalism of Australian literature is thus largely confined to those oppositional writers from strongly disadvantaged communities who pit themselves against a monolingual Australian (literary) history 'fraught with imperialistic assumptions and a nostalgic yearning for the metropolitan centre' (Hodge and Mishra 1990: 202). Other writers, including those traditionally associated with the combative nationalism of the Australian Legend, are held up instead as victims of 'pseudopostcolonialism' (PPC), a delusionary condition in which 'claims to [national] independence are exaggerated and the exercise of power within the society in terms of class, race and gender continues in a masked form' (Hodge and Mishra 1990: 216).

This dubious rhetorical manoeuvre allows Hodge and Mishra to stake a claim for the fundamental *doubleness* of the national literature and the various 'reading regimes' (Hodge and Mishra 1990: 217) that have been applied to it, both of which are perceived to alternate between confronting and concealing the multiple traces of Australia's colonial past. Meanwhile, the authors' idiosyncratic literary-historical survey doubles, in its turn, as a broad-based cultural diagnosis in which modern white Australians find themselves repeatedly driven to recycle the racialized fears and fantasies surrounding the figure of the cultural other that several of their colonial predecessors had attempted, unsuccessfully, to repress.

Hodge and Mishra's book is unremittingly negative in its appraisal of what its authors call the 'heroic inadequacy' contained in Australian literature (Hodge and Mishra 1990: 163). Attitudes towards the past are largely characterized by 'schizogenic processes' (Hodge and Mishra 1990: 142) of revelation and concealment; attitudes towards the land are mostly defined through negation and 'nomadic syntax', 'a form of consciousness which is rootless [and] fragmented', and which represents a distinctively 'Australian inflection of the modernist malaise' (Hodge and Mishra 1990: 154; see also Carter 1987). Hodge and Mishra's own particular variation on the 'gloom thesis' (Docker 1984) is marked above all by an insistence on the continuing history of racism in mainstream Australian society and culture. This is a history, in their eyes, that many of the nation's best-known writers and cultural commentators have proved only too adept at skirting, thereby confirming amnesia as 'a defining quality of the Australian mind' (Hodge and Mishra 1990: 14).

Diagnostic statements such as this are deliberately overstated, in keeping with the spirit of polemic in which *Dark Side of the Dream* was written; and in keeping with the book's remit as a revisionist alternative to dominant nationalist and/or eternalist visions of Australian literary history, both of which had reduced or even wilfully ignored the role of colonialism in shaping Australian attitudes towards other peoples, other cultures, and themselves. Postcolonial criticism, in this context, acts a valuable vehicle for literary and historical revisionism, even if it is by no means free from the neo-colonialist tendencies towards appropriation and assimilation that are characteristic of 'dominant settler culture[s] . . . with a colonized culture embedded within [them]' (Hodge and Mishra 1990: 71; see also Goss 1996).

This combination of ambivalence *towards* postcolonialism with the ambivalence arguably inscribed *within* postcolonialism can also be seen in later Australian applications of postcolonial theory, two good examples from the mid 1990s being Susan Sheridan's and Robert Dixon's aforementioned critical-historical studies, *Along the Faultlines* and *Writing the Colonial Adventure*, both published in 1995. Like Hodge and Mishra, Sheridan places particular emphasis on White Australia's continuing exclusion of Aborigines, which she sees as being crucial to

our self-constitution as 'Australian'—an identity, a unity, whose meaning derives from its discursive displacement of the 'other' race, just as its power as a nation state derives from the appropriation of Aboriginal land. In that respect, Australian culture is still colonial.

(Sheridan 1995: 121)

Postcolonialism, for Sheridan, is as much an extension of colonialism as a departure from it; she thus stands behind the notion of 'complicit postcolonialism', in part as an attempt to 'demythologize the heroism that [has been] repeatedly attributed to nationalist tropes' in Australian literary and cultural criticism to date (Sheridan 1995: 167). While Sheridan acknowledges the usefulness of postcolonial critique in challenging unitary myths and narratives of the nation—e.g. those allegedly enshrined in the national literature—she also emphasizes postcolonial critics' tendencies to reproduce and reify categories of the cultural other, even as they seek to open up the national narrative to a wide variety of previously marginalized voices, perspectives, and experiences. The heroic inadequacy that Hodge and Mishra had previously attributed to Australian literature is thus extended by Sheridan to the postcolonial modes of criticism that might be applied to it.

These reservations are shared by Robert Dixon, whose study of the turn-of-the-century ripping yarn, *Writing the Colonial Adventure*, similarly focuses on racialized constructions of the nation that post-colonial criticism is well placed to uncover, but also runs the risk of replacing with alteritist mythologies of its own. Dixon's book exemplifies a major strand of postcolonial literary/cultural criticism usually bracketed under the heading of 'colonial discourse analysis'. Colonial discourse analysis, often derived from the work of Edward Said (and strongly influenced, in turn, by the work of Michel Foucault), seeks to unpack the ideological contradictions in colonialist narratives of mastery and authority. What this means, in Dixon's case, is that late nineteenth/early twentieth-century adventure romance emerges both as the vehicle for an aggressively masculinist British imperialism and as an ideological site for the challenging of that imperialism in which underlying anxieties surrounding the imperial civilizing mission are involuntarily displayed.

Homi Bhabha's work on cultural hybridity and the construction of the colonial racial stereotype proves to be as influential here as Edward Said's on the imbrication of European culture and imperialism (Bhabha 1994; Said 1993). Not only is imperial adventure romance a hybrid form in Bhabha's sense that it generates anxiety about authority and national belonging; but this anxiety is mapped, more particularly, onto *Australian* texts that articulate a 'post-imperial paranoia about the loss of [British] metropolitan culture', texts in which the 'absorption of the English self by the land and by other races produces an Australian type that is a bastard or hybrid product' (Dixon 1995: 64; see also Hodge and Mishra 1990).

One of the advantages of Dixon's book is that it reconfirms the value of an inter- or transnational approach to the study of national literatures, a view supported in some of the more recent post-colonially inflected work on Australia, including Gillian Whitlock's broadly comparative study of the function of Empire in nineteenth- and twentieth-century women's autobiography, *The Intimate Empire* (2001), and Dixon's own later account of popular Australian literary and artistic constructions of the Asian/Pacific other, *Prosthetic Gods* (2001). Not all of this work is as international as it claims to be, and in at least some of it Australia is the unexamined hub from which global postcolonial analysis should radiate—an internationalized nationalism, as it were, rather than a genuinely cross-cultural concern. Still, more discerning critics such as Dixon and Whitlock make the valid point that Australian literature needs to be placed not just in a national but in a series of wider *imperial* contexts. Postcolonial methodologies provide the framework for an informed critical reading of these contexts, without Australian or other national literatures being reduced to mere epiphenomena of colonialism, instrumental conveyances for (anti-)colonialist ideologies, or accumulated bundles of (post-)imperial influences and effects.

The question of Australia's postcoloniality continues, in much current work, to be indefinitely bracketed, tentatively projected into a necessarily hypothetical future: 'Caught in that liminal, always undecided state between a colonial past and a possibly postcolonial future, "Australia" is a land, a society, a history neither colonial nor postcolonial' (Curthoys, qtd in Sheridan 1995: 167; see also Flannery 2003). No amount of attempts—and there have been several—to distinguish between the *historical* and the *discursive* dimensions of postcolonialism can eliminate this confusion, since it is a confusion born of the recognition that the 'epistemic project' of decolonization (Spivak 1987), in Australia and elsewhere, remains unfinished; that imperialism's work is far from done.

Postcolonial approaches to literature (for it should be clear by now that there is no singular approach, nor any uniformly binding methodology) are allied to this far-reaching epistemic project. Their twin objectives are to challenge, without simplifying, continuing histories of colonialism; and to celebrate, without fetishizing, contemporary cultural diversity, both within the parameters of the nation and across the wider world. These two objectives come together in the joint venture of literary/historical revisionism. Such revisionism mounts a challenge both to cultural *uniformity*, e.g. through the recovery of previously silenced narratives and histories, and to cultural *imposition*, e.g. through the multiplication of historical trajectories that often belie official records or accepted historical facts. In both cases, history stands at the centre of contemporary Australian contributions to the culture wars; and it is to the often heated debates over history, historiography, and their incorporation into established representational models—the literary canon, the historical record, literary history—that the book turns next.

2

Beginning Again

2.1 Some reflections on literary history

2.1.1 What is literary history?

There are few pursuits less fashionable yet more contentious than literary history. What is this outdated discipline that continues, in spite of itself, to be so up-to-date? And if literary history is seen, as it often is, as being an 'anachronistic reflex' (Pierce 1988: 88), then why is so much fuss being made about it, in Australia and elsewhere? One possible answer is that the current debates surrounding literary history are closely linked with those centring on the figure of the *nation*. If the nation can loosely be defined as a shared symbolic space invested with collective memories (Featherstone 1996: 53), then literary history charts that space, attempting to give it meaningful shape. Literary histories, it need hardly be said, are not intrinsically nationalistic; but they *are* national narratives of a kind, textual constructions of the nation: they are part, that is, of the negotiable field of meanings, signs, and symbols that is associated with national culture, national identity, national life (Bhabha 1990: 3).

Opinions are divided on the extent to which literary histories transcend the space of the nation, or whether their primary task is to monitor—to police the boundaries of—national culture. Before engaging with this debate and taking issue with some of its terms, I want to begin by dispelling a popular myth about literary historians. The myth runs something like this: literary historians, strictly speaking, are neither literary critics nor historians; instead, they are desiccated philologists, technically sound but theoretically deficient, whose elitist versions of the literary past resemble nothing so much as a rarefied form of ancestor worship. This myth, based on a view of philology that might itself be considered antiquarian, obscures the sophisticated, often theoretically refined work currently being undertaken in the field of literary history. Literary history, notwithstanding, is in a state of productive crisis, its traditional forms and concerns undermined by the new orthodoxies of postmodern/poststructuralist criticism; its authoritative, sometimes authoritarian syntheses displaced by the populist eclecticism of cultural studies. Developmental models of literary history are now widely seen, not least by literary historians themselves, as being terminally outmoded, while the twin fortresses of the literary canon and the historical period are increasingly under siege.

The prevailing view seems to be that the foundations of literary history need shaking; that its methods need to be rethought and its purpose reassessed. However, the facile millenarian rhetoric that might foresee an end to literary history overlooks the creative ferment that often accompanies a sense of crisis (Perkins 1991). New literary histories are emerging to supplant or update previous versions: histories which confront, rather than evade, ideological issues; which offer a pluralist view of literary/cultural production; and which acknowledge the mediating mechanisms—the institutional formations and regimes of value—through which representations of the past, in whatever form, are inevitably filtered and maintained (Frow 1991).

Let me return, though, to the notion of literary histories as national narratives. As Graeme Turner among others has suggested, national narratives are culturally generated; as such, they are both products and producers of concentrated ideological work (Turner 1991; see also Bercovitch 1986). National narratives, themselves conflicted, may open up the space of the nation: a space which Homi Bhabha—characteristically enough—has discovered to be conceptually ambivalent, to wear a Janus face (Bhabha 1990: 2–4). These narratives are just as likely, though, to share a consensus view of the nation, to legitimize nationalist sentiments underwritten by the dominant culture. Hence, in an Australian context, Ross Gibson's sardonic reading of the 1988 Bicentennial celebrations as part of a state-sanctioned attempt to 'authorize the nation as an *achieved fact*, as a society stabilized under the rule of compliant self-definition' (Gibson 1992: 195; his italics); or Sneja Gunew's critical analysis of the various, predominantly organicist Australian narratives that effectively reproduce and regulate a public sphere of Anglophone national culture (Gunew 1990).

Gunew refers specifically to those literary and cultural histories which essentialize national attributes, or which prescribe a pattern of development that closes off critical debate. Predictably perhaps,

Leonie Kramer's arch-conservative *Oxford History of Australian Literature* (1981) is top of Gunew's hit-list: not because it concerns itself—it doesn't—with myths of Australianness or national progress but, on the contrary, because it affects an Olympian disdain for those political credos and social changes that might interfere with enduring judgments of literary excellence and taste. The *Oxford History*, for Gunew, is universalist (or, as Hodge and Mishra would call it, eternalist: see Hodge and Mishra 1990) in its pretensions, meaning that it elides its own Anglo-Celtic cultural biases in the attempt to locate standards unconstrained by time or place.

For Gunew, among others, universalist and nationalist histories are alike in being dogged by expressivist concerns over the national literature and its capacity to articulate national values, beliefs, and attitudes. Literary histories, in this context, perform a predominantly policing function, either safeguarding lasting values presumed to be inherent in the national literature, or protecting the distinctiveness of literary expressions of national culture. It is difficult here at times to distinguish the critical discourse from the histories, since the metalanguage tends to mirror the dichotomous terms of the debate. Peter Pierce, for example, in his useful if by now dated 1988 survey of Australian literary histories, locates a 'melodramatic ethos' born of the 'fear of dispossession' (Pierce 1988: 88). This fear explains for Pierce why

the desire for a national literature (exhibiting national qualities, however these have been defined) has been so strenuously held by some, so contemptuously dismissed by others. The literary histories of Australia that invent different issues of debate, that abandon residual insecurities concerning the value of local materials (insecurities implied by the dichotomising habit and the melodramatic temper of debate) remain to be written.

(Pierce 1988: 88)

2.1.2   New literary histories of Australia

Have such histories since been written? This begs the question, first, of the collection in which Pierce's own essay was originally published: Laurie Hergenhan's *New Penguin Literary History of Australia* (1988). Along with the revamped *Oxford History* (1998), now under the more liberal stewardship of Bruce Bennett and Jennifer Strauss, the *Penguin History* represents the most progressively aware Australian literary history to date. Avoiding the high-handedness of earlier prescriptive histories and the illusion of coverage provided by serial lists of literary texts, the *Penguin History* is a bold attempt to reflect self-consciously on literary history, and on its formative role in the shaping of Australian national culture. While its multi-authored format cannot mask its own selectiveness and its varied essays are still contained within a chronological frame, the *Penguin History* shows its alertness to the meaning-making work of narrativity (Turner 1991), and to the constructedness of literary movements, genres, and texts as cultural forms. It at once reflects on the construction of national narrative and recognizes that such constructions are always interested, never value-free. Hence its focus on the currency of cultural perception, and on the semiotic circuitry of literary production and consumption in which national culture—the nation itself—circulates as commodified sign.

Emerging from the *Penguin History* is the sense that the symbolic value of Australian literature/culture is generated, at least in part, by outside sources and external agencies of support. This view, though hardly new, acts as a valuable corrective to the false dichotomies created by nationalist/universalist paradigms. Instead, the national literature, and its contending narrative histories, are understood as operating within an international, increasingly a transnational, framework. This last point emphasizes that literary histories are also geographies, and that their spatial reach extends beyond the boundaries of the nation. As Mike Featherstone among others has argued, '[I]t is insufficient to see the process of imagining the nation as purely the product of internal factors . . . [W]e should not consider [national] cultures in isolation, but endeavor to locate them in the relational matrix of their significant others' (Featherstone 1996: 57–8).

In addition, the very idea of a 'unique and integrated national culture' (Featherstone 1996: 57) is now considered by many to be questionable, even obsolete. The older anthropological conception of a distinctive (separate) culture has been largely replaced by a longer view—one which sees all cultural forms, interacting in a transnational context, as strands in a global, hybridized pattern of dis- and relocation. Roger Rouse states this view succinctly:

We live in a confusing world, a world of crisscrossed economies, intersecting systems of meaning, and fragmented identities. Suddenly, the comforting modern imagery of nation-states and national languages, of coherent

communities and consistent subjectivities, of dominant centers and distant
margins, no longer seems adequate.

(Rouse 1991: 8)

What happens to literary history in its guise as national narrative
when the idea of a national culture, even a 'culture', is under threat? The
logical move might be towards more experimental versions of literary
history, histories that might unsettle sedimented forms of national
narrative by highlighting multicultural dislocations and diasporic patterns of ebb and flow. But the question remains as to whether literary
histories, with their conceptual legacies of continuity and coherence,
can accommodate such postcolonial/postmodern disruptions, such
global flows and internal fissures. Are literary histories, even revisionist ones, condemned to being conservative? Do they participate, by
and large, in what D. A. Miller calls 'a general economy of policing
power'? (Miller 1988: 2). Can literary histories deliver themselves from
their exclusivist designs on literature; from their curatorial views on
history; from their essentialized notions of national culture? Should
the search be for new, revisionary, or alternative literary histories; or
should it rather be for alternatives to literary history as a record of
changing cultural forms?

Both the *Penguin* and the new *Oxford Histories* take up, and in
some cases refute, these challenges. Nonetheless, their effectiveness
is arguably dependent on a compromise between pluralist modes
of representation and the various policing mechanisms (periodiza-
tion, classification, etc.) that are characteristic of more traditional
literary histories. Hovering behind this compromise is a recognition of the logical impasse that ensues when synthesizing contexts
are used to link discrete events (Perkins 1991: 5–6; see also Frow
1991).

Homi Bhabha has located a similar split in the temporal logic
of national narrative, whereby the 'pedagogical' time that stabilizes
national identity confronts a 'performative' register that works towards
undoing identification (Bhabha 1990: 304). The increasing shift to
cultural studies at a number of Western universities might be seen as
an attempt to analyse, certainly not heal, this fracture. Cultural studies,
with its emphasis on the performativity of popular culture, is well
equipped to show how nations reinvent themselves, reconstituting
their own cultural mythologies. Cultural studies' national narratives
are rooted firmly in the present, with the chronologically ordered

taxonomies of the traditional literary history giving way to a congeries of contemporary cultural debates.

A good example here is Gillian Whitlock and David Carter's *Images of Australia* (1992), a wide-ranging introductory reader in Australian Studies which aims, in the words of its back-cover blurb, to chart the 'changing contours of Australian culture and identity . . . through contemporary debates on nationality, Aboriginality, multiculturalism, gender, the bush legend, and suburbanism' (Whitlock and Carter 1992: n.p.). Essays to this end, although to some extent historically inflected, are seen from the vantage point of the present, with a strong emphasis throughout (as in this book) on topical concerns and current events.

It might seem something of a category mistake to compare Australian literary histories with the kind of culturalist project represented by the Whitlock and Carter reader. Their methodologies are broadly dissimilar, their politics sometimes opposed. Yet they share, as I have suggested, an investment in the nation—not so much in the interests of nationalist legitimation as in the ongoing formation of a collective 'national imaginary' (Dixson 1999). The national imaginary is politically as well as conceptually ambivalent: it may serve very different masters, call upon more than one cause. The national imaginary, continually reconfigured, will surely survive into what Arjun Appadurai has prematurely called the post-national era (Appadurai 1996). It will be riven, as it always has been, with ideological conflicts. Cultural studies, revolving as it does—perhaps excessively—around national formations, will continue to chart the contours of Australian national culture. But so too will literary histories, whose exploratory national narratives (Hergenhan 1988) will need to remain critically aware of their own policing power. Nations, as previously mentioned, have the capacity to reinvent themselves. Literary histories also play their part in national self-invention. As Laurie Hergenhan says in his admirably modest introduction to the *Penguin History*: 'Each generation writes its own literature and should produce its own literary histories' (Hergenhan 1988: xiii). No doubt we can look forward to new new literary histories of Australia in the future.

2.1.3 *Literary history and the Australian canon*

A primary vehicle for the structuring of national literary history is the canon, which can be defined simply as 'a relatively short list of books or authors, ranging across several generations, which are taken to be the best and most characteristic of [a] nation's literature' (Buckridge 1995: 29). What is interesting in the Australian context is the relatively late emergence of a national canon, generally considered to be a function of the professionalization of Australian literature as a university discipline in the 1960s (Carter 1997; Dale 1997). Throughout the 1960s and 1970s, the Australian canon was alternately seen as celebrating national achievement and as 'denaturaliz[ing] local cultural values and aesthetics' by comparing these, often unfavourably, to imported British/European norms (Dale 1997: 47). By the 1980s, however, the emphasis had shifted from preserving the canon to diversifying or even dismantling it. Debate raged on the exclusivism of the canon rather than its imprimatur of excellence. Some saw a snobbish overemphasis on the 'metaphysicals' at the expense of the 'realists' (Docker 1984); others a sexist concentration on the male 'realists' at the expense of the female 'romancers' (Sheridan 1995).[1] New attention was paid to the creation of alternative canons, e.g. in women's writing and Aboriginal/multicultural/postcolonial literature, and to the widening of Australian literature into a more inclusive Australian studies, with an attendant emphasis on the diversity of national cultural forms (Bird, Dixon, and Lever 1997).

Such activity supports David Carter's materialist view of Australian literature as an institutional site of struggle in which its various, contending definitions are given social and material form (Carter 1997: 16). Many of these definitions, needless to say, have revolved around the canon, confirming the view of Australian literature as an ideological battleground 'for establishing cultural and intellectual authority . . . not least the authority to speak in the name of the nation' (Carter 1997: 20). Carter sees the Australian canon, accordingly, as an instrument of national self-examination—by which he often seems to mean nationalist self-congratulation—even when that canon itself is being subversively redefined, wholeheartedly resisted, or strategically ignored. What is at stake, in other words, in debates about Australia's canonical literature is 'the *nation* and the power to identify one's own interests with those of the national culture' (Carter 1997: 22; his italics). This investment in the nation, argues Carter, has continued in more recent 'post-canonical' times, when new literary histories have emerged that re-attach literary texts to the history of their making; when literary history is more usually seen as part of a wider cultural history; and when debates on canon formation are more likely to be found in the trivia pages of local magazines and newspapers than in the committee rooms of the nation's universities (Carter 1997: 22–3).

Carter's argument that the Australian canon has functioned as both receptacle for and mediator of 'national cultural capital' (Carter 1997: 22) is a good one, even if it overlooks important debates *beyond* Australia on what constitutes the national literature, and on which Australian authors are to be officially recognized and celebrated at any given time. (Canons, in this last sense, have always had more to do with historical contingency and ideological opportunism than with unchallenged continuity, the allegedly disinterested calculation of accumulated value over time: see, for example, Carter 1997; Guillory 1993; Herrnstein Smith 1988.) Thus, while Carter rightly stresses the increasingly important role played by corporate patronage networks (sponsorship, prizes, etc.) in mediating perceptions of what counts as high-quality Australian literature, he neglects to mention that these networks are often transnational/global in their range of institutional and commercial effects (for a self-corrective view see, however, Carter 1999).

Arguably, the internal debate over the national cultural capital of the canon has now given way to a globally disseminated argument about the appeal of individual celebrity writers and the degree of Australianness in, perhaps even the irrelevance of Australianness to, their work (Nile 2002). Meanwhile, the feeling has grown, both within and beyond Australia, that 'as an institutionalized canon, Australian literature [*per se* has become] outdated, irredeemably implicated in a conservative nationalist project that is out of tune with the younger generation' (Brown 2002: 17).

In Australia, this argument has been linked to 'bad-boy' social/cultural theorists such as McKenzie Wark and Mark Davis, who contend provocatively that the concern for preserving literary canons is merely a reactionary form of cultural gatekeeping in the age of global media, the unmistakable sign of a stagnant high literary culture's tedious 'preoccup[ation] with keeping things, unquestioningly, in their rightful place' (Wark 1999: 77; see also Davis 1997). Davis's and Wark's arguments, unsurprisingly, have been vigorously contested, not just by those they seem all too eager to dismiss as antediluvian traditionalists, but also by others who have accused them of making a virtue of not reading the authors they condemn as old-fashioned; as if 'literary canons [had acquired] such a bad name that any canonized writer [now] comes packaged with a health warning' (Brown 2002: 26).

As Ruth Brown suggests, it is one thing to say that canons, in Australia and elsewhere, are contaminated by cultural elitism, but quite another to imply that this is an excuse for not reading canonical literary works at all (Brown 2002). Part of the problem, according to Brown, is the diminishing role of literature in media-saturated consumer societies in which little time is given to in-depth reading, and in which university literature students can hardly be blamed for avoiding long and difficult literary works or relying on canned summaries, since 'their not reading the books is simply a part of the consumerist milieu in which they [currently] live' (Brown 2002: 27).

Another problem is the tendency, particularly marked in media-driven societies, to reduce complex literary/cultural debates to polemical 'either-or' positions: media-savvy 'gangsters' are duly pitted against literary-minded 'gatekeepers', and 'theory-loving' modernists against 'theory-bashing' traditionalists; willing participants all in the latest version of Australia's culture wars (Davis 1997; see also Callahan 2002). To some extent, such debates reconfirm what Peter Pierce among others has seen as Australian literary and cultural critics' 'melodramatic[ally] dichotomising habit[s]' (Pierce 1988: 88); certainly, by positioning themselves fair and square within the latest media-generated polemic, theorists like Davis and Wark have succeeded in attracting attention to themselves at the expense of more grounded understandings of the subtlety and multifacetedness of their work. Their own arguments, as Brown wryly suggests, are frequently reduced to soundbites and, as with the partly digested works they reference, the debates they raise are ironically based on an image of what they say rather than what is actually in their books (Brown 2002: 27).

Although Brown advances no particular solution to what she sees as an increasingly common predicament, she argues sensibly for the need to consider Australian literature in the context of its material conditions of production and consumption—a commodifying context to which literary/cultural critics outside Australia can and should contribute significantly, since after all the commodification of Australian writers, Australian writing and, indeed, Australia itself is often seen at its most pronounced offshore (Brown 2002: 32; see also Callahan 2002).

While debates about who should be included or not in the Australian canon are now generally considered to be anachronistic, fatuous even, it has become more imperative than ever to gauge the material conditions in which Australian literature is written, transmitted to its various national and international publics, and (not) read. These conditions include global patterns and processes of hypercommodification, with international celebrities doubling as international commodities, and with an easy celebration of cultural difference and diversity having a similarly commodifying effect, both on the mainland and offshore (Brown 2002: 33; see also Nile 2002). Clearly, the redemptive invocation of (multi)cultural difference needs to be held up to sustained critical scrutiny, even as the differential histories of Australian literary production and consumption, and the hierarchical evaluative mechanisms surrounding them, are periodically re-explored.

2.2 Founding fictions

2.2.1 Beginnings, origins, encounters

Australian literary history, mirroring the history of the 'discovery' and settlement of the Australian continent itself, engenders an unresolved conflict over beginnings. Where and when does Australian literature begin? This isn't just a question of specialist interest to literary historians, but to all those concerned with understanding Australia past and present within the fraught context of the contemporary 'history wars' (Macintyre and Clark 2003).[2] An ideological question, too, in which literary history is joined to a wider set of revisionist cultural processes, ongoing attempts to see a vibrant modern nation in the light of its often inglorious past.

Some of these debates have developed into unseemly public spats, e.g. between the prominent historians of white/Aboriginal encounter Henry Reynolds and Keith Windschuttle (see, for example, Reynolds 1996; Windschuttle 2002; also Macintyre 2003). Once again, dichotomizing tendencies, within academic as well as popular discourse, can be readily detected, prompting the critic Miriam Dixson to speak exasperatedly of a fundamental rift in Australian historiography between wide-eyed 'idealizers' and doom-laden 'demonizers' of Australia, equally self-absorbed opponents in the seemingly endless game of refashioning the present from the past (Dixson 1999: 1). The place of Australian *literature* within these debates, although it has sometimes been made to seem peripheral, has been an interesting one; not least because a number of contemporary Australian writers, in choosing to engage with variant forms of what might loosely be described as the historical novel, have made concerted efforts to tease out alternative ways of interpreting and inhabiting the past.

These efforts, some of which will be looked at in more detail later in this chapter, capture the interventionist as well as innovative spirit contained within the misleadingly simple word 'beginnings'. In his book of the same name, Edward Said—one of the leading figures of postcolonial criticism—distinguishes between 'origins' and 'beginnings'. The former, he suggests, are 'divine, mythical and privileged', while the latter are 'secular, humanly produced and ceaselessly re-examined' (Said 1975: xiii). Beginnings, suggests Said, are renewals rather than repetitions or recurrences; beginning, in this sense, is about the making or producing of differences, it is tantamount to beginning again (Said 1975: xvii).

Said's call for an anti-authoritarian approach to knowledge that facilitates what he calls 'the constant re-experiencing of beginning' (Said 1975: xiv) stands behind many of the recent revisionisms of (counter-)memory and the archive, allowing for the reaffirmation of previously suppressed histories: women's histories, non-European histories, histories 'from below' (Said 1975: xiii). These alternative narratives can also be found in most of the more recent literary histories. But despite numerous attempts to begin again, Australian literary history remains troubled, even haunted, by the problem of cultural origins. The laudable attempt, for example, to give emphasis or even precedence to Aboriginal production merely exacerbates the problem. For as Adam Shoemaker has observed,

[t]he historical dates which constitute what is known as 'chronological time' [the basis for literary history] have often been used to imprison Australia's indigenous peoples. Terms such as 'prehistory' and 'pre-literacy' carry with them the strongest possible sense of a time before—and a time after. Of course, these dividing lines have been imposed retrospectively upon Black Australians

by those who are not members of that culture. Such arbitrary demarcations also imply that the past begins when it is recorded in legible script, not when human beings began to commit stories to memory.

(Shoemaker 1998: 9)

Shoemaker's comments are highly relevant to the construction of Australian literary history, and to the perception of (Australian) literature in general. Here, he joins several other recent commentators on Australian literary/cultural history who have emphasized the centrality of memory (see, for example, Healy 1997); and who, insisting on the need to see historical events and their literary representations as being subject to the fluidity of imaginative processes, have enjoined their readers to construct their own creative histories of the present—in going back, to begin again.

However, Shoemaker admits that the desire to anchor the past in originary texts ('earliest poems', 'first letters', 'foundational narratives', etc.) remains extremely powerful. While the power of the foundational work is arguably common to all national literary histories, it might well be strongest in nations struggling to overcome the conceptual and material legacies of a colonial history. Two very different versions of this argument may be presented here. In the first, what we might call the postcolonial version, the foundational work is co-terminous with the establishment of the new nation, upsetting the entrenched hierarchies of metropolitan/European histories to create its own self-enabling vision of the future, as well as of the past (Bhabha 1990; see also Sommer 1991). In the second, the critical preoccupation with foundational works is rather read as the sign of a colonial persuasion. According to this version, the desire to locate 'first works' is the reflex of a threatened cultural nationalism; as in the wearisome, increasingly derisory task of identifying the Great Australian Novel, it implies that the national literature is to be measured against the yardstick of European canonical forms (Buckridge 1995; Dale 1992).

If the search for foundational works is characteristic of colonial 'canonical anxiety' (Buckridge 1995: 30), it may demonstrate a similarly colonial amnesia towards the prior status of indigenous cultural works. This status today is generally though still not comprehensively acknowledged. But problems of origin remain, tied in to the perception of what constitutes Aboriginal literature in the first place. Arguably the greatest of these problems is what to do about the transcription of

Aboriginal orality. As Penny van Toorn astutely observes, in speaking of the anthologization of Aboriginal material,

When the oral is reproduced in written form it becomes readable and culturally valuable in Eurocentric terms, as a sort of anthropological branch of the literary. Meanwhile early Aboriginal texts written in English are left out. When texts from the oral tradition count as literary writing but early Aboriginal-authored printed documents do not, the history of Aboriginal textual practice becomes absurd. As well as reinvoking colonial anthropological distinctions between oral and literate cultures, these apparently inclusive anthologies reinforce the line between literature with a capital 'L' and many so-called sub-literary modes.

(van Toorn 1996: 757)

In such a context, the attempt to pin down 'firsts' may be both inaccurate and patronizing. For example, David Unaipon's *Native Legends* (1929) is often considered to be the 'first work' of Aboriginal literature (see, for example, Beston 1979). But as van Toorn among others has shown, Aboriginal people were using a wide variety of written and printed textual forms from the early days of settlement; the problem is not that they didn't write but that that their writing wasn't acknowledged as 'literary' or seen as appropriate for in-depth critical study (van Toorn 1996: 754–5; see also Mudrooroo 1997, Muecke 1988).

An added problem, still heatedly discussed, is that of white/Aboriginal co-authorship (Hughes 1998; Kurtzer 1998). White textual practice, for good or ill, is very much a part of the history of Aboriginal literature, as indeed of several other indigenous literatures in English. In some cases, white transcribers were needed to take down the accounts of Aborigines who were functionally illiterate; in others, white editors collaborated, at times intrusively, in the production of the final published work. It is perhaps overstating the case to say that white transcribers and editors of Aboriginal texts have persistently walked the 'tightrope between collaboration and appropriation' (Shoemaker 1998: 14), although several individual examples might confirm this, but certainly not inaccurate to suggest that the history of Aboriginal literature reveals a tension between the individualist ethos of Western literary history and collective Aboriginal custodianship over literary/cultural forms.

Other tensions were to accompany the early stages—the first beginnings—of colonial Australian literature. Much of this writing was doubly marked, both by anxiety over the building of a new literature and by the nagging awareness of Aboriginal priority, an awareness often articulated in the manifest fear of the unknown (Gelder and Jacobs 1998). Recent critical work has consolidated the view of colonial writing as implicitly, sometimes explicitly anxiogenic, registering the tension between 'traveller' and 'settler' perspectives, and torn between the felt need to account for the passing strangeness of the new world and the contractual obligation to satisfy the exoticist predilections of the old (Bird 1998; Perkins 1998).

Primary vehicles for both were the diary/journal and the exploration narrative, both of which were addressed first and foremost to a metropolitan readership, and which arguably produced the strongest writing in a period during which most writers were from a middle- or upper-class English background, translating their experiences of Australia to an unfamiliar audience 'back home' (Webby 1989: xxi). Colonial writing, in this sense, can be seen as a congeries of 'fictions of factual representation' (White 1976)—letters, journals, diaries, sketches—that sought to pass off tendentious interpretation as reliable information, and that allayed their concerns about confronting the unfamiliar by couching their experiences in the reassuring language of the known.

This is of course a highly selective, even myopic view of Australian colonial literature, overlooking as it does significant work in poetry, fiction, and drama from the late eighteenth through to the turn of the twentieth century, as well as the intensifying public debate as to what constituted a properly Australian literature—what set it apart from the English models many of the nation's writers seemed so consciously to be imitating; and what building-blocks might be found for the development of a stronger national consciousness, for the more confident assertion of enduring presence in a country still not yet fully acknowledged as being one's own. It remains the case that non-fictional writing, from the epoch-making arrival of the First Fleet to the equally mythologized 1890s, acted as a valuable barometer for the changing literary sensibilities of the period; it also amply demonstrated the highly inconsistent, often explicitly divided or ambivalent attitudes the settlers expressed towards the land and their increasingly competitive social environment: attitudes that betrayed deep-seated uncertainties about proprietorship and belonging, together with a disquieting sensation of the unhomeliness of home (Gelder and Jacobs 1998).

These uncertainties are well demonstrated in what might loosely be termed the 'literature of encounter', in which the ever present fear of the cultural other is systematically counteracted by the attempt to control representation through discriminating strategies of racial classification and spatial containment (Carter 1987). Included in the early Australian literature of encounter are the so-called First Fleet annals, the wide variety of empirically oriented writings produced in the wake of Captain Arthur Phillip's historic 1788 entrance into Botany Bay. This originary moment gave rise to foundational fictions of a kind, even though the annals are more appropriately considered as non-fiction, testifying to most early colonial writers' preference for metonymic and descriptive prose (Bird 1998: 25).

Probably the best-known of the writers was Watkin Tench, whose *A Narrative of the Expedition to Botany Bay* (1789) has been held up as a shining example of 'the humanistic and Enlightenment heritage which has been [Australia's] since the time of the First Fleet' (Flannery 2003: 70). Perhaps so, but this doesn't stop Tench from indulging in fitful bouts of colonial racism, naturalizing white superiority even as he demonstrates his sympathy for the 'Indians' he and his party encounter during their exploratory forays around the headlands of the Bay. Tench's observations appear at first sight to convey an absolute epistemic authority, an unshakable belief in the transparency of the natives and in his capacity both to decipher their motives and to reassert his own. So friendly do they prove that 'we began to entertain strong hopes of bringing about a connection with them. Our first object was to win their affections, and our next to convince them of the superiority we possessed: for without the latter, the former we knew would be of little importance' (Webby 1989: 54).

On closer inspection, though, Tench's narrative betrays moments of significant interpretive anxiety. This anxiety is generally transposed onto the natives themselves, who are frequently presented as being at a loss to explain the behaviour of their European interlocutors, whom, it is implied, they will be warmly invited to appreciate but never granted the greater privilege to know. Hence the seamless continuity in Tench's narrative between the apparently incompatible alternatives of intercultural dialogue and physical/textual capture, well illustrated in the good-humoured sequence involving the abduction and education of the native Manly (aka Arabanoo). The sequence rehearses several of the standard ploys of what Bob Hodge and Vijay Mishra call, after Edward Said, hegemonic 'Aboriginalist discourse' (Hodge and Mishra 1990; see also Said 1978): the anthropologization of the (male) native as a test-case for reasoned enquiry into cultural difference; the spectacle of cultural otherness this entails; and the attempted conversion of the native into an emissary for the values of the polite white society that supports him (Webby 1989: 55–9).

Manly, named after the cove in which he was captured, is eventually persuaded to reveal a patois version of his Aboriginal name, Arabanoo. But this revelation merely confirms that the process of his assimilation is more or less complete. It has already been ascertained (a key word throughout the text) how much he knows and what place in the racial hierarchy he occupies: 'My observation . . . was (and it has been confirmed in a thousand other instances) that [these] people are as black as the lighter cast of African negroes' (Webby 1989: 56–7); he has already been convinced of the superior virtues of English cleanliness, courtesy, and decency; and he has already demonstrated his loyalty towards his captors by returning to them 'without testifying reluctance' (Webby 1989: 58), a pattern duly repeated when, after an unsuccessful attempt to escape at sea, he seems relieved in the end to have been rescued from 'an element of whose boundary he could form no conception' (59).

Not for the first time, the fixing of boundaries—geographical, cultural, epistemological—is effortlessly claimed to be the white man's prerogative. For all that, Tench's narrative remains persistently uneasy with what it doesn't know, seeking recourse in brave-faced conjecture: 'Our *ignorance* of the language prevented us from knowing much of what passed; it was, however, *easily understood* that his friends asked him why he did not jump overboard, and rejoin them' (Webby 1989: 58; my italics; see also Carter 1987: 35–42).

What the literature of encounter often ascertains, much to its own discomfort, are the limits of its own certainty; this may well lead it in some extreme cases to the demonization of an other it fearfully confronts across the gulf of mutual incomprehension, or to the avoidance of a potentially contaminating other, suggesting that 'encounter' and 'contact', far from being synonymous, may even be opposed. These distancing devices can be seen across a whole range of Australian discovery and exploration narratives from the late-eighteenth to at least the mid-nineteenth century. Narratives such as these are now often seen as constituting the first beginnings of an Australian literature. Yet at the time, they would hardly have been seen as constituting literature at all. As Delys Bird among others has suggested, the critical engagement with colonial writing demands a more capacious understanding of the literary than is frequently permitted; all the more so because '[s]o-called "serious literature", with its relatively rigid conventions and elaborated metaphoric and symbolic systems was ill-suited to undertake [the] process... of making sense through language of the new world' (Bird 1998: 24).

To some extent this is unfair to some of the more conventional writers of the period. Poets such as Charles Harpur, Henry Kendall, and Adam Lindsay Gordon were all wrestling, with admittedly varying degrees of success, to make sense of the new world, as were equally well-known novelists/romancers such as Marcus Clarke (of whom more later), Henry Kingsley, Rolf Boldrewood, and Rosa Praed. However, Bird's point still stands that colonial writing requires a broad view of literature often unlikely to be accepted back then, and still not always certain to be accepted today.

Colonial writing, as its own uncertain designation suggests, is a test-case for the hazards of literary category. One difficulty is to sift fictional from non-fictional forms of writing; another is to separate broadly oral from more ostensibly literary forms; while still a third is to distinguish English from Australian writing (Webby 1989). In each case, hard-and-fast distinctions are more likely to confuse than to clarify the picture. Hybrid genres such as journalism and travel writing cut across fictional/non-fictional demarcations, while demotic modes such as the yarn and the ballad obviously draw on both oral and literary sources, combining these into readily identifiable popular cultural forms.

Finally, most nineteenth-century writers, as previously mentioned, were from comfortable English social backgrounds; several were uncertain as to whether England or Australia was their sentimental home. As arguments developed over the course of the century about the rightful place and autonomous status of Australian literature, this last issue became contentious. If it was now accepted that there was a national literature, who were to be its official gatekeepers? Were Anglo-Australians, for instance, who identified as much with England as with Australia, to be considered as *bona fide* Australian writers? And if so, which Anglo-Australians? The émigré English journalist Marcus Clarke, widely acknowledged as one of the most gifted writers of his generation, stands at the centre of this controversy; and it is to Clarke's rumbustious convict novel *For the Term of His Natural*

Life (1882), one of the few undisputed classics of nineteenth-century Australian literature, that I turn next.

2.2.2   Cultural gatekeepers: Clarke, Gordon, Lawson, Franklin

For the Term of His Natural Life, first serialized as *His Natural Life* in the early 1870s, is commonly looked upon as 'the best novel produced in nineteenth-century Australia; in fact, the only one with claims to greatness, and arguably still the best one concerned with the convict system' (Hergenhan 1993: 47). Wildly popular on first appearance, the novel has been eulogized ever since: Brian Elliott, for example, in his gushing introduction to the 1984 Angus and Robertson paperback edition, goes so far as to call it a 'national monument', and 'in many ways the outstanding Australian work of the creative imagination' *tout court* (Elliott 1984: xi). However, while it is true that Clarke's novel 'became standard Australian reading, with a prestige on the colonial bookshelf equal to the Bible or Shakespeare' (Elliott 1984: xlii), Clarke himself has been periodically regarded with suspicion as an English immigrant to Australia whose work was carefully tailored to the metropolitan marketplace; and whose masterpiece, along with such well-known Anglo-Australian novels of the time as Henry Kingsley's *Geoffry Hamlyn* (1859) or Catherine Helen Spence's *Clara Morison* (1854), was sometimes adjudged to have been praised 'to the exclusion of more indigenous works' (Palmer, qtd in Wilding 1975: 95).

For the Term of His Natural Life is foundational in several different senses: as far and away the most influential convict novel of its generation (though not the first, an honour usually given to James Tucker's *Ralph Rashleigh*, posthumously published in 1845); as required reading on the iniquities of the Australian penal system, written from the double perspective of a gentleman convict who sees from within but is clearly positioned from without; and as a bridge between the well-established tradition of English adventure fiction and a distinctively Australian combination of committed realism and extravagant romance (Hergenhan 1993). Perhaps most of all, the novel operates as a foundational Australian victim narrative, with the disinherited protagonist, Richard Devine (aka Rufus Dawes), becoming an involuntary 'recruit to the ranks of [a convict] ruffianism' from which his gentlemanliness obviously distinguishes itself, but from which the circumstances dictated by the text will not allow him any opportunity to escape (Clarke 1984: 53).

The novel proceeds in like fashion according to a series of stereotypically antipodean displacements and inversions. It is a novel about civilization, but one which shows the tyrannies of English civilized society; about savagery, but one in which the convicts are co-opted into playing the 'savage' role. The antipodean law of inversion exposes the arbitrariness of the colonial social system; and yet the gentlemanly propensities of the narrator are never left in doubt (Hodge and Mishra 1990). The narrative thus constantly reminds us that Richard Devine is a true gentleman, while his nemesis John Rex is an impostor and a swindler; it also repeatedly shows us that although the convicts are 'the monsters that our monstrous system breeds' (Clarke 1984: 254), at their worst they are still 'savage beasts', representing 'all that is hideous and vile in our common nature' (Clarke 1984: 367). What makes a man a beast, the narrative suggests, is the lack of restraint that always threatens to undermine good breeding; yet good breeding itself remains imperative, even if its main exponent, Richard Devine, is destined to fulfil a tragic role.

The novel is thus an ironic transportation narrative in more senses than one. Australia becomes the place where Victorian models of Englishness are tested to their limits; the foundations of a transplanted settler society, like those of the System it creates in its own image, are portrayed as being rotten to the core. But in keeping with other nineteenth-century Australian adventure fiction, the novel is dogged by the very Englishness from which it seems to want to distance itself (Dixon 1995). The heroine Sylvia Vickers is inseparable from her fantasy-laden *English History* (until the book is unceremoniously burnt to attract the attention of possible rescuers); while the narrative itself seems similarly preconditioned to play out ironic versions of that other ultra-English colonial fantasy, Defoe's *Robinson Crusoe*.

For the Term of His Natural Life thus incessantly doubles back on itself: it is a Victorian novel pretending to be an Australian novel pretending to be a Victorian novel; it is a melodramatic historical romance which, for all its mischievous self-mockery, never quite succeeds in disowning its own status as a melodramatic historical romance (Clarke 1984: 213, 222). Perhaps the greatest irony is that its deserved reputation as one of Australia's foundational works only exposes it further to its own belated status; but that is an irony that arguably holds in common for several other Australian colonial texts.

Clarke's self-conscious Victorianism has not prevented him from being considered one of the greatest Australian writers; his reputation has more than withstood the test of time, which is more than can be said for his contemporary Adam Lindsay Gordon, sneeringly described as the 'rhyming jockey' with pretensions to being a 'second Byron' (Wright 1964, qtd in Elliott 1973: 2), who even enthusiasts like Brian Elliott have seen as waning from 'the most vital and representative of [colonial] Australian poets [into something of a critical] dead weight' (Elliott 1973: 1).

Perhaps the problem lies less with Gordon himself than with standard critical depreciations of the colonial period. 'There is a strong cleavage', Elliott suggests, 'between the colonial and the post-colonial spirit' and, as a result of this, previously admired writers have been summarily discarded as the exponents of a colonial art which is itself now 'voted below contempt' (Elliott 1973: 2). This is too defensive on Elliot's part—or perhaps just too critically early—given the post-colonial *recuperation* of colonial writing in Australia (see, for example, the restorative work of Susan Sheridan and Robert Dixon). However, even in more recent studies of Australian poetry, like Andrew Taylor's or Paul Kane's, Gordon runs out a distant second-best to colonial contemporaries like Harpur or, especially, Kendall; while his populism, unlike that of, say, Henry Lawson or Banjo Paterson, whose authenticity continues to some extent to be vouchsafed by the Australian Legend (see below), is now generally seen as striking a false note.

Yet even if once-famous poems like 'The Sick Stockrider' have not been fully nursed back to health, Gordon is a more interesting poet than he is usually given credit for. And what is interesting about him is, precisely, the gap between his colonial posturing and his proto-nationalist appreciation of Australia, particularly Australian landscape—a disparity which allows him to negotiate a position for himself as neither a British nor an Australian poet or, perhaps better, as both of these at once. Kane suggests, somewhat mysteriously, that Gordon's work shares with that of his fellow nineteenth-century poets Harpur, Kendall, and Brennan 'a radical duality in which the play of negativity inhabits a non-place of poetic inspiration' (Kane 1998: 45); what he probably means by this is that these poets were all inspired, in different ways, by Romantic poetic traditions whose uncertain transposition onto Australia resulted in either a productive awareness of conceptual inadequacy—an antipodean form of negative capability—or in a compensatory nativism which could not help but seem too early, even as its Romantic derivations could not help but make it seem too late.

Enter, on this wave of contested derivativeness, the nationalistic Legend of the Nineties, more commonly known as the Australian Legend. The Legend maintained, in the words of the historian Russel Ward, to whom the coinage 'Australian Legend' is usually attributed, that being Australian was definitely something to be fought for, and that its governing ethos was 'intimately connected with the bush and . . . . derive[d] rather from the common folk than from the more respectable and cultivated members of society' (Ward, qtd in Gelder and Jacobs 1998: 15). Literature had an important role to play in the creation and subsequent maintenance of the Legend, but not any kind of literature, rather that seen as upholding the combative values of radical nationalism and egalitarianism for which the Legend itself was seen to stand.

The Legend, although still periodically reinvented, now stands at something of a crossroads; it is increasingly seen as the limited product of an equally limited number of middle-class writers and intellectuals during the period roughly from the 1930s to the 1960s, who shared a somewhat inflationary sense of the justice of the national cause. The Legend's alleged radicalism has been exposed, as have its pretensions to egalitarianism. The modern consensus view is that it overprivileges white-settler experience by excluding Aborigines; male experience by marginalizing women; rural experience by ignoring the city. As Richard Nile puts it, pulling no punches, the Legend 'is exclusive, narrow and hierarchical, [even as it] gives the appearance of being wide-ranging and generously embracing, as a story whose heroes are the common stock of the nation' (Nile 2000: 1). In literary terms, the Legend has also been in steady decline since the late 1960s, although it continues to circulate widely in certain areas of popular culture (Martin 1998). Some of the writers associated with it, notably Joseph Furphy, are no longer widely read if read at all, while others such as Banjo Paterson and Henry Lawson, although enduringly popular, are no longer read unproblematically as matey stalwarts for the radical-nationalist cause.

Of the three writers, Lawson is the one whose reputation has best survived this critical onslaught on the Legend. His canonical status is not in doubt, but Lawson is much more than a canonical writer. The first popular cultural figure in Australia to receive a state funeral, Lawson has endured as a national icon celebrated in numerous memorials, festivals, and commemorative cultural events (Lee 1997). Lawson's popularity has made him available for a number of different cultural projects and initiatives; in this sense, he functions less as a literary/cultural gatekeeper than as the seemingly inexhaustible conduit for a series of alternative, often conflicting cultural myths (Lee 1997; Nile 2002).

Lawson himself was a highly accomplished self-mythologizer: the 'uncultured rhymer' pitted against a sneering colonial establishment; the 'shy, ignorant lad from the Bush . . . [with] a heart full of love for Australia, and hatred for wrong and injustice' (Lawson, qtd in Kiernan 1976: 209). He is constructed, and constructed himself, as the most representative of all Australian writers: one whose work set out to explain an emergent nation to itself; and whose gallery of ideal bush types—the drover, the selector, the swagman, the sharper, the undertaker—were instantly recognizable victims of a rough frontier society struggling for purchase in a conspicuously inhospitable space (Lawson 1976: xii). Lawson, in other words, was ideal fodder for the cliché-ridden Legend and its stock figure of the put-upon Aussie battler: sometimes wrong but more often wronged, resolutely anti-authoritarian, with 'values and ethics [that were] staunch and homespun and . . . inclinations [that were] communal rather than individual' (Nile 2000: 1; see also Curthoys 2000). Even 'post-Legend', this starry-eyed view can be found in a great deal of Lawson criticism, as can the notion that Lawson's poems and, especially, his stories express 'truth to life' and display an almost uncanny ability to capture 'how people really speak' (Kiernan 1976: xxi).

Lawson's work still suffers from being subordinated to the false authenticities of the Legend. However, the increasing tendency is to see it as having anticipated recent *critiques* of the Legend that focus on racial exclusivism, spurious appeals to solidarity, and a sexual division of labour that highlights the vanities and insufficiencies of men (Martin 1998). Sycophantic axioms such as A. G. Stephens'—'Henry Lawson is the voice of the bush, and the bush is the heart of Australia' (qtd in Lee 1997: 152)—are not actually borne out in Lawson's stories, many of which celebrate the decidedly unheroic exploits of those who have at best mixed feelings for the bush. The sentimentalism of the Legend is singularly ill-suited to the cheerful cynicism of Lawson's yarns and sketches, which function largely by negation, and in which sarcasm is developed, in accordance with the best traditions of the yarn, into a rarefied art form (Hodge and Mishra 1990; see also Reid 1977).

Nor, as these generic associations suggest, is there anything quintessentially Australian about them, apart from their obviously localized settings. Granted, there is an anti-colonial strain in Lawson's work, clearer perhaps in the poems than in the stories, that mocks the pompous rhapsodizing of some of his would-be nationalist contemporaries: 'If you swear there's not a country like the land that gave you birth, / And its sons are just the noblest and most glorious chaps on earth; / If in every girl a Venus your poetic eye discerns, / You are gracefully referred to as the "young Australian Burns"' (Lawson 1976: 147). But Lawson's own nationalism, like his much vaunted realism, is distinctly double-edged. He is perhaps more of an anti-ideologue—a 'lonely voice' (O'Connor 1962)[3]—than a champion of particular collective causes; a minimalist more adept at indicating what is not, or is missing, than in describing what is. A modernist, too, who joins other late nineteenth-century exponents of the short story in using the conventions of the genre—inference, impressionism, ellipsis—to highlight psychological uncertainties and deficiencies, as well as to effect targeted forms of social critique (May 1976; New 1987).

One of Lawson's most famous tales, 'The Bush Undertaker' (1887), provides an illustration of the inferential techniques used in many of his stories. The story, as is customary for Lawson, is disarmingly simple. Set on a broiling Christmas Day, it charts the verbal and physical wanderings of its solitary protagonist, the eponymous 'undertaker', the turning point being when he comes across the already stiffened corpse of the alcoholic shearer Brummy, and takes it upon himself to provide an honest burial for his far from honest friend. The story, like so many others Lawson wrote, is suffused with death, sardonically described elsewhere as being 'about the only cheerful thing in the bush' ('In A Dry Season'). It is also typical in being riddled with comically expressed anxieties: explicitly, about rapid decline and the dispiriting loss of mental and physical capacities, implicitly about the possible degeneration of the (superior) 'white race'. The racial subtext is none too difficult to decipher. Before stumbling upon Brummy, the undertaker digs up some bones from a 'blackfellow's grave', the race of the deceased nonetheless remaining unidentifiable to him (Lawson 1976: 105). The theft then comes back to haunt him in the shape of a number of marauding black goannas, who symbolically remind him of his past misdeeds and his own impending death. The 'great an' gerlorious rassaraction' wished upon Brummy, whose body is itself described as being 'blackened', thus seems to take on a rather different, racialized resonance to the one his friend apparently intends (Lawson 1976: 110, 106). For the 'grand Australian bush', ironically alluded to in the final paragraph, may be 'the home of the weird', but it is also the home of the Aborigines; and it has no racial preference for either the favours it grants or the lives it chooses, prematurely, to end (Lawson 1976: 111).

While it would be optimistic, to say the least, to convert Lawson into a surreptitious champion for Aborigines, stories like 'The Bush Undertaker' suggest that he was certainly aware, like most of his contemporaries, of the racialized anxieties underlying white-settler claims upon the land they selected for their own. These anxieties were often sexualized, too, as emerges in other Lawson stories, in which women become either vain upholders of a civility misplaced in such a thankless setting ('Water Them Geraniums'), or overdetermined victims of the brute indifference of the bush ('The Drover's Wife'). Lawson's focus in these and other stories is often on male failure and inadequacy, a very different picture from that drawn in the Legend's standard masculinist accounts.

This is not to suggest that the important feminist revisions of the Legend practised by Kay Schaffer, Susan Sheridan, and several others in the 1980s and on into the 1990s were redundant or unnecessary, rather that they exposed structural weaknesses already present in many of the writings they systematically debunked (Magarey Rowley, and Sheridan 1993; Schaffer 1988; Sheridan 1995). One of the alternative female 'bush writers' they championed instead was the previously but no longer neglected Barbara Baynton (*Bush Studies*, 1902); another was Miles Franklin, whose fledgling novel *My Brilliant Career* (1901)—fulsomely praised by Lawson, who wrote a preface and found a publisher for it—might well be seen to be as much a *part* of the Legend as an undermining of it from within.

Certainly, Franklin's aggressive pronouncements elsewhere about the need for an 'indigenous' Australian literature might come straight out of the Legend:

> Without an indigenous Australian literature people can remain aliens in their own soil. An unsung country does not fully exist or enjoy adequate international exchange in the inner life. Further, a country must be portrayed by those who hate or love it as their dwelling place, familiarly, or remain dumb among its contemporaries. The fuller its libraries, the louder its radios, the more crowded its periodicals with imported stories and sons, the more clearly such dependence exposes innate poverty.
>
> (Franklin 1956: 3)

Similar sentiments are expressed in the final chapter of *My Brilliant Career*, in which the sixteen-year-old narrator-protagonist, Sybylla Melvyn, takes it upon herself to deliver a stirring peroration on the virtues of the Australian national cause. 'I am proud that I am an Australian', she declaims, '[proud to be] a daughter of the Southern Cross, a child of the mighty bush. I am thankful I am a peasant, a part of the bone and muscle of my nation, and earn my bread by the sweat of my brow, as man [*sic*] was meant to do' (Franklin 1980 [1901]: 231).

This blatant appropriation of the masculinist discourse of the Legend comes across as being distinctly inappropriate in a novel that has little good to say about peasants or, for that matter, about men. The contradiction, though, is Sybylla's rather than Franklin's. Too much ink has been spilt on the extent to which the novel should be seen as autobiographical, too little on the extent to which it generates irony at its youthful narrator's expense. This irony extends to Sybylla's naive enthusiasm for the nineteenth-century Australian poets—Kendall, Gordon, Paterson, Lawson—the attempted emulation of whose 'nativist' work produces unintentionally hilarious results:

> I lay on the soft moss and leaves and drank deeply of the beauties of nature. The soft rush of the river, the scent of the shrubs, the golden sunset, occasionally the musical clatter of hoofs on the road, the gentle noises of the fishers fishing, the plop, plop of a platypus disporting itself mid stream, came to me as sweetest elixir in my ideal, dream-of-a-poet nook among the pink-based, grey-topped, moss-carpeted rocks.
>
> (Franklin 1980: 103)

Passages like this come straight out of the manual of bad colonial writing against which Lawson among others militated, and which progressive writers such as Franklin were equally determined to resist. The achievement of the novel, in fact, lies in its capacity for critical distance from its sympathetic protagonist, whose ambitions to be the next great Australian writer fall afoul of the worst excesses of the Legend, and whose early insistence that her novel is 'not a romance' gives away exactly what it is (Franklin 1980: 1).

However, *My Brilliant Career* is more than just a romance (which might account for its academic popularity). The novel straddles conventions in much the same way as it straddles centuries. While it is too romantic to be realist, it is at times too realistic to be romance; looking back to the nineteenth century and beyond (domestic melodrama, the governess narrative, the epistolary novel), it also looks forward to the twentieth (the fragmented modern novel as a pastiche of seemingly incompatible literary styles). *My Brilliant Career* is a watershed novel, foundational in its capacity both to locate itself within an 'indigenous' Australian tradition and to provide the grounds for that tradition's effective critique.

It is certainly not foundational, however, in the spirit in which the hapless *Bulletin* reviewer A. G. Stephens intended it when, in another fit of misplaced enthusiasm, he called it 'the very first Australian novel to be published, [since] there is not one of the others that might not have been written by a stranger or a foreigner' (qtd in Barnard 1967: 63). Nor is the novel uniformly progressive: its class politics are muddled and its racism is fairly typical for the era, even though it would be unwise in both cases to mistake Sybylla's attitudes for the author's own. Its feminism, however, leaving Sybylla's far behind, clears a space for the more accomplished work of Henry Handel Richardson, Katharine Susannah Prichard, and several other leading twentieth-century Australian women writers, while it also anticipates socialist-feminist critiques of an inflexible colonial class system that persisted well into the twentieth century, and that some would still see as being pervasive in Australia today.

2.2.3 Re-imagining history

The critical revisionism that has attended recent engagements with the Legend is part of a more general pattern of historical rewriting, much in evidence in contemporary Australia but equally prevalent elsewhere. Much of this is being done by a variety of freelance historians who either earn a living by writing commissioned histories—government history, corporate history, and so on—or who 'write local and family history as a labour of love' (Macintyre and Clark 2003: 21). More still is being done by a large number of creative writers, especially novelists, whose primary concern is perhaps less to recover than to re-imagine the past. The boom in 'neo-historical fiction' (Pierce 1992) in Australia in the last three decades is thus part of a much wider attempt to counteract the perceived 'cultural malaise of historical amnesia', and to 'reanimate the past in the present' by treating public and private, fact and fiction, as intersecting, mutually invigorating spheres (Pierce 1992: 305; see also Healy 1997, Macintyre and Clark 2003). This type of fiction is hardly a recent introduction to Australia. Many of the nation's best-known novels and romances have a strong historical component, from Marcus Clarke's convict novel *For the Term of His Natural Life* (1882) to Richardson's epic Gold-Rush trilogy *The Fortunes of Richard Mahony* (1917–29), to popular outlaw/bushranger romances like *Robbery Under Arms* (Rolf Boldrewood, 1888) and *Outlaw and Lawmaker* (Rosa Praed 1893).

One tendency of more recent work, however, has been an emphasis on 'the partiality and unreliablity of the sources from which formal and fictitious histories are constructed' (Pierce 1992: 310); another has been the global emergence of an identifiable kind of self-consciously hybrid historical fiction—Linda Hutcheon unwieldily calls it 'histori-ographic metafiction' (Hutcheon 1984–5)—which seeks to combine genuine and fake historical sources and, blurring the line between them, to produce ironic commentary on the ideologies of veracity and authenticity that govern official representations of the past. Histori-ographic metafiction, much like the postmodernism that inspired it, is now far less radical or transformative than it appeared, say, twenty years ago. Sometimes it is merely dull or formulaic, provoking the suspicion that it might now have reached its sell-by date. Still, at its best such fiction allows for a spirited re-engagement with the past that is both ethically responsible and aesthetically satisfying. It also has the potential to challenge the national/global memory industries from which it draws increasing sustenance (Healy 1997). After all, the commodification of memory is the function of a globalized late-capitalist society in which historical consciousness has been eroded by nostalgia—a society of the souvenir as much as of the spectacle, in which an ever-growing number of commercially viable memorabilia and pseudo-historical constructions has granted the illusion of access to, while effectively substituting for, the lived experiences of the past (Huggan 2002).

One recent neo-historical novel that clearly operates within this dual national/global framework is Peter Carey's self-reflexive account of the Ned Kelly legend, *True History of the Kelly Gang* (2000). Riding on the back of numerous other factual/fictional accounts of the famous Irish Australian bushranger, Carey's novel emphasizes the ambivalent and, above all, commodified status of Ned Kelly as national icon and anti-imperial resource. From the outset, the novel cheerfully acknowledges its debts by making a connection between the archival source on which it draws, a fictive version of the incomplete manuscript handed over by Kelly to the schoolmaster, Tom Curnow, who betrayed him, and the 'wholesale souveniring of [Kelly gang] armour and guns and hair and cartridges that occurred at Glenrowan on June 28th 1880' (Carey 2001 [2000]: 4). However, the written manuscript upon which the novel claims to draw can hardly be considered a reliable documentary item; rather, it acts as the trigger for a sequence of highly entertaining picaresque adventures in which the inscribed narrator, Kelly, doubles as comic 'remembrancer' (Burke 1989: 10) and tragic protagonist of his (mock-)heroic quest. Not for the first time in his work, Carey deliberately dissolves the boundary between oral and written, fictional and non-fictional sources, thereby maintaining a dynamic balance between competing versions of the historical past (see also Carey 1980, 1985).

Throughout Carey's novel, history slides imperceptibly into the more distant recesses of folk memory, while the documented discoveries of archival research converge with the fabrications of the adventure tale. This structural ambivalence is reinforced by the remarkable act of sustained ventriloquism by which Carey is able to give voice to Kelly's memories of his ancestral Irish, as well as his more immediate Australian past. The narrative is consistently doubled, as the subjective recounting of Australian colonial history encounters half-buried memories of an Irish ancestry—an ancestry that clearly causes Kelly as much pain as pride, and through which the repetitive patterns of a larger 'historic memory of UNFAIRNESS' (Carey 2001: 299; his capitals) can be seen inexorably to emerge.

In addition, Kelly's perception of ancestral memory itself is presented as being deeply riven. On the one hand, he scorns the attitude of those (such as his fellow gang member Steve Hart) who nourish themselves on the stories of the martyred Irish rebels, describing Hart witheringly at one point as 'like a girl living in Romances and Histories always thinking of a braver better time' (196). On the other, he is by no means immune himself from such forms of anti-colonial revenge nostalgia, as when he likens the gang to legendary Irish warriors such as the all-conquering Cuchulainn in his apocalyptic war chariot (326), or when he romantically enlists his latest recruits to a hallowed tradition of victims of British imperialism:

men who had been denied their leases for no other crime than being our friends men forced to plant wheat then ruined by the rust men mangled upon the triangle of Van Diemen's Land men with sons in gaol men who witnessed their hard won land taken up by squatters men perjured against and falsely gaoled men weary of constant impounding on & on each day without relent.

(Carey 2001: 328)

For Kelly, the superimposition of Irish folk memory onto recent Australian colonial history produces a double effect in which the fear of renewed betrayal lurks beneath the sanctioned pride of violent dissent. The contradictory desires to revisit and to purge the past are reflected in the text in a dialectical interplay between metaphors of burial/unearthing (49, 327, 352) and containment/expulsion (309). Through this interplay, a series of secret histories is temporarily brought to light only to be further suppressed. A paradigmatic example here is the buried trunk containing a dress worn by Kelly's father, which turns out to be a sign not of his effeminacy but, on the contrary, of his membership of a secret society of Irish rebels feared for their excessive use of force (17, 254).

These metaphors are reinforced by the idea of memory itself as a kind of malignant parasite, insinuating itself into the bloodstream and building its destructive force from within (12); and by the similarly embodied notion of memory as a bruise that slowly forms upon the body, providing evidence of recent affliction but also suggesting a much longer history of incubated anger now recorded on the surface of the skin (98, 309). These alternative metaphors—memory rising within the body, memory inscribed upon the body—mirror Carey's attempt to create an inner biography which gradually takes over Kelly's body, getting inside the historical character in an effort to articulate its pain, to make it speak. What is at stake here is not just a recovery of memory mapped onto the wild colonial body, but an implantation of memories designed to bring a collective history to the fore.

Thus, while Kelly prefers to envision himself as an actor in a violent history of his own making (245), he also seems to become the pathological host for malevolent forces which, nourishing themselves on his body, slowly destroy it from within. Memory, whether unconsciously absorbed or deliberately planted, is potentially lethal—literally so when the *Monitor*, the fondly remembered battleship that provides the inspiration for the gang's ludicrous armour, eventually becomes the symbol of invincibility that kills (327, 349).

It is highly ironic of course that Kelly entrusts his memoirs to the man who turns out to betray him, more ironic still that this same man painstakingly attends to the manuscript, his own personal 'keepsake of the Kelly Outrage' (4), only after its author's death. And most ironic of all is that Carey, who certainly can't be accused of not being aware of capitalizing on Kelly's legacy, seems himself to have taken on the role of a latter-day Curnow. The manuscript emerges in this context as another souvenir, perhaps the most valuable souvenir of all, from the siege at Glenrowan (350), lovingly restored by an owner who now brings back to life the very subject he himself had helped to kill.

This dialectic is maintained through the device of a fictional memoir that 'inhabits' its chosen subject. Is ventriloquism to be seen here as a related form of parasitism? Is 'speaking Kelly' to be understood as a sympathetic gesture of remembrance, or should it rather be seen as a surreptitious act of treachery and destruction? These are open questions; more certain is that Kelly's narrative, while idiosyncratic enough, is always inflected by other half-remembered narratives: the voice through which it claims to speak is never Kelly's own. Carey's strategy here is to offer a complex network of competing ventriloquisms in which the fiction of 'Kelly's voice' is projected onto other, equally fictional narrative voices, and in which the simulated memoir—the 'true history' with 'no single lie' (7) that Kelly has written for his daughter—ultimately pays tribute to neither history nor truth, but the generative mendacity of tall tales.

It seems fair to assume that for a growing number of Australians, the national narrative embodied in Kelly and, through Kelly, enshrined in the Australian Legend is embarrassingly exclusive, and that the

history of Aboriginal genocide and dispossession, increasingly institutionalized in a number of official events, museum exhibits and state
memorials, now constitutes the most important form of memory
work being undertaken in Australia today. All the same, there are
numerous signs that the folk memory associated with the Kelly gang
has made a recent comeback. Why is this? One reason might lie in
the current appeal of a variety of nation-based outlaw mythologies to
a transnational memory industry—an industry within which nostalgically rebellious figures such as Robin Hood, Jesse James, and Kelly
himself circulate as iconic representations of an oppositional history
that disguises other, probably more significant oppositional histories,
ensuring that these latter remain ignored or inadequately understood.

Another reason is the continuing usefulness of mythic narratives
like Kelly's as raw materials through which national(ist) struggles over
the uses of cultural memory can be expressed (Darian-Smith and
Hamilton 1994; Healy 1997). As ever, the crucial question is: who are
the 'we' of the nation? (Hamilton 1994: 25). Who is it exactly that
Kelly represents? And who is it that his memory has been made to
serve? It is tempting in the current postcolonial conjuncture to see
the resurgence of Kelly folklore as a form of collective repression that
shifts the problems of a rapidly changing multiethnic society back
into a romantically Celticized past. As the nation is forced to face the
pressures brought upon it by its own colonial history, so the status
of the national icon must be imaginatively reassessed. Fiction plays a
valuable role in such creative revisioning processes. Certainly, novels
like Carey's confirm the value of a sustained critical engagement
with the Kelly legend, joining it to a wider historical struggle to
counteract those nostalgia-ridden narratives of sanctified victimhood
which continue to block access to Australia's colonial past.

This struggle is also evident in novels like Kate Grenville's *Joan
Makes History* (1988), one of a number of recent feminist literary re-
imaginings of Australia that set themselves against self-aggrandizing
male accounts of the birth of the nation and the endured hardships
of the past. Published in the same year as the Australian Bicentenary,
the novel is explicitly anti-commemorative, ridiculing the 'bogus
grandeur' (Grenville 1988: 284) that attends foundational events such
as the landing of the First Fleet or the announcement of Federation,
and championing the humbler cause of those whose histories the
history books leave out (Grenville 1988: 258). Grenville's device for

this is 'ordinary Joan', a twentieth-century wife and mother of no great distinction, whose imagined lives—convict, navigator's wife, washer-woman, Aboriginal runaway, photographer—provide wry instances of histories lived against the grain, debunked, emptied out.

The novel alternates between Joan's 'real' life and these fabricated lives, challenging the boundary between them, and producing a collage of picaresque events in which differences of all kinds (social, cultural, historical) are levelled out. The operating principles for the text are bathos—'in the beginning was nothing much' (Grenville 1988: 3)—and gleeful, sometimes vengeful trivialization. 'Historic' events are exposed for the sham they are; 'discoveries' pre-empted; 'triumphs' either starkly relativized or brought rudely down to earth. Iconic figures from either side of the colonial divide (Captain Cook, Ned Kelly) are cut down to size and symbolically emasculated; inconsequential private histories—mostly female—are reinstated at public history's expense (Grenville 1988: 98).

It seems at times as if a huge grudge is being played out: against the English for their arrogance; against men for their vain pride; against History itself for its silencing of ordinary people's lives. At the centre of all this are the countless Australian women who have 'cooked dinners, washed socks and swept floors while history happened elsewhere' (Grenville 1988: 5). But the novel is too playful to be vengeful for long, and too knowing either to privilege the dull (which is often just dull) or to celebrate female achievement for its own sake. Rather, the novel recognizes that there are many different ways of making history, some more exciting but not necessarily more meaningful than others. As Joan says, after another of her imaginary escapades fizzles out into tame anti-climax, 'My history [will] reveal itself to me eventually, and I [will] have to embrace it, whatever humble form it might choose to take' (Grenville 1988: 154).

There are problems of course with this approach, not least those concerning Aboriginal history. Joan's sympathetic identification with Aborigines leads her to take on two Aboriginal roles: as a restless Aboriginal wife and mother during the time of Flinders' exploratory navigations in the late eighteenth century; and as an abused 'white boss's gin' (Grenville 1988: 171) when, during the course of the nineteenth century, developed transportation networks were finally beginning to 'open the country up' (Grenville 1988: 166). In both cases, it is clear where the narrator's sympathies lie; but in a text that multiplies the number of victim roles its narrator-protagonist takes on, these too are at risk of becoming emptied out. Joan's imagination enfolds the lives of suffering convicts and embattled settlers, as well as displaced and/or exploited Aborigines; gender becomes the 'common link' between alternative forms, and histories, of female exploitation that have nothing in common at all.

It seems best to counteract these narrative decontextualizations by recontextualizing Grenville's novel. Certainly, *Joan Makes History* makes most historical sense when read in the context of late 1980s' critiques of masculinist and/or elitist historiography, renewed resistance to a male-centred literary canon, and widespread perceptions of the Bicentenary celebrations as insulting to Aboriginal/migrant communities and, more generally, to women, reinforcing the notion of a normative white-male Australian historical subject.[4] These parallel developments were salutary at the time, galvanizing a number of valuable revisionist projects; but they also begged the question of whose revision was to be disseminated, to whom and by whom, and who had the authority to speak. *Joan Makes History* is well aware of these dilemmas, effectively de-authorizing its narrator-protagonist's narrative, even as she claims an all-encompassing authority at the beginning.as 'every woman who has ever drawn breath' (Grenville: 1988: 5) and, again at the end, as 'the entire history of the globe walking down the street' (Grenville 1988: 285).

After all, Joan counteracts the lies of others by concocting several of her own; her many lives are lies mortgaged against the continuing (self-)deceptions of Australian history, Australian literature, Australian art (Grenville 1988: 13, 39, 70, 237). In this sense, *Joan Makes History* is more an unmaking than a remaking of the Australian past, and an unmasking of its pretensions to a more equitable future. Perhaps that is why a novel that begins by making such grand claims about the transformative power of the imagination ends on such an unimaginative note, with clichéd intimations of mortality:

I am old and weary now, pushing the squeaking pram and considering my life, and what a paltry thing it is ... Soon I will be be part of the dirt, along with the other things that have had their day ... [T]his skull, that has been home to so many imagined lives, will become a receptacle for nothing more grand than another handful or two of dirt.

(Grenville 1988: 285)

If Joan has made history, the novel suggests, so have we all in our different ways—not much consolation for the dispossessed and excluded of history, who are hardly likely to be comforted by other people's re-imaginings of their past.

Grenville is less concerned in the end with the ways in which Aborigines and other excluded/marginalized groups have been written out of history than with their subsumption within dominant white male versions of history in which they are consigned to a restricted number of pre-designated roles. The text undermines this enforced roleplay by ironically restaging it, turning white male history into a series of mock-narratives of re-enactment in which the past is melodramatically replayed as both 'high' tragedy and 'low' farce. Similar tactics are adopted in Mudrooroo's 1983 novel *Doctor Wooreddy's Prescription for Enduring the Ending of the World*, which directly challenges the absorption of dying/dead Aborigines into the founding narrative of Australia as a new space of opportunity for tarnished members of a still-superior white race. The central figures here, both loosely based on nineteenth-century historical figures, are former bricklayer George Augustus Robinson, now crowned as Chief Protector of Aborigines in the new colony of Van Diemen's Land (Tasmania), and the title character Wooreddy, cast as Robinson's would-be earthly emissary, and charged with the sad task of playing out the last historical rites of a putatively dying race (Mudrooroo 1983: 134).

As its opening dedication to Bob Marley and the Rastafarian movement indirectly suggests, the novel cross-cuts between two radically opposed redemption narratives. The first of these is dependent on an erasure of the past that might allow for the dramatization of new beginnings (the revised white history of the colony), the second on a recovery of the past in which collective memory functions as a powerful cultural resource (Aboriginal retelling, in which stories of the more recent past are linked back, via the Great Ancestor, to 'known beginnings' and 'the origin of all things' (Mudrooroo 1983: 202)). Each of these narratives tries to incorporate the other: in the first case, through an evangelical rhetoric of reform that thinly disguises the reality of continuing destruction; and in the second, through a neo-Rastafarian reappropriation of the salvationist discourse of the Bible, in which historical experiences of displacement and dispossession are mythologically recoded, and indigenous rights to stolen lands and denied identities are defiantly reclaimed. The dialectic that results belies the 'ending' trope it invites the reader to consider, rejecting the metonymic connection between the death of Wooreddy and the inexorable extinction of his race.

The final paragraph of the novel is worth revisiting in this context:

Trugernanna stared towards the shore. The last male of Bruny Island was dead. There was a great hole in her which would never be filled. She tried to think of the people that might be alive at Wybalenna, but all she could see were the faces of the dead passing before their eyes. Each face passed, sunk in death and each face bore a name and once had been a living person. What was life? It seemed that all she had ever known was death. Now her husband was dead and lying in a shallow grave on that beach. She wished that she could have taken his corpse and burnt it in the proper way. Then she saw him with his *num* clothing covering his shrunken old man's body and his shaven head. No, the real Doctor Wooreddy had disappeared before they could get to him and inflict further humiliation upon him. She found herself sobbing and sought the arm of the tearful Dray. They clung to each other and let the tears roll down their cheeks as they watched the shore and the storm clouds clearing away. The yellow setting sun broke through the black clouds to streak rays of light upon the beach. It coloured the sea red. Then *Laway Larna*, the evening star, appeared in the sky as the sun sank below the horizon. Suddenly a spark of light shot up from the beach and flashed through the dark sky towards the evening star. As it did so, the clouds closed again and the world vanished.

(Mudrooroo 1983: 212–13)

The passage bitterly ironizes the white messianic rhetoric on which much of the narrative that precedes it had been founded. But in doing so, it also points to the possibility of a new beginning for Aborigines. Robinson's salvation was a fraud, his Promised Land a fetid prison, the new start he envisaged for his flock a sure means of propelling them towards their end (Mudrooroo 1983: 119, 36). He turns out to be a servant, not of God, but of a white colonial view of history, one into which the renamed Aborigines under his protection are ruthlessly absorbed (Mudrooroo 1983: 143; see also Carter 1987: 332). However, this absorption fails to clear a space for the playing out of a foundational white history. The absence Wooreddy's death creates sets the stage for a simulacral disappearance, as the world he had known vanishes temporarily behind the building clouds. But this white elegy for a dying race is overturned by the glimpse of black, red, and yellow that prefigures it: Wooreddy's death is accompanied, not by the ending of the world, but by the raising of the Aboriginal flag.

The novel thus ends by projecting history into the present and the future, as the collective vision of a continuing struggle for human freedom and indigenous land rights. At the same time, it acknowledges that the neo-historical novel—history itself—is largely a white rhetorical construct; and that, in Paul Carter's words, there are 'no [valid] grounds for presuming that aboriginal history can be treated as a subset of white history, as history within history' (Carter 1987: 325). In this sense, Doctor Wooreddy is less a counter- than an anti-historical novel, constantly struggling to de-authenticate the white historical discourses within which it is written and within whose space it is forced to co-exist (see also Johnson 1985). Its revisionism consists in gesturing towards a new beginning it can never fully articulate, a beginning which exists, somewhere beyond the confines of an assertive white history, in unoccupied space. These problems are by no means specific to Aboriginal writing. Indeed, Australian literature as a whole continues to play a significant role in challenging the white paradigms around which the idea of Australia itself is constructed—in (re-)imagining the nation, it often ends up by interrogating the category of whiteness itself.

3

Interrogating Whiteness

3.1 Whiteness and core culture

3.1.1 What is whiteness?

The last decade or so has witnessed the rapid development of a comparative cross-disciplinary scholarship on whiteness that has proved instrumental in building arguments against white supremacism, bigotry and racethinking at both local and, increasingly, transnational and global levels (see, for example, Dyer 1997; Frankenberg 1993, 1997; Hill 1997, 2003; Ware and Back 2002). The aim of this scholarship, particularly widespread in the US, has been to move beyond whiteness as a privileged racial category; its two main variants have been either to press for the abolition of whiteness as the shameful legacy of formerly segregated societies (Ignatiev 1995; Roediger 1994), or to forge more critically conscious understandings of whiteness as an empowering form of ethnic self-identity (Kincheloe *et al.* 1998). The whiteness to which these critics refer is not a given, ontological category but rather a 'normative structure, a discourse of power, and a form of [racialized] identity' (Ware and Back 2002: 13).

As a discourse of power, whiteness is less likely to be based on the perception of superiority than that of neutrality; for white people, as Richard Dyer wryly puts it, have always tended to 'colonize the definition of the normal' (qtd in Gale 2000: 271). What is striking about whiteness is, paradoxically, its degree of inconspicuousness. Whiteness is often invisible to those who continue to benefit from its privileges, while at the level of representation, 'whites are not of a certain race, they're just the human race' (Dyer 1997: 3). Similarly, white is both a colour and the absence of colour, both an assertion of ordinariness and a claim to extraordinary achievement (Dyer 1997: 223).

An extreme form that whiteness takes is, of course, supremacism, defined by Ware and Back as 'a set of beliefs, ideologies, and power structures rooted in a notion of natural, inherited, God-given superiority' (Ware and Back 2002: 5). Yet to equate whiteness with supremacism is to overlook the wide range of identitary options it offers; as Ware and Back suggest, whiteness is best understood as a 'relational [social and cultural] construct [in which its] primacy . . . is meaningful only in contrast with the qualities of other colors [and] can be rendered in different shades' (Ware and Back 2002: 5).

As a constructed category, whiteness is fundamentally unstable; its meanings alter significantly over time, and are redefined from place to place. Despite this, whiteness is routinely invoked to propagate the illusion of stability, cohesion, and homogeneity. Such appeals to commonality, now much more likely to be coded in terms of culture than in terms of race, mystify the conditions under which specific discourses of whiteness operate; they also overlook gradations and hierarchies within the register of whiteness, sometimes artful discriminations through which the category of whiteness itself may be expanded or contracted to suit particular political or ideological ends. The imagined solidarity of whiteness is thus contradicted by its conceptual instability as a racial/ethnic category, although as Dyer among others argues, the internal inconsistencies and constitutive paradoxes of whiteness usually have the effect of reinforcing, rather than weakening, its representational power (Dyer 1997: 40; see also Ignatiev 1995, Stratton 1999).

If contemporary whiteness is a discourse of power, it is also a discourse of fear, linked to the awareness of diminishing fantasies of cultural domination emerging out of the history of European imperial expansion (Hage 1998: 20). There are obvious connections between discourses of whiteness and those of imperial mastery, connections captured in that most volatile of historical fictions, the pre-eminent 'white race' (Hill 1997). As imperial authority breaks down and the discredited term 'race' is replaced with the more acceptable 'ethnicity', race increasingly becomes a signifier of culture (Stratton 1998). The fear of cultural decline, often laid at the door of unexamined globalization processes, may thus become a recodified form of post-imperial anxiety in societies which have long since given up official policies of racial discrimination, but which still remain haunted, even as they applaud themselves for their newfound commitment to interethnic tolerance and cultural pluralism, by the spectre of race (Hage 1998; see also Ang 2001, Ware and Back 2002).

One grotesque symptom of this, in keeping with Gramsci's theory of the pathologies of the interregnum,[1] is the so-called 'minoritization' of whiteness, the paranoid view that dominant white cultures are not only diminished, but are under active threat (Back 2002). Another, related symptom gives cultural form to whiteness's fear of reproductive inadequacy (Dyer 1997; McClintock 1993). The result is the anxiety that white culture may not have the capacity to regenerate itself. This anxiety, expressed at its most irrationally extreme, corresponds to the sense not just that white culture might be dying, but that it had never really existed in the first place; that whiteness might be a synonym for emptiness, signifying nothing at all (Dyer 1997: 39).

3.1.2   Legacies of White Australia

These fears arguably lurked behind the historical establishment of White Australia which, according to recent commentators such as Ien Ang and Ghassan Hage, continues to legitimate an at once 'self-empowering and self-protective parochialism' (Ang 2001: 13), a commitment to maintaining what are imagined to be the core values of an island continent 'set aside for the development of the white race' (Walker 1997: 33; see also Jayasuriya et al. 2003, Kane 1997). Whiteness emerged, it is generally agreed, in the late nineteenth century, as a function of the need to rationalize the racialized division of labour, e.g. in the tropical north (Stratton 1999). Federation then became the triumph for a particularistic, nation-based view of whiteness, as expressed in Prime Minister Alfred Deakin's affirmation of the 'desire that we [Australians] should be one people, and remain one people, without the admixture of other races' (qtd in Macintyre 1999: 142).

White Australia emerged, in Deakin's vision, as a 'reasoned policy' based on the maintenance of racial purity and aimed at securing the conditions for the 'idealized nation the Commonwealth was meant to embody' (Macintyre 1999: 143). Vital to the success of the White Australia Policy was to put an effective brake on non-European migration. This was duly implemented in the Immigration Restriction Act of 1901, which denied entrance to non-European migrants, as well as barring Aboriginal Australians from participating in the new nation's political life (Macintyre 1999). It is important to remember that the

White Australia Policy didn't designate specifically who was considered to be white, but discriminated rather on the basis of desirable and undesirable national migrant groups—a practice arguably revisited in current refugee policy. However, the most desirable of these groups—the British and the Irish—were also *de facto* the 'whitest', while the category of 'white' was expanded later to allow for the incorporation of eastern and southern Europeans into a swelling migrant workforce. European migrants were favoured because it was assumed that they shared certain core values, and that these values would facilitate their assimilation into a unitary Australian national culture (Stratton 1999: 178).

As the century wore on, the racial terminology surrounding migration patterns shifted, with the discriminatory 'Anglo-Saxon' eventually giving way to the majoritarian 'Anglo-Celtic', and 'ethnicity' coming increasingly to refer to southern and/or eastern European migrants, who occupied the discursive position of 'marginal whites' (Stratton 1999: 177). According to Jon Stratton, a twofold structure emerged through which ideologies of whiteness were maintained despite the formal abandonment of the White Australia Policy in the 1960s:

The first part of the structure [we]re the so-called real Australians who, the myth claim[ed], [we]re of British, and Irish, stock. This category provide[d] a nation-founding myth of Australia as having had a white population at Federation except for the indigenous people, the Chinese, and a few, small other groups, the Afghans, Kanakas and so forth, who ha[d] not been central to the production of the national phenotype. In this myth, the success of Anglo-Irish white Australia in excluding the indigenous people, and forcing out the Chinese, left Australia truly white and monocultural.

(Stratton 1999: 180)

The second part of the structure involved the absorption of 'ethnics' into what Stratton calls a 'white monomorality' (Stratton 1999: 181)—a shared moral order into which migrants were to be successfully inducted—consolidating the notion of the moral, rather than racial, homogeneity of the nation, and reconfirming the willingness of New Australians to subscribe to the unifying national cause. Whiteness emerged in this structure as both a management model for (white) cultural diversity and an unofficial means of keeping the moral diversity of an increasingly multicultural nation in check. Beneath the surface, race remained the language in which both of these forms of diversity were regulated, and in which 'the differentiation between

white multiculturalism and its morally distinct Other [was] expressed'
(Stratton 1999: 183).

Thus, while it has been claimed by some that the contemporary
rhetorics of multiculturalism and Asianization have mounted effective
challenges to white (Anglo-Celtic) hegemony, it remains largely true
that 'the boundaries of the [national] imagination are . . . Eurocentric,
cemented together around a core of white traditions' (Schech and
Haggis 2000: 236). The implication is that white (Anglo-)Australians
are still free to exercise different forms of race privilege, granting
themselves the right, for example, to choose between alternative
identitary options while continuing to see minority (migrant) and
Aboriginal Australians as having their racial/ethnic identities locked
in place (Moreton-Robinson 2000: 247).

Stratton's model, as he himself admits, is oversimplified. For one
thing, the White Australia Policy was not as systematic as he, and
several other contemporary critics, imagine; nor was the shared moral
order it sought to bequeath to subsequent generations of Australians
as comprehensive as policy makers would have liked. The policy also
needs to be seen within a wider, international/global context. Clearly
it wasn't unique, even if it is now almost universally regarded as
being distastefully xenophobic; to some extent, it was a sign of the
insularity of the times, and a symptom of the shared view, in Australia
and elsewhere, that national unity was all-important, especially in the
event of war (Blainey 1994: 136).

Several other settler nations—Canada, the United States, New
Zealand—were pursuing similar anti-Asian policies in the late nineteenth century; not that this condones the exclusionary attitudes
of White Australia, nor makes the policy itself 'understandable' or
'inevitable', as conservative historians like Geoffrey Blainey are keen
to have us believe (Blainey 1994: 136). It seems sensible, however, not
to treat the White Australia Policy as a purely local phenomenon,
nor to see the racism it instantiated as uniquely pernicious either
in form or in effect. Its demise, and the legacies it left, also benefit
from being seen comparatively. The dismantling of the policy, after
all, owed not just to internal reformist pressures but to the global
decolonization and emancipation movements of the 1960s. Similarly,
contemporary forms of xenophobia in the allegedly multicultural era
are not necessarily or even primarily national; as Les Back argues,
'[t]he Information Age is changing the relationship between time,

space, and form in racist culture. New territories of whiteness exceed the boundaries of the nation-state, while supplanting ethnocentric racism with new translocal forms of racial narcissism and xenophobia' (Back 2002: 132). A perception of the exceptional status of White Australia is perhaps just another form of Australian parochialism, while the undoubted negativity of many of the debates surrounding the legacies of White Australia deserves to be further discussed.

3.1.3 The core culture debate

One of the most vociferous recent critics of the negativity surrounding assertions of a racist White Australia has been the influential cultural commentator Miriam Dixson, in whose view a positively envisioned 'Anglo-Celtic core culture must continue to function as a "holding" centre for an emerging and newly diverse Australia' (Dixson 1999: 7). For Dixson, core culture gives valuable ballast to an increasingly pluralistic nation, one which has 'inherited many of the best aspects of British and Continental European traditions' (Dixson 1999: 13; see also Malouf 2003). This core culture, in keeping with the spirit of the times, is strategically deracialized; whiteness gives way instead to a colour-blind but culturally homogeneous 'Anglo-Celticism', which is seen as playing a vital 'cohesive role' in an era of increasing cultural pluralization and social fragmentation (Dixson 1999: 3).

Dixson's argument is that core culture allows diversity to flourish; but why should diversity need a core culture? And to what extent does the obvious historical fact of Australia's relative ethnic homogeneity guarantee the notion of a core culture, operating under the sign of what Dixson nostalgically calls the 'old Australia'? Dixson's stated fervour for a continuing core culture exceeds her enthusiasm to spell out what that culture actually consists of. An unexplained core culture is allowed, nonetheless, to hijack an inclusive national imaginary; conceived of at the same time as being indeterminately threatened, this originary culture is granted the authority to lament its own perceptible decline and likely eventual loss (Hage 1998).

What is this core culture? To a large extent, it seems to correspond to what Jan Larbalestier calls 'the imagined space of White Australia': 'the cultural centre from which all other ways of being in the world are evaluated, and understandings of assimilation, integration and diversity are accommodated' (Larbalestier 1999: 147). Core culture, understood this way, has as much to do with older, reactionary ways of thinking about White Australia as it does with the cultural pluralism of a newly multi-ethnic Australia—not that these two apparently contending ideologies are necessarily opposed (Hage 1998; Stratton 1999). In fact, much of Dixson's argument inadvertently rehearses the central tenets of global White Power movements: the idea of whites—especially white women—as bearers of national cultural identity; the minoritization of white culture; and the fetishization of the 'ordinary people' in whom whiteness, as a valuable set of social and cultural attributes, most appropriately rests (Dyer 1997; Roediger 1994; Ware and Back 2002).

Core culture is apparently informed by the view of ethnicity as 'a cultural collectivity of persisting resonance, one framed in terms of historical and symbolic–cultural patterns, including religion' (Dixson 1999: 56). As the inclusion of religion suggests, core culture isn't just an 'ethnic substratum which...underpins identity and community' (Dixson 1999: 55), it is also a distinctly moral entity that draws sustenance from a reservoir of allegedly shared values and beliefs (Stratton 1999). The locus of this morality is the nation, to which Dixson applies so many of the arguments she associates with core culture that it becomes quickly understood that the bearers of core culture are also the primary symbolic representatives of national life (Dixson 1999: 53). These representatives are required to hold the fort against 'the fragmenting experiences of modernity and postmodernity', with academic poststructuralism coming in a close second as a potentially destabilizing force (Dixson 1999: 159, 167).

The scenario is a depressingly familar one: for here once again is the indomitable (and indomitably anti-intellectual) spirit of the Australian Legend, writ large this time in the generous language of modern liberal–humanist/cultural–pluralist thought. In an interestingly counter-intuitive move, Dixson accuses Australian intellectuals of turning their back on modernity:

The response of Australian intellectual culture to race . . . is actually embedded in and coloured by a thumbs-down verdict on the whole modern project, in a debate in which that culture itself declines to join. The consequent self-doubt bleeds silently into our feeling about race. And beyond race into a general negativity about identity I believe is more pronounced here than in comparable countries.

(Dixson 1999: 126)

While Dixson's appeal for a more comparative approach to Australian racism is welcome, her populist insistence on counteracting the 'flat imaginary' and 'weak identity' of contemporary Australia seems like a throwback to such hoary colonial notions as the 'antipodean inferiority complex' and the late, unlamented 'cultural cringe'.[2] Anglo-Celtic ethnicity, similarly, is found to be 'potent in effect but muted in expression' (Dixson 1999: 93), weighed down by the guilty sense of historical irreparability and a self-flagellating view of Australian race relations as being 'uniquely bad' (125). Core culture steps in here as a necessary corrective, a reminder that Australia shares the strengths as well of the weaknesses of other so-called fragment societies (Canada, the US, New Zealand), all of which 'took shape around a core culture formed by Western European settlers' (63).[3]

I have dwelt too long perhaps on one particular version of core culture, but Dixson's argument has been an influential one, reappearing as it has in many, not necessarily politically compatible guises: as a renewed defence of cultural nationalism; as an apology for 'real Australians'; and, in its most paranoid form, as an effect of what Ghassan Hage has grimly called 'the Hansonization of white [Australian] culture', an overriding sense of 'cultural decline from which neo-fascism is [also] being fed' (Hage 1998: 247, 26; see also Markus 2001). It remains to be seen to what extent Australian literature has upheld these and other notions of core culture, or whether it has been more effective in challenging unitary myths of national culture and the dominant, though often fearful, white discourses within which such myths are given shape and corresponding ideas of the nation are born and bred.

3.2 Extra/ordinary whiteness

3.2.1 Ordinariness and the suburban imaginary

As Richard Dyer argues, '[w]hites are the one particular group that can take up the non-particular position of ordinariness, the position that claims to speak for and embody the commonality of humanity' (Dyer 1997: 223). The link between ordinariness and whiteness, featuring mostly as an unmarked racial category, has been explored by a number of different twentieth-century Australian writers, whose work can be seen alternately as a critique of the deadening effects of modern life—conformity, domesticity, and so on—and as a celebration of the experiential diversity of the everyday.

In much of this work, ranging from the fiction of White and Ireland to the poetry of Slessor and McAuley, there is a distinct, sometimes virulent strain of anti-suburbanism. In their most extreme form, these literary critiques comprise a contemptuous reaction to the boredom and banality of the suburbs, or a horrified recoil from the relentlessly standardizing practices of suburban or, more generally, modern life (Gerster 1990; Kirkby 1998). More usually, however, Australian literature has complicated crudely simplistic notions of suburbia as either a 'euphemism for normality' or a sanctuary for self-deluding fantasies of a 'falsely reconciled world' (McCann 1998: 56, 71). Instead, the suburb features much more ambivalently as both a real and imagined space within which the contradictions of Western industrial/capitalist modernity are negotiated; it is at once a conformist site within which everyday cultural practices are performed and regulated and a fantasized symbol of the desire for escape from 'mundane cycle[s] of work, consumerism and domesticity' into a liberated space (McCann 1998: vii).

The Australian writer who stands out most for his double-edged literary explorations of suburbia is the contemporary poet Bruce Dawe, whose suburban poems are good examples of his self-declared attempt to 'celebrat[e] the commonplace without merely rephrasing existing stereotypes' (qtd in Kuch 1995: 81). As befits the title of one of his poems ('Contrarieties': see Dawe 1995: 7), there are numerous contrary selves co-existing in Dawe's poetry: at different times, sometimes simultaneously, he plays the part of the undogmatic moralist, the sentimental pragmatist, the *faux naif.* These various selves come together in his suburban poems, which offer glimpses of the hidden depths lying beneath ordinary gestures, events, and people; poetry can help bring these to the surface, even if they can't always be properly expressed. What results, to some degree, is a wry celebration of the inarticulate, touched with more than a hint of the 'romantic fatalism' often seen as characterizing Dawe's verse (Kirkby 1998: 18).

A touchstone poem here, from the collection *Beyond the Subdivisions* (1969), is 'Homo Suburbiensis', which offers '[o]ne constant in a world of variables / —a man alone in the evening in his patch of vegetables, / and all the things he takes down with him there' (Dawe 1969: 96). This solitary man, 'lost in a green / confusion, smelling the smoke of someone's rubbish', seems both directionless and aimless, unsure of himself and removed from the day-to-day realities of social life. Yet, in a characteristic twist, Dawe suggests that the apparently empty space this man's life occupies is actually filled with vital presence; what the man provides is '[n]ot much but as much as any man can offer / —time, pain, love, hate, age, war, death, laughter, fever' (Dawe 1969: 96). Suburbia features here both as attenuated site and as comforting repository of the unexceptional; it is revealed at the same time as hopelessly inadequate and constricting and as a surprisingly capacious forum for the diverse routines and rituals of everyday life.

A similarly double-sided view of the ordinary is provided by Australia's most technically accomplished contemporary poet, Les Murray, whose wide range of poetry is incorporated into what he calls a 'vernacular republic', accented by the repeated actions and readily identifiable speech rhythms of 'common life' (Murray 1984). Although the scope of Murray's poetry is greater than Dawe's, and the setting for many of his poems is rural rather than (sub)urban, there are similarities of vision. Both poets are aware of the 'sacramental nature of everyday life' (Kuch 1995: 81), which lends a quasi-religious quality to their poetry. Both are also concerned with the various means by which the everyday can be transformed and defamiliarized; and by which ordinary experience can be transfigured into extraordinary patterns of insight and perception, allowing for a (re)discovery of complex modern elements within the apparently 'simple' and 'traditional', as well as an almost mystical apprehension of ancient, sometimes arcane traditions buried beneath the surface structures of modern working life (see, for example, poems such as Murray's 'The Milk Lorry' or the myth-saturated 'Walking to the Cattle Place': Murray 1998: 253–4, 55–77). Both poets, finally, articulate a vision of Australia that is largely though by no means exclusively white, male, working-class. In Murray's case, whiteness is the unacknowledged marker of an amalgamated pre-Athenian civilization which incorporates elements drawn from Greek, Christian, Celtic, and Aboriginal Australian spiritual/material traditions, strongly aligning these 'with a deep belief in the abiding and traditional virtues of rural life' (Taylor 1987: 141).

This civilization, which Murray suggests is best seen in terms of a merging of Aboriginal spirituality and Celtic Boeotianism, is rural, traditional-minded, family-oriented, and conscious of the value of rootedness and the sacredness of place (Murray 1984; see also

Taylor 1987). However, in spite or, perhaps better, because of the 'black [Aboriginal] thread' (Murray 1984: 27) he sees as running through his poetry, Murray's poetic vision belongs to a longstanding tradition of redemptive European primitivism in which the attempted convergence between 'black' and 'white' cultural sensibilities is instrumentalized for a variety of white aesthetic and ideological ends (Goldie 1989; Torgovnick 1990). Aborigines are co-opted to the cause of poor-white, rural Australians, victims both—in Murray's eyes—of the urban-liberal prejudices of the present and the colonialist high-handedness of the past (Murray 1984: 5).

Murray's position is made clear in his astonishing 1994 attack on the 'political correctness' of the Australia Council. 'The ruling elite of Australia', he fulminates,

are excluding people like me from their Australia—the country people, the rednecks, the Anglo-Celts, the farming people—they have turned their backs on us . . . They denigrate the majority of Australians who are born in this country, those that have mainly British ancestry . . . We Old Australians, not necessarily Anglo but having no other country but this one, are now mostly silenced between the indigenous and the multicultural.

(qtd in Vasta and Castles 1996: 571)

While this position, as one might expect, is complicated in Murray's poetry, it helps explain the bitterness of satirical poems like 'A Brief History': 'Our one culture paints Dreamings, each a beautiful claim. / Far more numerous are the unspeakable Whites, / the only cause of all earthly plights, / immigrant natives without immigrant rights. / Unmixed with these are Ethnics, absolved of all blame.' (Murray 1996: 11). Poems such as this are more, of course, than simple mission statements, and the depth and range of Murray's poetry endorses his horror of all 'isms' and his distaste for fashionable jargon and political cant. All the same, they provide insight into the contingent connections in Murray's work between racism, sexism, and nationalism, the 'claimed privilege[s] of ordinary whiteness' (Gale 2000: 265), and the anxieties surrounding the perception of a destabilized Anglo-Australian core culture, articulated as a fanfare for the common (white) man.

These themes are also taken up in a wide range of twentieth-century Australian drama, as in the work of Australia's most popular playwright David Williamson, whose plays have been seen as 'a battle between New Australia and Old Australia for the heart, mind and body of the next generation' (Harrison 1995: x). Like Murray, Williamson has little time for the blandishments of what he sees as a tyrannical 'political correctness enforced on [contemporary Australian] society by the "holy" ideologies of post-structuralism, radical feminism and multiculturalism' (Williamson 1995: ix). Instead, he has done much to popularize the 'aggressive vernacular' of the so-called Ocker Aussie: normatively white, relatively uncultivated but ambitious and self-confident, often fiercely nationalistic (Carroll 1995: 220; see also Harris 1974). However, Williamson's plays are as likely to be critical as celebratory of the stock figure of the Ocker, and his satire homes in on a wide variety of social and political targets: abuses of authority; the frailties of mateship; the hypocrisies and entanglements of working- and middle-class family romance.

These elements come together in one of Williamson's most controversial plays, *Dead White Males* (1995), a vitriolic satire on the excesses of academic poststructuralism, focusing on the literary and cultural wars surrounding Shakespeare and his work. The play relentlessly mocks its main character, the predatory university professor Swain, who contends self-righteously that 'the masterpieces of liberal humanist literature have been [complicit] in the process of depriving women, people of colour, people of non normative sexual orientation, and people of the non industrialised world, of power' (Williamson 1995: 3).

For Swain, the study of literature isn't about the accumulation of wisdom, but rather the acquisition and maintenance of power —mostly his own. He cuts short or mocks those who don't share his views on the privileging of 'white middle class anglo celtic males' (Williamson 1995: 7), while using 'slimy sophistry' (Williamson 1995: 4) to justify his lustful pursuit of one of his brightest students, Angela, who is duped into reproducing his clichéd 'multiculturalist' agenda: 'I am so happy to be able to make the choice to step outside the narcissistic self-centredness of liberal humanism and as a conscious *choice* join you in the constructivist feminist multiculturalist project' (37; Williamson's italics).

Over and against this milksop rhetoric Williamson counterposes a hard male world of survivalist confrontation, in which men *are* warriors and women *are* nurturers, and aren't simply 'constructed' as such (73, 82). The blatant racism, sexism, and homophobia of Williamson's most 'sympathetic' characters (Angela's rambunctious grandfather Col, her eager fellow-student Steve) are thus tacitly endorsed as they become embodiments of 'ordinary', 'common-sensical' attitudes in a play whose anti-intellectualism is hardly rescued by self-mockery, and whose unabashed conservatism underpins its shrill attack on the moral self-satisfaction of academia and the gender confusions produced by (pseudo-)liberal self-love.

Williamson's wry analysis of the homespun virtues of the 'ordinary Australian' harks back to the equally influential work of Ray Lawler, whose 1955 play *Summer of the Seventeenth Doll* is sometimes seen as Australia's only dramatic classic, 'the masterpiece against which all other theatrical attempts to interpret universal truths in terms of specifically Australian situations must be judged' (Jillett 1977, qtd in Fitzpatrick 1979: 19). Like several of Williamson's plays, *Summer of the Seventeenth Doll* explores white Australian masculinity in crisis. Lawler's larger-than-life protagonists Barney and Roo, seasonal cane-cutters from Queensland down south for the annual five-month lay-off, are presented as living on borrowed time and trading off increasingly anachronistic bush myths. Barney has already lost 'his' girl, while Roo's physical pre-eminence is successfully challenged by a younger, fitter fellow. While the two men—especially Roo—are treated with affection, the play pokes fun at their post-adolescent aptitude for turning themselves into victims of the circumstances they themselves have helped create.

The play's self-destructive rehearsal of white-masculinist bush stereotypes confirms the exhaustion of the Australian Legend that some critics—unaccountably—see as being upheld (see, for example, Fitzpatrick 1979). The seasonal cycle provides only illusions of regeneration and replenishment, while—again as in Williamson's work—a scarcely controlled violence underlies the surface of domestic harmony and back-slapping bonhomie (Lawler 1957: 50, 127–8). The play rapidly turns into an exhibition of white male (and, to a lesser extent, white female) vulnerability, in which the rituals of mateship offer only temporary cover, and alcohol, in particular, operates as destructive catalyst and false personal/social panacea. In sum, Lawler's play presents a powerful challenge both to outdated mythologies of rural white Australia and to the fictions of civility that uphold its (sub)urban counterpart, as the breast-beating machismo of the former and the cultivated respectability of the latter are exposed as little more than tawdry sham.

3.2.2 White death

Whiteness suffers both from its associations with banality and inadequacy and from its tendency to overreach itself, raising ordinary action to the level of extraordinary art. At its most extreme, whiteness becomes the colour of suffering itself, as articulated through the mock-heroic figure of the white (male) failure, even if this figure—a common one throughout the history of Australian literature—is simultaneously held up to critique (Bliss 1986; Kane 1998). Failure has both a small and a capital 'f', alternately mocking the pretensions of the irremediably small-minded and deflating the heroics of the would-be visionary: the great man, leader, chief. White failure, in this last sense, is the gendered effect of absolute white power confronting its own inevitable limits; its correlative is the impulse to destruction, as captured at its most extreme in the double-edged trope of 'white death' (Dyer 1997). White death is double-edged in so far as whiteness contains within it the capacity for both victimage and agency: death suffered, but also death inflicted; the helpless emptying out of one's own life, but also the wilful extinction of lives other than one's own (Dyer 1997: 209).

To some extent, the spectral figure of white death is a by-product of the worst excesses of a twentieth-century modernity haunted by barbarisms practised in the name of a 'superior' civilization, and by genocides predestined to secure the lasting supremacy of a 'master race'. To say that much post-war literature in the West—and not just the West—emerged out of Hitler's shadow might be too obvious to mention, but it certainly reminds us that many of these writers were actively engaged in an international struggle against modernity's contradictions, a struggle that narrowly nationalistic approaches to literature, Australia's included, have been reluctant to address. Whatever the case, the two World Wars had more effect on the development of a modern Australian literature than any of the national events of the twentieth century although, as in other Western countries, it remains moot whether modernism itself was a response to or a reaction against the experienced immensities of global transformation and social/cultural change.

As Fredric Jameson among others has argued, literary modernism is inextricably entangled with the material struggles of colonialism (Jameson 1990; see also Said 1993). Evidence of this entanglement is ample in Australian literature, as in other postcolonial literatures.

The aesthetic properties of modernism often carry connotations of metropolitan cultural elitism. Such self-privileging 'white mythologies', as Robert Young in a different context calls them (Young 1990), are vigorously challenged in the work of modern Australian poets like A. D. Hope, Judith Wright and James McAuley, as well as in the experimental fiction of writers like Randolph Stow, Patrick White, and Christina Stead.

I shall restrict myself here to a closer analysis of two prominent novelistic examples of literary modernism, White's *Voss* (1957) and Stead's *The Man Who Loved Children* (1941). Both are canonical works by canonical writers, although the fluctuating fortunes that accompany the literary politics of recognition have seen both writers fall more recently from favour, if not necessarily from grace. White and Stead, at first glance, seem a most unlikely pairing. The former is generally considered to be a 'metaphysical' writer—as Simon During calls him, a 'late-colonial transcendentalist' (During 1996: 17)—with decidedly misogynistic tendencies; the latter to be a feminist realist, albeit one with an idiosyncratically romantic/symbolic/mythic bent.

However, the distinction, like that between Australian 'metaphysicals' and 'realists' in general, is as tendentious as it is tenuous.[4] White and Stead have much in common. Both writers spent substantial periods of their lives abroad, and were well attuned to international aesthetic and political movements. (Like her predecessor Henry Handel Richardson, Stead is primarily thought of as an expatriate writer, although perhaps Ann Blake's term 'transnational writer' is more appropriate given Stead's congenital restlessness and her multiple, often conflicting attachments to place (Blake 1999).) Both had contemplated Nietzsche, that quintessential philosopher of modernity, and had probably read too much Freud and, especially, Jung for their own good.

Not least, both shared a displaced European modernist sensibility. This manifests itself in the heightened self-consciousness, at times the Gothic extravagance, of their work, which makes good use of what T. S. Eliot called 'the mythical method' (Eliot 1975: 177); in their situated engagement with many of the stock dilemmas of modernity (bourgeois materialism, spiritual emptiness, estrangement, the repressed violence of everyday domestic and social life); and in their ambivalent search to transcend the constraints of 'ordinary' life, either by radically defamiliarizing it or by pushing beyond the boundaries of the known to alternative territories of consciousness, often acceded to via experimental forms of verbal/visual performance: writing, theatre, music, art. Yet if both writers are withering in their onslaught on ordinariness, what White savagely called 'the exaltation of the "average" ' (White 1994: 270), they are equally harsh on its extraordinary counterpart—the felt conviction of individual greatness, and the willed subjection of the perceptibly weak to the demonstrably strong.

Voss and *The Man Who Loved Children* emerge here as hallucinatory studies of the devastating effects of white (male) monomania: on the family unit, on society at large, and on the fractured individual who, driven by barely controlled compulsions, allows these to legitimize his twisted impulses to domination and destruction. The German explorer Voss, in White's novel, and the American family patriarch Sam Pollitt, in Stead's, have both been seen with some justification as Hitler figures (Brydon 1987; During 1996). Certainly, both White and Stead had publicly recoiled from the atrocities of German Nazism, and had been explicit in their acknowledgement of its baleful influence on their work. Both were also incensed by the violence brought about by residual colonial/imperial authoritarianism, an attitude satirized in the grotesque—simultaneously ridiculous and terrifying—figures of the nineteenth-century explorer Voss, intent on willing an entire country into existence (' "The map? . . . I will first make it." '—White 1958 [1957]: 26); and the twentieth-century conservationist Sam Pollitt, whose experiences with the Smithsonian in Malaya cast him as a latter-day Livingstone, penetrating 'into the heart of the darkest unknown' (Stead 1966 [1941]: 225).

In both cases, colonialism/imperialism and Nazism coalesce in the absolute figure of pure whiteness. For Voss, 'standing in the glare of his own brilliant desert' (White 1958: 96), whiteness is an emanation of pure will, a confirmation of the greatness of his own European philosophical inheritance, even if that inheritance later becomes the altar on which he sacrifices himself to ensure that his story passes into self-glorifying myth (White 1958: 182, 475). Whiteness is duly sanctified, not by achievement but by an allegorical instance of radiant failure in which European Man, stripped of his pretensions to godhead, is metaphorically 'decapitated' in order that he might return after all, redeemed, to God (White 1958: 411).

For Sam Pollitt, similarly, whiteness functions both as a principle of perfectibility and as an agent of destruction. The two come together in his deadly fascination for eugenics, which holds out the promise of universal brotherhood, but only at the cost of weeding out perceived 'degenerates' and 'misfits', the operating principle being that whoever/whatever doesn't fit into the system must be summarily destroyed (Stead 1966: 49–50). It is the brutal logic of eugenics, rather than patriarchal family dynamics, that provides the ideological underpinnings to Stead's novel, although the one certainly informs the other, as 'free-thinking' Sam, entertaining his beloved children on a diet of racist/sexist innuendo, draws them inexorably into a noxious conspiracy that enslaves them as well as his browbeaten, increasingly suicidal wife.

For Sam, whiteness is originary, both superior and primary; as he tells his Indian secretary in Malaya, 'even the very darkest [races] are descended from whitish or pale people like the ancient Persians. The Chinese are almost white, too, for the most part. The black man is rather rare. Do you really think . . . that primitive man was black? Do you think he was black and got white?' (Stead 1966: 219). Sam's derision makes a mockery of his philanthropic aim 'to penetrate into the hearts of dark, yellow, red, tawny and tattooed man', and to bring them all together 'into a world fellowship, in which all differences of nationality, creed, or education will be respected and gradually smoothed out' (Stead 1966: 49).

This is protection by destruction, a motto that also underlies White's colonial allegory of redemption, in which Aborigines are consigned to play a bit-part as comic witnesses or shadowy antagonists in a mock-drama of white torment and sacrificial self-love. They may not be killed off, but then they don't need to be, since separate existence is withheld from them. In keeping with the conventions of European primitivist aesthetics, the Aboriginal world exists in parallel to the white man's world and is a function of it; not that this makes the novel racist, or condones the white-supremacist ideologies that drive it, but it is still apparent that White is a prisoner of the very white-settler mythologies his novel ostensibly debunks.

The point is well made by Simon During, who situates White's work at the cusp of an emergent postcolonialism in Australia, a postcolonialism towards whose alternative view of the history of national race relations it symbolically gestures but, bound up as it is by the prejudices of its time, it cannot quite bring itself to endorse. For During, this helps explain, not only the ambiguities of White's work, but also those of the so-called 'metaphysical ascendancy' that arguably characterized Australian fiction and, to a lesser extent, poetry at around mid-century (Docker 1984). The metaphysical ascendancy, argues During, was in part a nationalist attempt to counteract the negative European stereotypes of antipodean 'emptiness' and 'ugliness' by filling them with local, historical meaning. However, this attempt was itself indebted to European ontologies:

Invoking the universal tragedy of the human condition (a classic Eurocentric theme) was ... seductive locally because it expressed the travails and horrors of white settlement while simultaneously concealing them ... The break with realism ... happened not as a turn to explicit postcolonialism but as an internationalism whose tragic orientation predated modernism and whose most articulate recent instance [surrealist apocalypticism] was developed in pre-war France.

(During 1996: 18)

Objections might be raised here to the notion that experimental novels like White's represented a radical departure from the dominant conventions of social realism, a break belied by the enduring popularity of realist fiction in Australia throughout the twentieth century and right up to the present day. Similarly, the notion of a 'postcolonial turn' in Australia/Australian literature that 'marks a switch from colonialist to postcolonial cultural politics' (During 1996: 15–16) seems unduly oversimplified, even if it helps explain some of the more reactionary impulses behind White's canonization in the 1960s and 1970s, as well as the rather more muted appreciation of his work today.

All the same, During's historicization of White's work, and of the formidable cultural mythologies that came to surround it, usefully suggests the faultlines running through ostensibly progressive, anti-colonial modes of twentieth-century 'white writing' (Coetzee 1988) that remain uncannily beholden to the colonialist sympathies and prejudices they otherwise seek to uncover and contest. Hence the paradox that white failure, however abject, can work towards evoking European colonialist nostalgia, a paradox at its most apparent when that failure is made to assume mock-purgatorial dimensions: 'Perhaps true knowledge only comes of death by torture in the country of the mind' (White 1958: 475).

And hence the lasting fascination with the victimized corpse of the defeated white-male colonial explorer, whose sanctified remains lie scattered across an improbably large number of Australian novels, stories, poems, and plays. In Australian literature, nothing becomes the explorer in his life like the leaving it, even if the death-of-the-explorer theme has long since become fodder for parody, as in a number of works, like Peter Carey's *Oscar and Lucinda* (1988), where its delusions are no sooner melodramatically displayed than they are viciously debunked. Australian exploration literature, however, doesn't need fashionable postmodernism to deflate it, as attested in numerous self-parodic homages to white European explorers and navigators: from Kenneth Slessor's 'Five Visions of Captain Cook' (1932) to James McAuley's 'Captain Quiros' (1964); from Douglas Stewart's 'Worsley Enchanted' (1952) to Francis Webb's 'Eyre All Alone' (1961).

Narrative poems such as these are as likely to be self-doubting as celebratory; they are either disabused of the visionary mysticism that initially inspires them or quietly uncertain about the potential of present memory to recapture the imagined heroics of the past. They may not challenge whiteness or the ideologies it embodies explicitly, but they do suggest that the extraordinariness of figures like Eyre, or Cook, or Worsley is at least in part a function of the collective race privilege they exercised in pursuit of their individual ends. And of the race privilege exercised, as well, by their legion of white (historical) followers and (literary) commemorators. For, returning once more to *Voss*, white death is a sure sign of the desire for white regeneration; and disembodied whiteness—the transmutation of the body after death into pure spirit—a sure sign of the desire for continuing white control (Dyer 1997: 24–5; see also White 1958: 472).

3.3 Shades of white

3.3.1 Reconfiguring the bastard complex

For Richard Dyer, 'concepts of race are [first and foremost] concepts of different bodies' (Dyer 1997: 24). What allows white supremacists to think of themselves as different is their felt 'closeness to the pure spirit that was made flesh in Jesus' (Dyer 1997: 25)—a spirit made apparent in their imagined mastery over their own and other people's bodies, and in their belief in the potential 'to transcend their raced bodies', a potential conspicuously withheld from members of all but the chosen 'master race' (Dyer 1997: 25). However, the potential to transcend the white raced body is also contingent on the ability to protect it, to guard it from contamination by other, 'alien' bodies, and from infiltration by members of another, 'lesser' race.

The most obvious instance of anxiety over the policing of the white body is the discourse of *miscegenation*, in which the living proof of an 'illicit' mixing of different races becomes a shifting ideological mechanism through which the fiction of 'race' itself is socially tested and strategically remade (Lemire 2002; Sollors 1997). Miscegenation discourses are as much about desire as about fear, clinching the link between whiteness and sexual race preference (Lemire 2002). In this, as in other respects, they are relentlessly doubled; posing a symbolic threat but also a material opportunity, miscegenation effectively demonstrates both the 'ambivalent driving desire at the heart of racialism' and the deep entanglement of colonialism in the machinery of sexual and economic—sexual *as* economic—transaction and exchange (Young 1995: 181).

The negative term 'miscegenation' has long since been replaced by its more positive equivalent, 'hybridization'. But both of these terms remain closely tied to colonial histories of racial violence and exploitation, even if the latter, now arguably rescued from its earlier, race-tainted connotations ('half-breed', 'half-caste', etc.), is now more likely to prompt 'questions about the ways in which contemporary thinking has broken . . . with the racialized formulations of the past' (Young 1995: 6). The break is perhaps not as absolute as several postcolonial theorists, notably Robert Young, like to imagine. But Young is honest enough to note that hybridity, for all its utopian potential, has not entirely lost its negative capacity to signal the disruption of a dominant society, even if he would no doubt shudder to compare this to such falsely 'genetic' processes as the dilution or degeneration of a putatively superior race (Young 1995: 24; see also Brah and Coombes 2000).

Notwithstanding, cultural discourses of hybridity, like biological discourses of miscegenation, are historically conditioned, and vary widely in their range of institutional and material effects. Miscegenation discourses, in particular, invite a whole host of invidious cross-cultural distinctions, e.g. between the 'indelibility' of black blood, as enshrined in the American 'one-drop' rule, and the 'dilutability' of red/indigenous blood, suggesting its amenability for absorption into a dominant white stock (Wolfe 1994). These of course are ideological, not biological notions closely linked to discrepant colonial histories of dispossession and enslavement, although a comparative treatment of these histories can certainly help bring their material specificities into relief. Such discourses are likely to be phrased and gauged quite differently depending on whether their primary material objective is the expropriation of land or the exploitation of labour (Wolfe 1994). But they are nearly always shadowed by the stigma of colonial racial deviance, indicating that race 'is defined not by its purity, but rather by the impurity conferred upon it by a system of domination. Bastard and mixed-blood are the true names of race' (Deleuze and Guattari 1987: 379, also qtd in Young 1995: 180).

In postcolonial Australia, the remnant figure of the 'bastard'—the child of mixed race—serves as a living reminder that the nation's assimilationist/eliminationist racial policies have been unsuccessful in diluting or eradicating the traces of Aboriginal blood. This figure has discernible links to specific genocidal policies in Australia. But it also belongs to a larger structure of national illegitimacy—one which reconfirms that colonial racism is 'unfinished business' (Hage 1998, qtd in Hodge and Mishra 1990: 23); that no treaty has yet been signed; and that the word 'Aborigine' itself implies a tacit recognition of prior rights (Hodge and Mishra 1990: 23–4).

This structure of illegitimacy, centring on the unresolved issue of stolen land, is referred to by Hodge and Mishra as 'the bastard complex', and it has wide ramifications for all kinds of Australian literary and cultural production, in the nominally postcolonial present as well as in the documented colonial past (Hodge and Mishra 1990). For Hodge and Mishra, the bastard complex is precisely *not* a confrontation of indigenous entitlement; rather, it is a strategy of avoidance and displacement that allows 'shared illegitimacy' to be affirmed 'in order to evade a [continuing] anxiety about origins', and that masks the 'symbolic management of Aborigines' by claiming to respect indigenous territorial rights (Hodge and Mishra 1990: 25–6). The bastard complex, like the discourse of whiteness to which it belongs, has both self-exonerating and incriminating aspects. It lies behind the self-given 'right of the (white) founding fathers to beget bastards without responsibility', enlivening the myth of Aboriginal sexual availability; and behind the eliminationist notion that the mixed-race child must be protected in order to be destroyed, anchoring the myth of Aborigines as a 'dying race' (Hodge and Mishra 1990: 37, 44).

These myths are critically dissected in two landmark literary works in the history of white-Aboriginal relations, Katharine Susannah Prichard's *Coonardoo* (1929) and Xavier Herbert's *Capricornia* (1938). The two novels are usually read as passionate attacks on exploitative patterns of Aboriginal socialization or, in Prichard's case especially, as sympathetically observed if self-consciously over-romanticized portraits of Aboriginal cultural life (see, for example, Hodge and Mishra 1990; Lever 1993; Sheridan 1995). These two readings are linked, or rather locked, in a violent relationship of mutual contradiction encapsulated in the troubled figure of the 'half-caste', whose potential to fashion a new mixed race in postcolonial Australia is symbolically foreclosed (Mudrooroo 2002 [1990]).

The novels thus explore, in different ways, the impossible desire to create a new interracial dispensation, an alternative to the tainted world of White Australia. This impossibility is *material*, signalling the unchallenged reign of a white ideology of domestic control and property ownership, but also *aesthetic*, suggesting the inadequacy of accounting for the social and cultural specificities of Aborigines by using modified white-European representational codes (Lever 1993: 24–5). In fact, both novels indicate that continuing white control over Aborigines is material *and* symbolic, as the Jungian/Lawrentian undertones of Prichard's novel and the Melvillean/Stevensonian overkill of Herbert's, both of which might be seen as practising variations on Hodge and Mishra's 'Aboriginalism', implictly attest (see Hodge and Mishra 1990).

This view supports a tragic or fatalist reading of the novels, for which there is certainly abundant evidence (Morse 1988; Mudrooroo 1990). As Ruth Morse suggests, novels such as *Coonardoo* and *Capricornia* are inherently contradictory, weighing the 'demand that the races blend, [which] seems to be an impossible necessity . . . [against] the wish for that other impossibility, that they remain separate but equal' (Morse 1988: 96). A parallel reading suggests, however, that both novels kick—with however little effect—against their own fatalistic tendencies; and that both provide a metaracist critique, mediated through the ambivalent figure of the 'half-caste', of the white desire to claim and control an Aboriginal point of view.

Perhaps 'mediated' is the wrong word to use for characters such as Prichard's Coonardoo and Herbert's Nawnim/Norman. For in so far as both are bound by the ideological terms of the bastard complex, they are actively *prevented* from mediating between 'black' and 'white' symbolic universes, and are obliged instead to fulfil a series of pre-designated functions whose terms are largely dictated by the white 'masters of mankind' (Herbert 2002 [1938]: 504). In *Coonardoo*, the idea of Coonardoo as a Jungian 'shadow soul' or symbolic partner to the station-owner Hugh Watt belongs to the ideology of displaced white-colonial mastery that the station represents to him (Prichard 2002 [1929]: 74). Sentimentality and brutality are the alternating faces of this ideology; is it the submissive Coonardoo, or rather the predatory Sam Geary, who is better fitted for the role of Hugh's symbolic twin?

This secondary alliance is supported by the symbolic interplay between Classical (Hugh) and Old Testament (Sam) mythologies. The former draws on the idealized heritage of the noble savage; the latter looks back to a patriarchal genealogy that legitimates the sexual subordination of the black woman as concubine, servant, wife. These turn out however to be related, not incommensurable symbolic legacies, both of which are used to justify sexual opportunism and domestic exploitation (Prichard 2002: 121, 235). There is thus a paradoxical sense in which the novel's symbolic regime of reconciliation—obviously primitivist in inspiration—complements rather than counteracts its material regime of social hierarchy and division, a pattern confirmed in the appropriation of Aboriginal lore by Hugh's mother Mumae, which invokes white mastery of the symbolic, as well as the material realm (Prichard 2002: 96–7).

In *Capricornia*, similarly, few alternatives can be found to the discourse of white mastery. Savage irony undercuts, but also underscores, this discourse throughout the novel. The inhabitants of Capricornia—a thinly disguised version of the post-Federation Northern Territory—are a motley bunch of small-time crooks and big-time blunderers, blaming their incompetence and loose morals on the 'depraving influence of the Wet' (Herbert 2002: 400). It is as if natural selection had chosen the site to produce a particularly unedifying cross-section of humanity, none more unedifying than Krater, the monstrous embodiment of Fatal Contact with whose legendary brutalities the novel's ironic staging of the war between 'Stone-Age Man and Anglo-Saxon' begins (Herbert 2002: 44).

Krater and his men initially charm the local Yurracumbungas, who take them not for 'the brown-men who used to come upon them from the North', but rather for *bona fide* 'supermen who had come to stay and rule' (Herbert 2002: 4). Needless to say, this originary tryst ends in appalling violence and destruction, leaving behind the remnants of its more amorous entanglements—the latter-day white 'combo' and his black 'lubra', together with the 'half-caste' who provides unwanted evidence of their union, and who is constituted as a menace to white ascendancy in a region where 'the half-caste population was easily three times greater than the white' (Herbert 2002: 27).

Herbert's novel deploys the conventions of the yarn to display a fierce contempt for the misplaced nationalism of 'Australia Felix' (Herbert 2002: 59), projected here onto a forgotten backwater in which third-raters pose with pride as the country's 'true Australians', and the white-male boast of radical egalitarianism dumbs down an already dim-witted population while naturalizing a system of flagrant racial injustice and abuse (Herbert 2002: 376, 470). Within this system, the maligned figure of the 'half-caste' can at best become white, if he or she is skilful enough at racial 'passing' (Fabi 2001; Sollors 1997), but is at worst 'neither black nor white, a drifting nothing' (Herbert 2002: 96), consigned to routine abuse and the strong likelihood of an early death. Norman, abandoned son of good-for-nothing adventurer and acquitted murderer Mark Shillingsworth, is thus guaranteed some measure of civilized (i.e., white) existence only if he continues to forswear his racial origins, internalizing the epithets that were previously used against him and applying them to other 'half-castes' in his turn (Herbert 2002: 291–2, 300).

In a novel in which the idea of Aboriginal pride is treated as a joke and the exchange of racial insults becomes further cause for throwaway humour, it is hardly surprising that those who do most to challenge the dominant white order should meet a variety of less than dignified ends. Hence cruel deaths are meted out to the novel's most enlightened (or, shall we say, least hypocritical) racial pedagogue, Peter Differ; and to 'half-caste' Tocky, whose suicide not only robs Norman of the wife and child he had always coveted but also appears to foreclose on the possibility of an alternative racial future (Mudrooroo 2002 [1990]: ix). Those who help or care are marked out to die or suffer, as is also the case with Coonardoo who, sacrificed in a kind of ritual punishment for the socially impossible, is impaled on the contradictions of Hugh's self-serving desire to 'see and think black' in a social environment where it would have been much wiser to 'marry white and stick white' (Prichard 2002: 153, 56).

The enactment of this rite makes a mockery of the novel's symbolism of reconciliation:

White cockies were settling to roost in the big gum-tree beside the house. Mumae was there, Coonardoo told herself. Mumae would see her and know that she, Coonardoo, had done as Mumae bade her for Youie [Hugh]. She had looked after and obeyed Youie, although in some way she had displeased him so; brought down the torrent of his anger upon herself... Little feet of the kangaroos were doing their devil dance in the twilight. Coonardoo's voice fluttered out; embers of her fire were burning low. Crouched over them, a daze held her. From that dreamy and soothing nothingness Coonardoo started suddenly. The fire before her had fallen into ashes. Blackened sticks lay without a spark.... She crooned a moment, and lay back. Her legs and arms, falling apart, looked like those blackened and broken sticks beside the fire.

(Prichard 2002: 247)

The return of the white cockies (cockatoos) takes us back to the moment in the text when Mumae's death is seen to unleash a curse on the community, a curse associated with the legend that 'white cockies were once blackfellows', and are now celebrated by local Aborigines in a corroboree held in the creatures' name (Prichard 2002: 22). This might be seen as evidence of the indigenization of white-settler mythology; the novel suggests that it is more likely the reverse. Aboriginal characters in white-settler novels are often seconded for the task of cultural haunting (Gelder and Jacobs 1998; Goldie 1989). Here, however, it is the hybrid figure of Mumae—the resolute white overseer with the respectful subaltern moniker—whose ghost affirms an originary white presence in the novel, suggesting that its various boundary-challenging alternatives (Coonardoo as fair-haired Aborigine, Hugh's 'manly' daughter Phyllis, etc.) are contained, in the end, by white representational and legislative codes. Hybridity is manipulated in the interests of consolidating whiteness; it masks the potentially threatening racial/sexual differences whiteness seeks, largely successfully, to control. In this context, Mumae's position as the false friend who dominates the Aborigines she forces to respect her is perhaps not so different from that of the various benevolent racists in Herbert's novel, including the self-incriminatingly named Andy McRandy, the shameless 'combo' who is enthused by the idea of

Aboriginal citizenship, but also by the idea that Aboriginality should eventually be 'bred out' (Herbert 2002: 373).

Coonardoo and *Capricornia*, both novels ahead of their time, both motivated by a keen sense of racial injustice in post-Federation Australia, are thus themselves haunted by a problem for which there is no ready answer. The problem is not, as some might see it, how to turn the prohibitionary rhetoric of 'miscegenation' into the permissive possibilities of 'hybridity'. It is rather that hybridity itself is an inadequate mechanism for counteracting a white-colonial racial imaginary; indeed, hybridity might well be seen as a part of the very white-colonial racial imaginary it is often called upon to dissolve (Brah and Coombes 2000; Young 1995).

This problem, integral to the dilemma of postcoloniality, can also be seen in the contradictions of contemporary reconciliatory multi-culturalism. For Prichard and Herbert, writing in the 1920s and 1930s, hybridity was a front for—if also an affront to—a still dominant White Australia; whether this remains the case today is, for many, unresolved (for alternative views, see Hage 1998; Turner 1994). The time has surely come, at any rate, to revisit the postcolonial fetishiza-tion of hybridity, to retrace its historical origins more carefully, and to interrogate its continuities with the 'racialized formulations of the past' (Young 1995: 6; see also Puri 2004; Spivak 1999).

3.3.2 *Reclaiming Stolen Generation narratives*

For all the efforts of a Prichard or a Herbert, the widespread perception of 'half-castes' as a social menace was to constitute the crux of the 'Native Problem' by mid-century. 'Children of mixed parentage', write Quentin Beresford and Paul Omaji, 'were widely thought [at the time] to present the worst characteristics of both races . . . It was feared "half-castes" would be more black in their outlook than white; that they would constitute a numerically strong population to threaten white interests; . . . and [that] they would threaten white moral and social standards' as well (Beresford and Omaji 1998: 34).

As the menace appeared to mount, two solutions were proposed to the Problem. The first of these was to wait things out, since there was (concocted) evidence that pure-blood Aboriginal populations, especially in the far North, were dying; the second was to accelerate the process by absorbing mixed-blood Aborigines into the 'master race'. (This racial engineering was far from a uniquely Australian phenomenon. Similar plans were being hatched, at similar times, in several different parts of the world: Nazi policies towards Jews and Gypsies are well known, but it also bears reminding that in postcolonial countries such as Canada, a newly instituted residential school system was forcibly removing Native children from their families and educating them to be white with the ultimate purpose of 'killing the Indian in the child [until] all the Indian there is in the race should be dead' (Canadian Royal Commission 1996, vol. 2, ch. 10, qtd in Beresford and Omaji 1998: 59).)

A. O. Neville, one of the architects of what are now generally known as the Stolen Generations, advocated a three-step approach to racial policy, involving the forced removal of 'half-caste' children from their mothers, the control of marriage among 'half-castes', and the encouragement of intermarriage with the white community (Beresford and Omaji 1998: 46). These measures would in time correct what Neville saw as 'incorrect mating' practices among 'half-castes', ideally leading to a situation in which it would be possible to forget that there had ever been any Aborigines in Australia at all (Neville 1947, qtd in Beresford and Omaji 1998: 48).

The Stolen Generations, long peripheral to the Australian national imaginary, have in the last couple of decades become central to it, as the crucial plank in a highly public memory project anchored by the 1997 *Bringing Them Home Report*. The report, one in a large number of recent transnational reconciliation initiatives, has been brilliantly analysed by John Frow in terms of 'the clash between an assimilationist project that assumes the inevitable absorption or extinction of the indigenous population, and the resistant survival of a dispossessed and disoriented people living on stolen time' (Frow 1998: 360). To this might be added a proliferating number of diverse Stolen Generation narratives—books, plays, films, exhibitions, TV programmes, newspaper articles, magazine stories—in which the merging of written and oral, documentary and (auto)biographical sources confirms the crucial role of imagination in reconfiguring the historical past (Attwood 2001; Healy 1997).

For the historian Bain Attwood, these narratives provide examples of the 'necessary surfacing of a hitherto silenced or submerged history' (Attwood 2001: 183); but they are also marked by 'narrative accrual' as an effect of a white-controlled commodity culture, operating both within and beyond the parameters of the national culture, that recognizes the commercial viability of alternative narrativizations of the national past (Attwood 2001: 183). One danger this commercialization poses is that Stolen Generation narratives might be absorbed into a generic, all-encompassing Stolen Generation Narrative that provides the historical template for Australian race relations, and that entails a corresponding neglect of other, equally important narratives of Aboriginal destruction and dispossession in the context of Australia's contemporary history wars (Attwood 2001: 204). It is uncertain, Attwood suggests, whether the Stolen Generation Narrative is a 'talking cure' or a white containment strategy; whether it is one or the other, or both, depends on the different contexts in which individual narratives are created, and on their combined effect on the constituencies they are intended to serve (Attwood 2001: 204; see also Frow 1998).

In what follows I want to look briefly at two examples of Stolen Generation narratives. The first of these, Sally Morgan's *My Place* (1987), was not seen until recently as a Stolen Generation narrative but rather as an Aboriginal life-story, a 'dialogically generated' form which usually combines the traditional techniques of collective Aboriginal storytelling with autobiographical individualism and a measure of white editorial expertise (van Toorn 2001: 13; see also Brewster 1995, Nettelbeck 1997). Whether it qualifies as a Stolen Generation narrative is, of course, as much an ideological as an aesthetic question; as Attwood points out, it was not originally seen as one by its first critics and reviewers although, co-opted since through the process of 'narrative accrual', it is much more likely to be seen as one today (Attwood 2001: 204).

The second is a more clear-cut case in some respects, a limit case in others. For Kim Scott's *Benang* (1999), sometimes loosely seen as a 'sequel' to *My Place*, is, for all its extensive use of sources, clearly a work of fiction: a novel. However, whether Stolen Generation narratives require factual accuracy is an irresolvable issue; rather, like the wider historical debates into which they have been drawn, the factual and fictional elements of the accounts often cut across one another in such a way as to draw attention to the flimsiness of historical evidence, to challenge the fixed temporalities of official histories, and to cast history itself into dispute so that 'past realities . . . can be changed in and for the present' (Frow 1998: 363), rather than being sealed into a neatly compartmentalized past.

My Place and *Benang* are both attempts to piece together an Aboriginal inheritance from the broken shards of memory. This attempt is held back in Morgan's text by shame, the need or desire to keep Aboriginal identity hidden; in Scott's, shame is redirected, hurled back in white faces as a means of confronting them with their own disgrace. Both texts are concerned to reclaim a history that has been discarded by others, literally in some cases in the figure of the unwanted 'half-caste', rejected by a white father unable or unwilling (like *Capricornia*'s Mark Shillingsworth) to take responsibility for what he has done. The recovery of family history in such circumstances is complicated by memory gaps and disputes over likely parentage; these disputes, in Scott's text especially, are then used as the means by which an originary history of white settlement in Australia can be unravelled and undone (Scott 1999: 183, 476). Thus, while *My Place* insists on the need for Aboriginal people to claim a rightful place in history, *Benang* goes further, setting itself aggressively against the white man's history, and reversing the processes of geneaological barbarism by which Aboriginal histories have been systematically superseded or suppressed (Birch 2004).

At the centre of these processes in the novel are the twin figures of the (historical) Chief Protector of Aborigines, A. O. Neville, and the narrator's (fictional) white grandfather, the improbably but appropriately named Ernest Solomon Scat. Scat, a nightsoil remover, joins Neville in the project of diluting Aboriginal bloodlines, a eugenicist experiment eventually aimed at the total absorption of the Aboriginal race. The project recasts genocide ('breeding out') as generosity ('breeding up') by preaching the doctrine of racial uplift, and by providing the twisted rationale by which an elaborate caste system legislates across the range of Aboriginal livelihood and identity, assigning to each and every individual his or her 'proper' place.

The planned removal and resettlement of the town's sizeable 'half-caste' population is an important part of this horrific genetic experiment, providing an opportunity for interbreeding along the lines of animal husbandry (Scott 1999: 91), while furthering the wider agenda that foresees the extinction of the Aboriginal race. *Benang* operates, in this context, as a Stolen Generation narrative on several different levels. At one level, children are taken from their parents in the interests of re-educating them; at another, agency is taken from the Nyoongar in all aspects of their daily lives (Scott 1999: 216, 337–8).

At still another, the text operates as a counter-narrative of reclamation, symbolically recapturing what had previously been stolen, hidden, lied about, repressed. A similar point might be made about *My Place*, whose intergenerational narratives are contained within the macronarrative of Aboriginal dispossession, a narrative of multiple removal—birthright, family, freedom, humanity—that mirrors the history of Australia itself as an act of territorial theft (Morgan 1990 [1987]: 213).

The Stolen Generations are thus seen as a sad episode in a longer, sadder history of stealing—a history of whiteness that must be *dissociated* from whiteness if future generations of Aboriginal Australians are to succeed in sustaining the spiritual and material connections they need to (re)build their identity, their family, their place (Morgan 1990: 306). This dissociation is difficult given the ideological force that whiteness still exercises over Aborigines: several of Sally's relatives admit to the temptation to 'pass' as white in order to protect others from the implications of their ethnicity, and to remember only those aspects of their past that are most likely to win them acceptance in mainstream society, while others are deliberately repressed (Morgan 1990: 98, 107, 122). This willed separation from one's own heritage, when extended to others, is yet another form of removal—a denial of access to shared cultural memory that prevents the childhood Sally from knowing where she belongs and, in a fundamental sense, who she is (Morgan 1990: 105, 141).

Trawling back through time in search of place, Sally later becomes a detective piecing together the clues of her own family history (Morgan 1990: 238). But, as in *Benang*, this is genealogy against the odds: against black shame, against white indifference or hostility, against the virtual impossibility of reconstructing a past whose access routes are blocked by traumatic memory and marked by mysteries that will probably never be solved, gaps never filled, stories never told. Both texts confront the need to recapture memories without being destroyed by them—a dilemma by no means restricted to Aborigines, as graphically illustrated in Sally's white father's eventually fatal alcoholism, a side-effect of his inability to come to terms with his harrowing experiences of having been a prisoner of war.

In *Benang*, this trauma extends to an entire landscape scarred by death and memories of abject poverty and destruction, a landscape of corpses in which more than one of the narrator's Aboriginal ancestors is moved to wonder 'if it were true, that the white ones were the dead returned; brains askew, memories warped, their very spirit set adrift ... Those who had been closest to her were gone. She felt surrounded, almost, by the dead' (Scott 1999: 246). In such a landscape, history stinks, like the rubbish tip that abuts the Aboriginal reserve; or like the sanitary role of Ernest Scat who, when not attending to the racial hygiene of Aborigines, 'crouched behind the white bums of the town and took what they left behind' (Scott 1999: 118).

How is this dreadful legacy to be transformed? In part, by disrupting white historical chronology, weaving between different generational accounts that replace the teleology of a 'beginning-and-ending' story and that upset attempts to resurrect an originary white-pioneer mythology by breeding 'the first white man born' (Scott 1999: 10). And in part also by insisting on the continuation of a Nyoongar inheritance contained in the stories buried beneath the detritus of white history—recovered stories which are dredged back to the surface and spoken, as they must be, from the heart (Scott 1999: 357).

In *My Place*, similarly, Morgan insists on the value of stories which, exchanged across the generations, maintain a vital link to the more recent as well as the more distant ancestral past (Morgan 1990: 354). While these are stories that cross the 'colour line', they are not necessarily stories of cross-cultural reconciliation, despite attempts to frame *My Place* as a national reconciliation narrative or to repackage it as a New Age tale of collective healing for an international liberal readership, complete with statutory acknowledgement by Alice Walker, who mystically intuits 'the oneness of spirit between all "Aboriginal" peoples' and appeals to the commonality of their ancestral racial past (Walker, cover blurb for Morgan 1990; see also Waring 1997). Still less is *Benang* a reconciliation narrative; rather, the fallacy of separating out white and Aboriginal bloodlines is matched in the novel by the impossibility of reconciling them, and the figure of the 'embarrassed reader' at the end—an implied reader throughout the novel—is repeatedly accused rather than temporarily absolved (Scott 1999: 495).

The packaging of *Benang* and, particularly, *My Place* indicates that one link between Stolen Generation and (trans)national reconciliation narratives is their shared tendency to be co-opted to mainstream projects in which they run the risk of being stolen all over again (Birch 2004). This is not to say that reconciliation narratives have no part to play in national projects of self-reckoning, or that reconciliation should be dismissed as just another self-serving vehicle of white power. However, as Ken Gelder and Jane Jacobs argue in their book *Uncanny Australia* (1998), 'reconciliation' co-exists uneasily with 'difference' in postcolonial Australia.[5] The authors liken this condition to the experience of the uncanny, in which 'one's place is always already another's place and the issue of possession is never [settled, never] complete' (Gelder and Jacobs 1998: 138). In rediagnosing the condition of the unsettled settler, Gelder and Jacobs's study arguably bears most relevance to white Australia. But their point is that there is no clean break between alternative visions and versions (e.g. 'white' and 'Aboriginal') of Australia; rather, as conventional colonial distinctions between self and other become increasingly indeterminate, 'a certain unboundedness' takes over: at different times, 'each inhabits the other, disentangles itself, and inhabits it again' (Gelder and Jacobs 1998: 138).

While it is tempting to read *My Place* and *Benang* from this postcolonial optic, it is equally tempting to read them for evidence of the opposite—of the desire, against all odds, to find cultural stability and coherence, and to retrieve a lasting and mutually empowering sense of identity and place. Perhaps certain kinds of postcolonial reading can be as assimilative as the overarching Stolen Generation Narrative; and as inadvertently colonizing in their effect of turning Aboriginality to their own (white) political needs and historical ends. *My Place* and *Benang* are most useful, in this context, not as an unmasking of mythologies of whiteness, but as a reminder of alternative, Aboriginal epistemologies: epistemologies which are no less powerful for being bound up in—subject to but not subordinate to—whiteness, and which are experientially self-sustaining even if they are deemed to be categorically 'incomplete'.

3.3.3 Coda: passing thoughts

Aborigines' desire to assert the specificity of their own cultural heritage is often matched by their practical need to accommodate to the white world; sometimes extreme measures may be called for, as in the surreptitious attempt to pass as white. One survival strategy among others, passing is often less a means of assuming white authority than of avoiding it; possibly a means of eroding it too, in so far as it exposes the myth of whiteness as being racially unmarked (Fabi 2001; Ginsberg

1996). Whatever form it takes, however, passing is always more than just a theoretical exercise in identity subversion. Depending on the context, it may be seen as an attempt to gain freedom and mobility, or a sign of cultural alienation, or both of these at once (Fabi 2001). In literature, it may also be seen as a narrative strategy, mirroring the choice of racial indeterminacy as productive, and/or disruptive, disguise (Fabi 2001). Last but not least, passing is a way of asking awkward questions about cultural authenticity—questions that may raise doubts about the stability of the relationship between the genuine and the fake (Eco 1990; Haywood 1987).

Anxieties caused by passing are a staple of Australian literary history. From Ern Malley to Helen Demidenko, from B. Wongar to Mudrooroo, questions have been asked about the motives for passing, the peculiar susceptibility of the Australian literary establishment to fraudulence and fakery, and the link between settler culture, the beautiful lie, and the literary hoax (Daniel 1988; Flannery 2003; Nolan and Dawson 2004).[6] In the case of Aboriginal fakes—and there have been several—some important distinctions need to be mentioned. The first of these distinctions is between passing (black-to-white) and reverse passing (white-to-black), which often have entirely different motives (Manson 2004). The second is between a writer who consciously passes (B. Wongar) and one who believes, however problematically, that his racial/ethnic identification is sincere (Mudrooroo). The third is between a writer who wishes to pass as either white or Aboriginal—to claim a specific racial/ethnic identity—and one who wishes to conscript the (imagined) trappings of whiteness or Aboriginality to his or her particular cause. Finally, a fourth is between the historical practice of passing and the literary trope of 'going native'. These distinctions will be borne in mind in the following, strictly passing thoughts on passing, thoughts which provide further evidence of the power of whiteness in (literary) Australia, and of the greater 'ethnic options' (Moreton-Robinson 2000) available to writers who happen to be white.

Australian literature is replete with images of going native, encapsulated in the cross-over figure of the white blackfella (Healy 1997; Schaffer 1998). Going native is a standard colonial trope and is by no means restricted to Australia (Goldie 1989). Not really an example of passing at all, it comes closest in spirit to reverse passing in the loose sense that it is a temporary performance of alterity that leaves white subjectivity intact (Manson 2004). As Terry Goldie puts it, going native is about the acquisition of indigeneity, not about becoming indigenous: 'The indigene is acquired, the white is not abandoned. The title character of [Canadian writer Robert] Kroetsch's *Gone Indian* has clearly "gone" too far. The task is to go native, not to become gone native' (Goldie 1989: 215). Going native, in other words, is about the performative exercise of identitary options. In a trope predicated on return, the white blackfella may be suitably chastened by his experiences among the natives, but these will rarely prevent him, once he is home, from thinking of himself as white.

Going native thus offers a simulacrum of change that reinforces white privilege; its conditions, needless to say, rarely operate in reverse. To some extent, as Goldie suggests, going native appeals to a white-settler need for the grounded connection to an unfamiliar country. Goldie attaches this need to what he calls the process of indigenization, 'a peculiar word [which] suggests the impossible necessity of becoming indigenous' (Goldie 1989: 13). In this context, the figure of the white blackfella may be disruptive after all, a sign of the split consciousness of the unsettled settler (Gelder and Jacobs 1998; Hodge and Mishra 1990). Operating under the sign of the uncanny, the white blackfella is estranged from himself, but nonetheless strangely familiar; the repetition of the trope—its transformation into a colonial commonplace—then serves to make this strangeness more familiar still.

A good recent example of a reworking of the trope is David Malouf's 1993 novel *Remembering Babylon*. The novel is set in mid-nineteenth-century Queensland, but its primary frame of reference (possibly modulated by Malouf's 'hybrid' status as half-Lebanese) is the late twentieth-century reconciliation debates. Within this frame, the question asked is: is it possible for white Australia to transform itself; is it possible for whites, 'crossing the boundaries of [their] given nature', to submit to 'the [other] side of things'? (Malouf 1993: 132, 140). Enter the figure of Gemmy Fairley, a living embodiment of the imaginative power of transformation, whose sixteen-year spell with an Aboriginal community appears to have changed him irreversibly, despite some of the villagers' attempts to wean him slowly back. Malouf uses the figure of Gemmy to reflect ironically on the process of settlement, on settlers' 'garrison mentality' (Frye 1965: 830), and on a place that is largely defined by being seen as threatened and is still some way from being seen as home (Malouf 1993: 38, 63).

Gemmy's consecutive metamorphoses are also used to reflect on the tension between essentialist and performative conceptions of identity (Butler 1990). Is Gemmy 'black' or is he 'white'? What are the criteria for 'blackness' and 'whiteness'? The novel, as one might expect, provides no definite answers. Gemmy's eventual return to the Aborigines suggests, however, that this is no mere white blackfella who has temporarily gone native; rather—and the novel's reversal of terms is significant—he is a black whitefella who was born as white but has since been resocialized as black. Malouf has been criticized for offering Gemmy's irresolvable hybridity as a solution after all (Perera 1994). But it is clear that the novel spurns solutions, and Gemmy proves as resistant to being read in terms of postcolonial settler ambivalence as he does to being interpreted within the reassuring parameters of the Reverend Frazer's 'Colonial fairy tale' (Malouf 1993: 19).

Nor is it any easier to see Gemmy in terms of the dynamics of racial passing. At times he seems to be the 'parody of a white man' (Malouf 1993: 39), at others the simulacrum of a black one. The various changes he undergoes are less passing by design than metamorphosis by default; and although the evidence suggests that he goes back to the Aborigines, it also mocks Frazer's pompous sentiment that '[o]ur friend Gemmy is a forerunner . . . no longer a white man, or a European, whatever his birth, but a true child of the place as it will one day be' (Malouf 1993: 132). Gemmy's apparent death at the hands of pastoralists allows the novel in its last section to reflect elegiacally on a missed opportunity; the realities of public office now take over, and the institutional fashioning of White Australia has begun. This suggests that the whiteness the villagers had always feared losing is never really lost, despite the tragic consequences; *Remembering Babylon* thus reads, in the end, more as a pastiche of failed romantic transcendence than as the sentimental reconciliation narrative it is sometimes taken to be.

This brings me to my second example, the Jindyworobaks, also operating ironically within a European Romantic lyrical tradition, despite the poets' collective denial of it and their assertion of a 'Dreamtime nationalism' in its place (Elliott 1979: xliv). The Jindy-worobak movement of the 1930s and 1940s, despite occasional support from mavericks like Les Murray, who has self-mockingly described himself as 'the last of the Jindyworobaks' (Murray 1984), has often been regarded with affectionate embarrassment as so much visionary dog-gerel: 'Jindy jingles', A. D. Hope once nastily called them, performed by poets belonging to 'the Boy Scout School of Poetry ... [with] a boyish enthusiasm for playing at being primitive' (qtd in Elliott 1979: 248). It has been fashionable for some time now to see 'Jindyworobakism' as a kind of misguided antipodean primitivism, loosely adopting half-digested theories about Aborigines and other 'primitive' peoples and incorporating these into a white-dominated nationalist aesthetic (see poems, for example, like W. Flexmore Hudson's 'Song of an Australian' or Ian Mudie's 'This Land').

Brian Elliott, in his influential introduction to the 1979 UQP *Jindyworobaks*, sees their poetry as 'annexing' both white and black worlds in the service of a new national idiom. This idiom could be seen uncharitably as seeking to rid itself of pseudo-Europeanism, only to install pseudo-Aboriginalism in its place. But to be fair, as Elliott suggests, the Jindyworobaks were neither attempting to pass as Aborigines nor to become indigenous; theirs was poetry by whites for whites in which a nostalgic European Romantic aesthetic was given modern national form.

Certainly, many of the poems display ironic awareness that they aren't, and can't be, Aboriginal: in Rex Ingamells's 'Forgotten People', for instance, the speaker is moved to admit: 'I can but guess their pain, and guess the white / And exquisite laughter of their lost delight'; while other classic Jindyworobak poems are either given to ironize their own idealizations (Ingamells, 'Black Mary'), to critique their own incursions (Mudie, 'Intruder'), or to acknowledge the irreducible otherness of the indigenous people whose society and culture they seem to want to emulate (William Hart-Smith, 'Nullarbor'; Roland Robinson, 'Kimberley Drovers'). The ubiquitous irony to be found among the Jindyworobaks suggests an alternative view of their poetry than that of naive idealism; rather, their nostalgia is harder-edged along the lines of Renato Rosaldo, who sees modern white elegy as affecting mourning for what it has itself destroyed (Rosaldo 1989).

If Jindyworobak poetry remains misunderstood, such misunderstandings still reflect usefully on competing claims to Aboriginality today. In some of these claims, Aboriginality slides into an instrumental Aboriginalism, appropriated and adapted for white aesthetic and political purposes (Hodge and Mishra 1990). Aboriginality, seen this way, is not an anthropological concern for indigenous societies and customs, but rather an intuited panacea for a white Australia lapsed into cultural servility and philistinism and in desperate need of spiritual release (Elliott 1979). Perhaps the most obvious fake to turn to here is not Australian at all—the American pop guru Marlo Morgan, whose risible spiritual odyssey *Mutant Message Down Under* (1994) illustrates some of the continuities between romantic primitivism and the ransacked bag of religious *idées reçues* that is modern New Age thought. New Age thought also intrudes into contemporary (mis)understandings of Australian multiculturalism—a cultural phenomenon that has also given rise to its own fair share of fakers, as the next chapter will suggest.

However, neither Aboriginality nor multiculturalism can always be co-opted for white needs, material or spiritual. Flirting though it does with New Age ideas, literary works like Sally Morgan's *My Place* show this. Aboriginality, as a specific set of ways of knowing and looking at the world, is not always accessible to whiteness, still less an imagined counterpart to it. This is something that generations of white Australians have known, but not necessarily acknowledged; and that others have acknowledged, to their credit or their cost, without necessarily placing their own whiteness itself in doubt.

4

Multiculturalism and its Discontents

4.1 Demidenko, before and after

4.1.1 The end of the affair?

In 1994, the previously little-known writer Helen Darville published her first novel *The Hand that Signed the Paper*, and almost immediately hit the headlines. *Succès d'estime*—the novel won a stash of literary prizes—came to be accompanied by *succès de scandale* as it emerged, not only that it had played fast and loose with Holocaust history, but also that it had been published under a false Ukrainian name. The 'Demidenko affair', as it all too quickly came to be known, raised unanswerable questions about its infamous progenitor. Was Demidenko/Darville to be seen as a pathological attention-seeker, or rather as a canny manipulator? Was she to be treated in her own right, or rather to be added to an already impressive list of Australian literary hoaxers, tricksters, frauds?

As the affair grew, much media attention was given to the ease with which Demidenko/Darville had tricked a politically correct Australian literary establishment, seemingly fixated on commandeering writers for the nation's multicultural cause. 'The early players in the Demidenko affair', asserted Luke Slattery with more than a hint of *Schadenfreude* in the conservative daily *The Australian*, 'were easily duped because, for various reasons, they wanted to be seduced by the siren voices of multiculturalism. And, in a dramatic sense, they were' (Slattery 1996: 273). As the revelations broke, some persisted in defending the indefensible; others, turning, enthusiastically joined their numbers to the attack. Demidenko/Darville duly found herself at the centre of a fiercely contested, and of course highly mediated, morality play in which liberals wavered between the acceptance of a certain artistic licence and the condemnation of unethical cultural appropriation, while conservatives felt themselves bound to analyse the moral symptoms of a nation's inexorable cultural decline.

Was Demidenko/Darville cynically manipulating the valorization of literary multiculturalism in Australia? Critics like Vijay Mishra certainly thought so:

> She knew that an otiose settler tradition needed the multicultural writer. And she knew that naivety (the unmediated, raw style of the author) would be seen as the characteristic of a multicultural writer not quite in control of her intertexts. This is the judgement not only of the official judges (Vogel, Franklin and ASAL) [for the prizes the novel won], but of the common reader as well. Whatever the origin of the name, the effect is that of confirming that the 'ethnic' enters Australian culture as an already read text. This is the essence of postmodern racism.
>
> (Mishra 1996: 350–1)

There is some support for Mishra's view that Demidenko/Darville knew exactly what she was doing (see, for example, Gunew 2002: 67–78). However, the consensus, a decade on, now seems to be that hers was as much a misguided act of hubris as a calculated attack on 'the ethics of [literary] passing' (Mishra 1996: 19), or a cunning sideswipe at the 'liberal racism' (Brennan 1997: 115) that frequently accompanies the reception of designated 'multicultural' texts. Meanwhile, the text itself continues to raise pertinent questions about the authenticity attributed to ethnic authorship and the market value of multiculturalism; it points, that is, to multiculturalism's availability as a conceptual mechanism through which ethnicity is turned into a commodity, made subject to the changing rules that govern global cultural exchange (Gunew 2002; Huggan 2001).

All the same, few now believe that the Demidenko affair, bright though it burned, constituted an important moment, let alone a turning point, in Australian literary history. Several reasons might be cited here. One has to do not so much with the short-lived as the cyclical nature of literary scandals. Scandals have a tendency to disappear and reappear according to the whims of any given cultural moment or, perhaps better, cultural market; at the time of writing, 'Ern Malley' seems to be making something of a comeback (see, for example, Carey 2003), while Demidenko, shunned by the media as well as by her publishers, has all but vanished from view.[1]

A second reason is the recent critical turn from individual trick-sters/hoaxers to the genealogy of fraudulence that seemingly co-exists with the historical development of Australian literature itself (Nolan and Dawson 2004; Ruthven 2001). A third reason—more pertinent to my argument here—is the evidence of what might cynically be called 'multiculturalism fatigue' in Australia. Multiculturalism fatigue is more than just a convenient alibi for the reversal of earlier government policies, although it is certainly true that the last decade has witnessed a considerable 'downsizing' of multicultural departments and committees in Australia, if not necessarily a formal abandonment of the project of multiculturalism itself (Jupp 2002; Markus 2001).

Such fatigue is connected, no doubt, to the popular backlash against strategies of cultural advocacy and social equalization previously associated with multiculturalism, and to the rationalization of 'race-blind' theories of human capital based on the disingenuous claim that it matters less where people come from, or are perceived as coming from, than what they are worth. But it has as much to do with an increasing exasperation, registered at both ends of the political spectrum, with the conceptual inadequacies of that infuriatingly ambiguous term 'multicultural', and with a widespread rejection of the equally reductive, even unintentionally racist terminology it fosters across a wide range of literary production and the arts.

4.1.2 Multiculturalism, the nation, and beyond

To some extent the perception of multiculturalism fatigue involves a deliberate misunderstanding of the historical effects of multiculturalism in Australia, from its semi-official inception in the early 1970s to its unofficial dismantling in the present day (Castles *et al.* 1988; Lopez 2000). As Ghassan Hage among others points out, there has been a subtle difference throughout this period between descriptive ('lifestyle') and prescriptive ('life-chance') models of multiculturalism in Australia; between multiculturalism 'as a marginal reality in a main-ly Anglo-Celtic society and multiculturalism displacing Anglo-Celtic culture to become the identity of the nation [itself]' (Hage 2003: 59; see also Ang 2001; Stratton 1999).

Before asking whether multiculturalism is over in Australia, it might therefore be worth asking whether it has ever really begun. Certainly the crucial problem of unequal socio-economic access to the institutions of Australian society has not been solved—some extreme critics wouldn't even see it as having been raised—by multicultural- ism, while even the most basic of comparisons between policy-making in different, nominally multicultural societies, e.g. Canada, makes a mockery of the breast-beating assertion that Australia is the most multicultural society in the world (Jupp 2002).

James Jupp, in his recent book on the history of Australian immi- gration, dismisses this populist view unceremoniously:

The often repeated and incorrect claim that Australia is the 'most multicultural society in the world' does not bear close inspection. It is certainly much more multicultural than it was fifty years ago when the post-war immigration program began. It is even more multicultural than it was at Federation in 1901, when 20 per cent of its people were overseas-born and it had large German and Chinese minorities. But it is still much more a 'British' society than either Canada or the United States in terms of origins. Nor can it compare with such truly multicultural societies as India, Russia, Indonesia, Papua New Guinea or most of the states of Africa. Its social, intellectual, business and political élites are still overwhelmingly of British origin; three-quarters of its people speak only English; and a similar proportion subscribe, however nominally, to Christian denominations.

(Jupp 2002: 5–6)

While Jupp's categories—'British society', 'true multicultur- alism'—raise doubts of their own, they also make dear the double- edged association of multiculturalism with nationalism. Apparently the rhetoric of multiculturalism can be deployed with equal effect either to assert a nation under threat or to celebrate national unity (Jupp 2002; see also Hage 2003; Turner 1994). This is especially the case in settler societies like Australia, where multiculturalism has histor- ically been linked to the project of national unity, rather than—as in South Africa—to the development of cultural distinctiveness or—as in the United States—to the promotion and protection of individual civil rights (Jupp 2002: 84–5).

Australian multiculturalism can be distinguished in several ways from related developments in other white-dominated settler soci- eties. Its distinctiveness consists primarily in the long-term initiative to create a diverse immigrant society through 'planned policies of resettlement' (Jupp 2002: 101)—policies more concerned with the practicalities of immigration settlement than with the ideals of cultural maintenance, and usually conceived, implemented, and administered by a centralized state (Jupp 2002: 93). These resettlement initiatives have aimed throughout to promote social cohesion at the national level, for example through the provision of language education, and through the extension to new immigrants of rights and privileges 'already enjoyed by the native-born' (Jupp 2002: 101). While more recent policy suggests an increasing devolution of resettlement programmes to the individual states, partly as a reflection of the shifting place of Australia's immigrant workforce within a globalizing economy, Australian multiculturalism from the outset has been a *national* project, for all its perceived connectedness to free-ranging cosmopolitan elites (Jupp 2002; see also Castles *et al.* 1988, Lopez 2000).

It has also been, until relatively recently, a predominantly *white* project. Multiculturalism is often viewed as a viable alternative to the ideology of White Australia that dominated immigration policy until at least mid-century. Yet the fact remains that most of Australia's immigrants are white, despite marked increases in the numbers of Asian migrants since the early 1980s. Although officially 'race-blind', multiculturalism can easily be seen as a form of white cultural managerialism, no longer revolving around the exclusion of non-whites, but still motivated by collective anxieties about 'non-assimilable non-Whites' (Hage 2003: 56; see also Vasta and Castles 1996). Multiculturalism, this view suggests, is both an index of racial anxiety and a structure of racial repression, systematically ignoring the reality that '[r]ace is, in the end, the language in which the differentiation between white multiculturalism and its morally distinct Other is expressed' (Stratton 1999: 183).

The positive view of multiculturalism is that it is a 'workable model for civic tolerance' (Hutcheon, qtd in Huggan 2001: 126) in settler societies, like Australia's, that are still struggling to free themselves from the shackles of their white-supremacist past. The negative view is that it is complicit with both new and residual forms of white domination, including the 'well-grounded disposition to imagine Australia as a place where white Australians should reign supreme' (Hage 1998: 232). This latter view, while perhaps exaggerated, cannot be dismissed so easily. It suggests that multiculturalism co-exists with, and is to some extent fed by, colonial racism, and that the 'racialized developmental difference' (Hage 2003: 113) that characterizes racism influences multiculturalism as well. It also suggests a national 'culture of suspicion' (Jupp 2002) driven by the sometimes invented demands of economic rationalism, or even a culture of 'paranoid nationalism' (Hage 2003) registered in draconian border-control and defensive housekeeping, and signalling 'the history of White paranoia in Australian culture which has structured Australian nationalism from the time of its birth' (Hage 2003: 47).

Paranoid nationalism is more in keeping with revulsion than respect for multiculturalism, and there are many who support the central tenets of multiculturalism while abhorring the licensed xenophobia that surrounds, say, the criminalization of 'illegals' in Australia and elsewhere. Multiculturalism, however, is not necessarily antithetical to such national(ist) policing mechanisms; after all, as Jupp, one of its greatest advocates, confesses, Australian multicultural policy has always been an instrument of restriction: a means both of marking and controlling internal 'ethno-specificity', as well as of channelling external population flow (Jupp 2002: 5).

If Australian multiculturalism is a national project, its effectiveness has always depended on wider, transnational understandings—of population movements and (un)stated immigrant preferences; of international markets and global cultural/economic flows. Multiculturalism at large is very much an 'epiphenomenon of globalization' (Bennett 1998: 2), even if it still tends to be seen—and not only in Australia—as an intra- rather than an international affair (Bennett 1998: 2). Not that global awareness necessarily counteracts some of the more parochial tendencies associated with multiculturalism; on the contrary, a symbiotic link can be posited between globalization, multiculturalism, and the 'culturalization of racism' (Essed 1991: 14) through which 'new' racisms can be surreptitiously legitimated, and not-so-new ones can continue with impunity to be observed (Essed 1991; Vasta and Castles 1996).

Globalization, like multiculturalism, is double-edged, acting as a check on Australian cultural insularity and provincialism while providing an anxiety-inducing reminder that the privileged 'isolation of Australia, based on distance and immigration control, is under increasing threat' (Jupp 2002: 204). Both terms are invoked as much to mystify as to clarify international political relations, and both just as routinely enlisted to conjure up simple causes for complex socio-cultural processes and effects. These contradictions also carry over into the sphere of economics: hence globalization can be seen, according to perspective, in terms of a generously inclusive or a mercilessly exclusive fiscal policy, while multiculturalism can either be viewed as threatening to national productivity or as essential to the nation's economic health (Bennett 1998: 17).

For all their obvious global resonances, nation-based multiculturalisms may end up by sanctioning a surface appreciation of internal cultural diversity rather than fostering deeper international awareness. As Maria Koundoura admonishingly argues, 'we must negotiate between nationalism and globality [if we are not to] allow the ethnocentric politics of multiculturalism to stand in for a study of the world' (Koundoura 1998: 82; see also Gunew 2004).

Unduly narrow or non-relational understandings of multiculturalism are also likely to endorse the compartmentalization, even fetishization of ethnicity, as in mainstream constructions of 'multicultural literature' in which writers who are perceived as coming from different, preferably disadvantaged backgrounds are engaged to perform, usually for a limited season, within an equally restricted repertoire of pre-set cultural roles. Ethnic compartmentalization is further strengthened by the perception that the multicultural writer's primary role is to bear witness and, in so doing, join history to fiction, especially if the history of a real or imagined community is involved (Gunew 2004: 6). Multicultural writing thus comes into being as a horizon of literary/cultural expectations in which the standard *cultural* requirement (ethnic particularity) is duly linked to the preferred *literary* option (autobiography and/or social realism), and the literary text becomes inextricably bound up with the life of its writer in a prescriptive set of critical gestures that are as sociologically overdetermined as they are aesthetically underplayed.

4.1.3 Preliminary thoughts on multicultural literature

The fundamental questions remain: what is 'multicultural literature', and is the designation useful? Sneja Gunew's introduction to *Framing Marginality* (1994), while dated, remains helpful here. Gunew begins, as well she might, by noting the terminological inconsistency with which definitions of migrant writing, ethnic literatures and, more recently, multicultural literature have been supplied and traded in Australia, but finds in each a common element that signals 'the alterity of various writings produced in Australia but perceived as 'other' (*alter*) than the Anglo-Celtic norm' (Gunew 1994: 3).

All of these terms, however, carry several problems with them, adding critical insult to experiential injury. 'Migrant writing' implies impermanence, as if migrant writers had no proper place in Australia; it also invites a treatment of the literature in terms of an applied but thoroughly unprofessional sociology, as the distillation of a homogenized 'migrant situation' in which one writer's experience, transparently mirrored in his/her writing, is made to stand in metonymically for all. 'Ethnic literatures', meanwhile, deploy a selective understanding of ethnicity in which some writers are strategically perceived to be more ethnic than others, and others—so-called 'Anglo-Celts'—are perversely perceived, not least by themselves, not to be ethnic at all (Hage 1998). The highly problematic term 'Anglo-Celt' is elevated to the norm and serves as a convenient straw category, while 'ethnic' writers are automatically propelled into an oppositional role. Aboriginal writing is usually left out on the reasonable grounds that Aborigines have consistently and categorically refused to see themselves as 'ethnic'; but one can only wonder how many of the 'non-Anglo-Celtic' writers dubbed as 'ethnic' would willingly accept the label, or would freely allow themselves to be co-opted into a representational role.

'Multicultural literature' avoids some of these problems, only to substitute others of its own making. The term 'multicultural' is theoretically more inclusive than 'migrant' or 'ethnic', but it still has the ring of alterity to it. It implies a primary relationship to the nation, albeit a highly complicated one, that potentially underestimates the equally complex transnational networks in which both the writers and the writing are enmeshed. It reinforces the dominance of English, either by assuming the centrality of English-language writing, or by performing what Gayatri Spivak calls, in another context, 'the act of wholesale translation into English' (Spivak 1993: 182)—a homogenizing act that levels out differences between nominally distinct cultural groupings, so that (to adapt Spivak again) the literature of an Italian–Australian woman begins to resemble, 'in the feel of its prose', the writing of a Vietnamese–Australian man (Spivak 1993: 182). Finally, it confers a political advocacy on the writers which is unshared, possibly even unsought, but nonetheless makes them collectively liable to accusations of special status, or to the broader reactionary argument that multiculturalism panders to an 'ethnic lobby' that places serious strain on the resources of the state (Jupp 2002; Markus 2001).

Gunew, however, is only too well aware of the ideological hazards of literary category. As she suggests, 'the very term, "multicultural literature", already conjures up the spectre of homogenization', while the recent reception of such writings has tended to 'swing between primitivism (or nativism) and Eurocentrism—the endorsement being offered in both cases by emissaries from the "civilized" centre' (Gunew 1994: 22–3; see also Huggan 2001). As Gunew admits, no amount of terminological sleight of hand can solve these contradictions, which are endemic not only to the Australian culture industries, but also to the continuing disparity between 'lifestyle' and 'life-chance' multiculturalisms in the Australian welfare state (Hage 2003).

While the term 'transcultural', now increasingly used in the critical literature, is perhaps a more accurate reflection of the fluid conditions of globalization under which contemporary Australian writers operate, it is arguably no more free of patronizing or even racist connotations than the term 'multicultural' itself. Whether multiculturalism has a future in Australia will obviously depend on more than the wranglings of a handful of literary and cultural critics. But these can play a valuable role in analysing discrepant or, as Gunew in her more recent work calls them, 'situated' multiculturalisms—multiculturalisms which are not only carefully compared and internally differentiated, but are also appropriately 'contextualized in relation to [national and transnational] geopolitical and cultural dynamics' in an increasingly interconnected global space (Gunew 2004: 1). Such criticism needs to perform the near-impossible task of being attentive to cultural differences without simultaneously reifying them. It also needs to be attentive to historical change; otherwise it risks remaining bound to an earlier discourse of migration, centred on post-war immigrants in Australia, which makes claims about cultures that effectively no longer exist (Langer 1998: 176).

4.2 Discrepant multiculturalisms

4.2.1 Multicultural anthologomania

The primary medium for the dissemination of multicultural litera-ture, in Australia and elsewhere, has been the anthology. A spate of multicultural anthologies appeared in Australia during the period from the late 1970s to the early 1990s; the receding number since then is less a sign of growing disenchantment with multiculturalism in general than a more specific awareness of the diminishing value of ethnic/migrant/multicultural literatures as descriptive label and marketing tool. During the heydays of the 1980s, multicultural literature was part of a widespread 'anthologomania' (Eliades 1995) encompassing disparate forms of perceptibly 'marginal' or 'minority' writing—including the writing of migrant women, often hastily considered to be doubly marginal—and aimed at undermining mainstream literary hegemonies and the universalist criticism they looked to for support.

Such revisionist anthologies, designed as much to raise awareness of social as literary issues, were always in danger of becoming their own worst enemies, further marginalizing the very writers whose visibility they wanted to increase. They might thus be seen as having courted the media backlash their publication almost inevitably created, one typical response being that they fulfilled a compensatory function—that minority was usually also minor writing, and that its recognition was essentially a form of positive discrimination based more on the guilty desire to redress social inequality than on any felt need to reward the literary merit of the works themselves (Eliades 1995; see also Huggan 2001).

The play of frequently contradictory perceptions that surrounded the emergence of multicultural writing in Australia indicated the residual conservatism of the literary establishment while also pointing to the more specific contradictions of the anthology as a literary-historical form. The decontextualizing effect of literary anthologies has been well noted, as has their paradoxical tendency to level out the very differences they are designed to bring to light (see, for example Brennan 1997; Guillory 1993). Anthologies are tailored to the not-always-stated agenda of their editors, who, however catholic their intentions, are encouraged to find commonalities in the writing for which the individual texts sometimes offer precious little grounding or support. Finally, they perform a canonizing function even if the writing itself is constructed as counter- or anti-canonical (Guillory 1993). While they may undoubtedly play a valuable role in finding a home for lesser-known or even unknown writers, they are just as likely to reward writers who have long since been acknowledged; thus it is that, like literary prizes, anthologies often have an establishment feel to them: they are like 'a life belt thrown to swimmer[s] who [have] already reached the shore' (qtd in Winegarten 1994: 65; see also Bourdieu 1993).

The best anthologizers, of course, are well aware of these dilemmas and, in several cases, will actively attempt to incorporate them into their own introductions or the structure of the collected work. In what follows, I will look briefly at the contents and editorial framing of four Australian multicultural anthologies, two of them published in the halcyon 1980s, one in the early 1990s, and the last in the late 1990s, a period during which such anthologies already seemed to have gone into terminal decline. A basic distinction will be observed throughout between the *integrationist* anthology, whose primary function lies in the celebration of national cultural diversity, and its *interventionist* counterpart, which takes a much more critical view of the notion of diversity and the construction of the nation itself. Into the first category come Peter Skrzynecki's *Joseph's Coat: An Anthology of Multicultural Writing* (1985) and, half a decade later, R. F. Holt's *Neighbours: Multicultural Writing of the 1980s* (1991); while in the second are Sneja Gunew and Jan Mahyuddin's *Beyond the Echo: Multicultural Women's Writing* (1988) and, more recently, Paula Abood, Barry Gamba, and Michelle Kotevski's *Waiting in Space: An Anthology of Australian Writing* (1999).

Skrzynecki's and Holt's anthologies are framed as exercises in social and cultural awareness, directed partly against those latter-day Australian bigots still determined to bask in the limelight of 'an irretrievable past' (Skrzynecki 1985: 14). For all the aggression this implies, the two anthologies are conciliatory rather than confrontational, with Holt's, in particular, offering itself in a spirit of self-congratulatory optimism designed to celebrate Australia's 'continuing achievement in social integration' (Holt 1991: x). Humanist sentiments abound, as in Skrzynecki's assertion that 'this compassionate and humane collection . . . is indicative of the changing nature of our society'—by which the reader cannot fail to grasp that these changes are for the general good (Skrzynecki 1985: 13).

Still less equivocal is Holt's understanding of Australia's slow but inexorable progress towards intercultural harmony, as traced in the movement of the anthology's subsections from 'Rejections' through 'Transitions' to 'Connections', a questionable corollary to the editor's equally questionable suggestion that during the 1980s 'so-called multicultural writing became increasingly accepted as a natural, valid part of mainstream Australian literature—at least in the pragmatic sense of it being increasingly and routinely published, reviewed and read' (Holt

1991: ix). Such misleading progressivism is supported by the elision of dates, although a quick glance at the Acknowledgements page confirms the suspicion that the pieces are not in chronological order, and in any case a strong feeling of sometimes mutual rejection, evidenced in such powerful work as George Papaellinas's portrait of working-class xenophobia, 'Christos Mavromatis is a Welder' (1984), or Ania Walwicz's much-anthologized tirade against suburban small-mindedness and banality, 'Australia' (1981), remains.

To be fair to Skrzynecki, his anthology cannot be accused of suggesting, as Holt's does, that prejudice and discrimination are on the wane in an increasingly diversity-conscious Australia, nor can he be blamed for including the egregious B. Wongar (aka Sreten Bozic) in the Biographical Notes as a Stolen-Generations Aborigine fleeing from the likelihood of separation from his parents and relocating overseas (Skrzynecki 1985: 224; see also Nolan 1998). To some extent, like later anthologizers, Skrzynecki is motivated by a keen sense of the continuing discrimination from which writers from non-English-speaking backgrounds suffer and which their writing insistently registers, along with a studied reluctance to 'sever the linguistic roots from which they grew' (Skrzynecki 1985: 13). Still, Skrzynecki's insistence on the shared experience of discrimination elides obvious differences in social status which, when added to the miscellany of his selections, cannot help but exacerbate what we might call multicultural anthologies' doubly decontextualizing effect.

This double effect—decontextualization of content (multiculturalism) and of form (the anthology)—is addressed in only slightly later but far more critically conscious anthologies, a good example being Sneja Gunew and Jan Mahyuddin's *Beyond the Echo: Multicultural Women's Writing* (1988). The editors are over-concerned to distance themselves from the sociological 'case-study' approach that posits multicultural writing as a confessional account of the problems of the so-called 'migrant experience'; as if literature, oral history, and sociology were entirely separate categories, or life and literature had no reason to overlap. Likewise, they are too keen to see 'non-Anglo-Celtic' perspectives on living in Australia as inevitably differing from those of the self-designated mainstream, thereby co-opting multicultural writing for an oppositional imperative—the interrogation of national unity, for instance, or the idea of fixed cultures and identities—which the writing itself may not necessarily support.

Still, Gunew and Mahyuddin deserve credit for assembling a collection that is not only of high literary quality but also energetically engages with the complex adjudicative mechanisms by which literary quality, and the conspicuously uneven social systems in whose name it often operates, is monitored and assessed. This entails a watchful eye for premature celebrations of a 'boutique multiculturalism' (Fish 1997) that stands in for undifferentiated otherness—a cosmopolitan gloss on the dominant culture (Gunew and Mahyuddin 1988: xvii)—or one that, operating remedially, applies only to those perceived as belonging to 'the multicultural world' (Gunew and Mahyuddin 1988: xvii).

In contradistinction to Holt and, to a lesser extent, Skrzynecki, Gunew and Mahyuddin make no attempt to hide behind notions of compassionate humanism or reconciliatory universalism, staking a claim instead for 'positive discrimination' as a means of confronting and resisting 'racial and gender bias and inequity in every aspect of our society, including the public arenas of writing, publishing and reading' (Gunew and Mahyuddin 1988: xiv). At the same time, they emphasize the literariness of the writing they present as well as its political instrumentality, particularly in the opening section of the anthology, where formal experimentation is at a premium (sometimes to the point where cultivated unconventionality itself becomes a kind of orthodoxy, as in the seemingly obligatory use of the first-person pronoun in lower case). All in all, though, *Beyond the Echo* illustrates that it is possible to show respect for difference without advertising—precisely by *not* advertising—respect for it, as in the juxtaposition of different language-versions of the same poem, or the inclusion of a poem in Russian that has no English translation at all.

An altogether noisier version of the interventionist anthology is Paula Abood, Barry Gamba, and Michelle Kotevski's *Waiting in Space: An Anthology of Australian Writing* (1999) which, despite its confrontational directive, is much more oblique in its critical terminology, as in the editors' cryptic claim that the collection provides opportunities for emerging writers 'to reflect the textual realities that live in and out of the margins' (Abood, Gamba, and Kotevski 1999: viii). The anthology is firmly committed to the idea of multicultural writing as a site of resistance, though it is sometimes unclear exactly what is being resisted, and the overblown language of the editors ('the erasure of diversity remains a feature of the Australian literary canon'; 'it is near impossible to locate the voices of diversity in the public sphere'; etc.) scarcely supports their heartfelt claim that 'the expressive voice of the other is an act of resistance against the monolingual nation' (Abood, Gamba, and Kotevski 1999: viii).

In fact, it might be possible to see some of the writing itself, an oddball assemblage of occasional prose and poetic fragment, as resisting some of the general claims the editors make on behalf of it, as well as reinstalling some of the foundational categories they reject: the collection is 'not intended to be read as autobiographical', but it is often highly likely to be; it is 'not a site of quirky offerings of the disgruntled second generation', but it is often precisely that (Abood, Gamba, and Kotevski 1999: viii). However, looking beyond the editors' inflationary rhetoric, the collection certainly bristles with hostility, providing a valuable antidote to bland versions of a multicultural Australia in which the fantasy of mutually respectful cohabitation is realized, and social and political conflict is conveniently emptied out. From Andrew Ma's ironic homage to KFC to Rihana Sultan's tongue-in-cheek invocation of household curiosities, the collection upsets exoticist expectations of the dutifully different and the 'good ethnic story' (Nahlous, qtd in Abood et al. 1999: 13). Instead, a strong sense of dis-ease, instability and even mutual paranoia prevails, as in Nushet Yilmaz Comert's fantasmatic poem 'The Veil': 'You can see my flesh of pleasure I am in your dream / I exist behind the veil / You search for me / Touch me / You can / I cannot touch you / Untamed / Dangerous I might be' (Comert, qtd in Abood et al. 1999: 87).

Interventionist collections like *Waiting in Space and Beyond the Echo* reject the notion of a unified national culture, a country at ease with its own burgeoning cultural diversity, without necessarily threatening the dominant paradigm of the (Australian) nation itself. Indeed, as *Beyond the Echo* in particular makes clear, multicultural writing potentially revitalizes the nation, creating 'new Australias' more in tune with contemporary realities (Gunew and Mahyuddin 1988: xiii). More recent work, including Gunew's, has uncoupled the link between multiculturalism and the nation, offering alternative models of multiculturalism—'multi-multiculturalisms', Gunew calls them (Gunew 2004: 132)—in which more play is given to transnational networks and alliances, and in which 'transculturalism' is identified as 'the latest term in a continuum to which multiculturalism belongs' (Gunew 2004: 127).

While Gunew's formulation implies that multiculturalism has been imaginatively transformed rather than institutionally superseded, it has undoubtedly lost a good deal of its earlier social urgency and affective force. The cluster of defensive qualifiers that tended to accompany earlier versions of multiculturalism has given way to an increasing awareness that the paradigm is terminally afflicted with Eurocentrism, even racism, and that it risks imploding from its own internal contradictions, even if it has not yet ceded its right to counteract 'the vicious denigration of minority . . . cultures that is so rampant in many parts of the world today' (Bharucha 2000: 11). What are the alternatives, however, to multiculturalism as social vision and literary vehicle? One possibility is still another form of culturalism, *inter*culturalism, and it is to this phenomenon, most widely applied in literary circles to the theatre, that the chapter turns next.

4.2.2 *Multiculturalism, interculturalism, and the theatre*

The Indian theatre critic Rustom Bharucha makes a useful if over-schematic distinction between multiculturalism and interculturalism in his book *The Politics of Cultural Practice: Thinking through Theatre in an Age of Globalization* (2000). While interculturalism, for Bharucha, is 'a voluntarist intervention circumscribed by the agencies of the State and the market, multiculturalism is increasingly identified with the official cultural policies of western democracies like Australia, Canada, and Britain' (Bharucha 2000: 33). Intercultural practitioners, according to Bharucha, are at an advantage insofar as their interventions are not strictly bound to state authority; unlike multiculturalism, which is generally 'concerned with the cohabitation of different cultural and ethnic groups negotiating a common framework of citizenship' within the context of the nation, interculturalism has 'a greater flexibility in exploring—and subverting—different modes of citizenship across different national contexts, through subjectivities that are less mediated by the agencies of the State' (Bharucha 2000: 33).

In the domain of the performing arts, this understanding of the intercultural as (1) potentially disruptive of state formations and (2) largely transnational in orientation has informed the work of several prominent theatre practitioners, included among them the American Richard Schechner, the New Zealander Christopher Balme, and Bharucha himself. Schechner's influential view is that the 'real exchange of importance to artists [is] not that among nations, which . . . suggests official exchanges and artificial kinds of boundaries, but the exchange among cultures, something which [can] be done by individuals or by non-official groupings, and . . . doesn't obey national boundaries' (Schechner, qtd in Pavis 1996: 4).

Several objections might be raised here. Understandings of culture have shifted considerably in the wake of postcolonial and globalization theory, neither of which sees cultures as bounded entities subject to knowledgeable exchange and informed comparison, but rather as negotiable components within a highly mobile global system of diasporic networks and transnational commodity flows (Appadurai 1996; Hannerz 1996). The economization of culture, often manipulated in state interests, is more likely to be supported than subverted by intercultural practice, which also has an unfortunate tendency to assume a naive, falsely reciprocal relationship between the different cultures of the world. Unreflective interculturalism, at worst, is blatantly ethnocentric and exploitative, disregarding individual and collective property rights in its effort to create a shared mixture of cultural elements drawn, frequently out of context, from different corners and countries of the world (Bharucha 1993; Gilbert and Tompkins 1996).

Then again, it would be just as naive to equate syncretic mixing with cultural cannibalism or imperialist appropriation, while globalization has brought with it an acknowledgement that 'cultures' (the scare-quotes seem to be increasingly necessary) have the capacity strategically to reinvent themselves, drawing from a global-cultural repertoire that can be adjusted to a variety of local interests and concerns (During 1998; Hannerz 1996). Free exchange this is certainly not, any more than globalization presupposes reciprocity. Interculturalism, in this sense, is a symptom of the uneven global exchange in cultural commodities rather than a compassionate alternative to it or a utopian gesture, beyond the push-and-pull of market forces, towards the 'dialogical redefin[ition] of the world' (Bharucha 2000: 3).

Like multiculturalism, interculturalism is dependent on the market or, perhaps more accurately, markets; it is clearly a function both of the economization of culture under current conditions of late-capitalist globalization and of the mediating role that continues to be played in cross-cultural dialogue and interaction by the modern nation-state (Bharucha 2000; Gunew 2002). This might help explain why the two terms 'multicultural' and 'intercultural' are sometimes blurred in current usage, or easily confused with the link term 'transcultural'; for while each of these terms, as I hope to have suggested, has a non-identical prefix, all are involved in continuing processes of negotiation between the shifting interests of the global economy and the equally unstable political requirements of the nation-state.

A more specific instance of interculturalism in practice is so-called 'syncretic theatre'. Syncretic theatre, as Christopher Balme explains, is not to be confused with theatrical exoticism, which has a long history in the Western performance arts. Theatrical exoticism, suggests Balme, 'involves the use of indigenous cultural texts purely for their surface appeal, but with no regard to their original cultural semantics'; in syncretic theatre, by contrast, these cultural texts 'retain their integrity as bearers of precisely defined cultural meaning' (Balme 1999: 5). Syncretic theatre is intercultural, for Balme, less in its attempt at aesthetic rejuvenation (which, depending on the context, is often wilfully exoticist) than in its conscious effort to combine surface elements of different signifying systems while enquiring into the deeper semantic structures underlying each. The result is often conflictual, especially in the case of theatre arising out of a context of colonialism. Balme cites examples of the counter-appropriation of Western theatrical models by colonized people, in which the dominant system is not necessarily eclipsed but is certainly confronted, and in which the possibly insurmountable problems of cultural conflict are brought to crisis and acted out.

A contemporary Australian example is the Aboriginal playwright Jack Davis's multi-layered historical play *No Sugar* (1985). (It seems worth noting that interculturalisms rarely observe the distinction between indigenous and migrant writing that often characterizes multiculturalism; indeed, indigenous writers are often the first to be co-opted to the intercultural cause.) *No Sugar* revolves around the day-to-day struggles of two Nyoongah (Western-Australian Aboriginal) families in the 1930s—a time of severe economic depression during which a hypocritically protectionist government, intent on tackling the so-called 'Aboriginal problem', saw fit to shepherd its wards, irrespective of tribal affiliation, into a number of often less than salubrious state-run missions and reserves.

The play reveals the link between intercultural theatre and the postcolonial drama of contestation, in which historically documented experiences of dispossession and dislocation are symbolically re-enacted on stage (Gilbert and Tompkins 1996; see also Gilbert 2001). The primary grounds of contestation in Davis's play are spatial, with several of its Nyoongah characters 'flaunt[ing] their non-compliance with the rules of the spaces assigned to them by [repeatedly] venturing "out of bounds"' (Gilbert and Tompkins 1996: 156). These acts of defiance are thrown into relief by the open-plan staging, which deliberately creates an impression of dispersal while also reinforcing the interconnectedness of the play's symbolic (mythological) and everyday (historical) events (Balme 1999; Gilbert and Tompkins 1996). *No Sugar* accords well with the view of Aboriginal drama as a mode of 'symbolic realism' in which there are no clear lines of demarcation between the realms of the everyday and the spiritual-mythological (Balme 1999: 62). It also squares with the view of intercultural theatre as a site of performative tension between alternative worldviews, although these worldviews are neither as ontologically separate nor as ideologically incompatible as might at first sight be supposed.

A key role is played here by the government tracker, Billy Kimberley, a mediating figure who occupies 'black' and 'white' worlds simultan-eously, and whose split consciousness emphasizes hybrid potential, as well as internal division, within the drama as it unfolds. In one symbolically charged scene, Billy performs a corroboree with members of other Nyoongah tribes that reveals as much about the differences as the solidarity between them. Many of these differences have been artificially brought about by recent government impositions—forced relocation, the removal of children, racial engineering—which, for all the euphemistic vocabulary that accompanies them, bear the tell-tale marks of older legacies of sanctioned colonial/imperial violence.

In the scene, as in much of the play, a thin line separates cultural exchange from mutual incomprehension. In his recuperative reading of the scene, however, Christopher Balme suggests that the gruesome story Billy tells about the massacre of his tribe occupies three mutually enriching discursive spaces: (1) a true story passed down to him by his brother, and now recounted according to the protocols of Nyoongah oral tradition; (2) a fictional story, performed within the context of Western theatre; and (3) a documented historical account (Balme 1999: 164–6). For Balme, it is in the productive tensions opened up between these narratives, as well as in the supportive combination of semiotic registers (verbal, gestural, musical, etc.) available to perform them, that the intercultural dimensions of the scene are revealed and acted out.

Balme's larger point is that there is no 'pure' cultural space from and within which Nyoongah identities can be performatively renegotiated, rather a series of partly connected spaces that allow for the dominant historical narrative of white-settler ascendancy to be strategically recoded and undermined. This reworking/unworking of the white man's terms is described using the white man's theoretical vocabulary, a banal but nonetheless viable criticism that has been levelled at both interculturalism and postcolonialism, which are often seen as being torn between their desire to rehabilitate non-European perspectives and epistemologies and their awareness of their own complicity in the continuing dominance of European aesthetic forms (Bharucha 1993; McClintock 1992).

However, it would be too simple just to accuse intercultural/postcolonial practitioners of perpetuating a long tradition of anti-Eurocentric Eurocentrism, since the two related critical practices have historically generated much of their momentum from their acknowledgement of precisely this double-bind. The critical vocabularies of interculturalism and postcolonialism, to a greater extent than those of multiculturalism, are aware of the unevenness that accompanies their own cultural exchanges, and of the tenuousness of the claims they might be persuaded to make on behalf of indigenous alterities—claims sometimes more likely to be theoretically ingenious than practically informed.

4.2.3 Representing refugees

The give-and-take between 'multicultural' and 'intercultural', 'migrant', and 'indigenous' is further complicated by conflations within each of these descriptive categories. Consider refugees, usually seen as a subset within the general category of migrants. If a basic distinction can be made between *proactive*, in the main economically motivated, and *reactive* or forced migration, then refugees occupy the second of these categories in so far as the circumstances of their migration are nearly always beyond individual control (Richmond 2002). Although legal definitions vary, refugees are generally considered to be people fleeing life-threatening circumstances: ethnic cleansing, religious persecution, war (McMaster 2002: 21). In the aftermath of political independence in several regions of the so-called Third World and the collapse of communist regimes in what used to be known as the Second, new and often violent forms of nationalism have emerged that have resulted in the victimization and/or expulsion of large numbers of ethnically stigmatized peoples (Richmond 2002: 708).

As Don McMaster argues, refugees are the embodiment of the political identity crisis of the modern global era:

In their homelessness and statelessness refugees are the unwilling representatives of a cosmopolitan alternative to the idea of a homeland. The ideal homeland can be seen as unrealisable, or alternatively recognised as the site of struggle against the reductionism of national identity.

(McMaster 2002: 21)

The functionalization of the refugee as a negative mirror-image of the cosmopolitan tacitly acknowledges the political expediency underlying contemporary, usually Western-driven myths of a 'borderless world' (McMaster 2002: 36; see also Maley 2002). In fact, refugees illustrate the obvious truth that national borders are now policed—at least for certain categories of people—more stringently than ever. Similarly, the utopian rhetoric that often surrounds such (neo-)liberal projects as an integrated world economy and global citizenship is counteracted by the realities of a double social exclusion, with asylum seekers falling afoul not only of the tyrannical regimes of the Third World countries they wish to flee from, but also of the increasingly authoritarian policies of First World immigration control.

In addition, refugees are often subject to a national 'politics of fear' (MacCullum 2002; Manne 2004), eagerly fanned by populist governments and a sensationalist media, and sometimes linked to memories of colonialism and decolonization that 'alter the definition between individuals and states whose cultures . . . construct the host and guest in radically incompatible ways' (Rosello 2001: vii). A common (mis)perception of refugees, that they are the beneficiaries of a legislated form of hospitality, can easily lead to the reactionary argument that they constitute, like hospitality itself, either an 'impossible luxury' or an 'unacceptable risk' (Rosello 2001: 7; see also Derrida 2000). This also encourages a jaundiced view of refugees as potential threats to national security. As McMaster puts it:

Displaced persons and refugees are the 'other' in the realm of national politics; they represent all that is foreign, strange and alien. This discourse assumes that refugees present a problem: they are not ordinary people but represent, rather, an anomaly requiring specialised correctives and therapeutic inventions. Refugees are suspects in their new lands, perceived as amoral criminals or even terrorists. This politics of fear separates refugees from citizens.

(McMaster 2002: 37)

Current perceptions of a 'refugee crisis' in Australia—out of all proportion to the small number of actual refugee intakes (Mares 2001; McMaster 2002)—provide an unwanted reminder of the cultural isolationism and, at times, the overt racism underlying multicultural Australia's postcolonial present, as well as White Australia's (neo)colonial past. Despite a well-documented series of international scandals—the *Tampa*, the Pacific Solution, the Children Overboard affair[2]—government policy toward asylum seekers has hardened noticeably over the last decade, revealing a clear split between the relative if hardly unrivalled generosity shown towards official 'offshore' claimants and the hardline stance taken up towards undocumented arrivals 'onshore'. At the time of writing, 'onshore' arrivals are automatically quarantined in isolated detention centres while their claims are being processed, and are thus taken out of sight of the public and—so the government hopes—out of harm's way (Crock 1993; Mares 2001).

Current refugee policy in Australia is difficult not to see as a form of race-based political opportunism, directly playing on populist perceptions of refugees as the nation's significant other and linked, in turn, to irrational historical fears of alien invasion, particularly by the undifferentiated hordes of the 'Asiatic' North. While it would be exaggerated to describe such policy as intentionally racist, the recent evidence suggests a hierarchy of opportunity favouring (white) European refugees over their (non-white) counterparts from Africa, Asia, and the Middle East. Meanwhile, the representation of asylum seekers, particularly in the mainstream print and visual media, has remained at best unnuanced and, at worst, unremittingly negative, stressing the drain on national resources that refugees produce and the strain they place on the nation's collective goodwill. Such unreflected nationalistic representations tend, once again, to confirm the status of refugees/asylum seekers as collective objects of finite public generosity, rather than as individual subjects with their own life-stories and their own, not necessarily convincing, reasons for seeking protection from a foreign state.

Counter-images can be found in the shape of refugees'/asylum seekers' own life-narratives, a number of which, mostly in the mode of oral histories or testimonies, have recently found their way into print (see, for example, *Tales from a Suitcase* (2002) or the earlier collection *Refugee* (1982)). In a sign of the times, these experience-based narratives share space with revived white fantasies of alien invasion (e.g. Eric Willmot's *Below the Line* (1991) or John Marsden's adolescent-fiction trilogy *Tomorrow, When the War Began* (1995)), offering, in the last case, a perhaps unwelcome reminder of an influential if critically neglected Australian popular genre. A third literary strand consists of assorted re-enactments and dramatizations, several of them in the genre of workshop theatre, and fronted by such high-profile figures as Louis Nowra (see, for example, *Displaced Persons* (1985), Nowra's controversial TV play).

In the remainder of this section, I want to look more closely at a recent compilation of refugee/asylum seeker testimony, gathered by the Australian journalist-activist Heather Tyler and melodramatically entitled, *Asylum: Voices Behind the Razor Wire* (2003). The accounts, drawn from asylum seekers serving time in Australia's various euphemistically called immigration detention centres, are presented in such a way as to touch the heart while also stimulating outrage. A particularly virulent example is the following letter addressed to asylum seeker/activist Aamer Sultan, a highly educated doctor presented in the text as being untiring in his efforts to defend the human rights of his fellow detainees:

Like you, I believe asylum-seekers should not be detained for long periods of time. They should be sent back to where they came from in 5 to 10 days preferably in a body bag with a bullet between the eyes. All Muslims should be sterilised at birth. All boats with boat people should be sunk. You are a guest in this country so you should keep your opinions to yourself. Hitler should have done us a favour by exterminating the Muslims rather than the Jews.

(Tyler 2003: 150–1)

Equally chilling is the opinion of an experienced immigration lawyer, who when asked whether there is any likelihood of an amnesty being granted to those asylum seekers who remain in detention, responds summarily: 'There will be no amnesty. They will stay there till they rot' (Tyler 2003: 218).

These are of course minority views, even if they indicate a groundswell of xenophobia in Australia, apparently encouraged by some of the more crudely flag-waving sections of a cultural-nationalist press. However, this shouldn't detract from the reinforced sensationalism created by books like Tyler's which, however honourable their motives, co-opt their foreign subjects as friends and allies in a mighty battle against the continuing tyrannies of the Australian state. Very different asylum seekers, with very different histories and objectives, are enlisted here for a white-liberal salvation narrative that demonizes asylum seekers' countries of origin even as it seeks to rescue them from their own demonization by an often hostile Australian press. In addition, Tyler's interviewees are rarely allowed to speak for themselves, with the author mostly content to reproduce bite-sized chunks of transcribed text which are then inserted into a master-narrative of heroic resistance—a twinned resistance that collapses differences between persecution (in the home country) and punishment (in the host state).

To some extent, these pitfalls are common to other forms of activist or advocacy literature, which tends to slide into a kind of melodramatics of victimage in which unsung heroes are pitted against dehumanized/dehumanizing villains in an allegorical struggle to lift the burden of the oppressed. This raises the vexed question of whether such texts can be politically effective while remaining aesthetically satisfying or, alternatively, whether a subgenre—call it 'refugee literature'—can ever escape from being crudely functionalized for global commercial ends. The commodification of victim narratives has recently been seen as a by-product of contemporary global 'wound culture' (Seltzer 1998)—a function both of the postmodern retailing of disaster and, paradoxically, of a 'postemotional society' (Mestrovic 1997) that insulates itself from such harrowing 'real-life' accounts (Lennon and Foley 2000; Phipps 1999).

It is perhaps too early to tell whether refugee testimonials, in Australia and beyond, will feed the maw of the global memory industry, although there are signs that they are already being absorbed into the tourism of suffering, through which death and disaster are routinely transformed into commodities 'for consumption in a global communications market' (Lennon and Foley 2000: 5; see also Rojek 1993). What is clear is that 'refugee literature' can easily be turned into another marketable form of cultural voyeurism, capitalizing on the endangered, the impoverished, and the needy, and manipulating the vicarious experience of suffering as a means towards establishing a false solidarity with the oppressed. As with other kinds of multicultural writing, there is exoticist mystification at work here. The liberal championing of refugees suggests the violence, not just of overt racial protectionism, but also of covert ideologies of benevolence—ideologies in which kindness towards foreigners doesn't necessarily make them any less foreign, and insufficiently differentiated narratives of survival and resistance mystify the condition, even as they advertise the suffering, of the oppressed.

4.3 Demystifying 'Asia'

4.3.1 Looking West to the East

If refugees are the latest version of white Australia's 'utterly distrusted Other' (Ang 2001: 130), then Asians have long grown accustomed to occupying this demonizing role. Negative stereotypes abound in Australian representations of Asia, many of them motivated by the anxious recognition that Australia, while clearly situated in an Asia–Pacific geography, has historically defined itself against Asia as a fundamentally 'different' (often meaning 'alien') part of the world (Ang 2001; Walker 1997). While the pendulum continues to swing between those who see Australia as physically distinct from or as psychically attached to Asia, both positions are conditioned by the same essentializing logic. According to this logic, 'Australia' and 'Asia' are totalized entities locked in a relationship of 'mutual exteriority' (Ang 2001: 131). This relationship persists even if strategic enthusiasms are periodically encouraged to express themselves: 'Australia no longer turns its back against "Asia" (because it can no longer afford to), but is now for "Asia" (because it thinks it has to be)' (Ang 2001: 131).

In this sense, the so-called 'turn to Asia' in the 1980s and 1990s—a tide now observed by some as having gone back out—is not uncharacteristic of Australian responses to Asia since the colonial period, which have often oscillated between the widest of extremes (Broinowski 1998: 440). Phobic representation has returned, of the paranoid type in which the nation's 'genocidal past is [now being] replayed as its apocalyptic future' (Morris 1998: 247; see also Hage 2003). Then again, this might just be seen as an exaggerated version of the racial/spatial anxieties that have permeated the history of Australian–Asian relations, anxieties that are arguably constitutive of a country conceived as a 'white European enclave in an alien, non-European part of the world' (Ang 2001: 130).

As might be expected, literature has played a major role in articulating these racialized anxieties. For much of the colonial period, Asia could be counted on to provide a gallery of outlandish racial stereotypes, ranging in intensity from inept comic villains to ravening barbarian hordes (Broinowski 1992). Twentieth-century representations could hardly fail to be more subtle, and several writers took on a more positive engagement with the region. In the best of this writing, Asia featured as spiritual lure or philosophical challenge, while granting more limited opportunities for cultural–political analysis or experiment with non-European aesthetic forms.

Still, Asia has yet to live up to its claim as Australia's most fertile imaginative territory, a territory that the nation's writers 'may well do a lot to define [and] even perhaps to give configurations it didn't have before' (Koch 1987: 104; see also Tiffin 1984). To be sure, contemporary literary encounters between Australia and Asia are more self-conscious, more sophisticated, and better researched than the vast majority of their often crudely exoticist predecessors. Many of them, however, continue to be plagued by Orientalist myths and stereotypes; as David Myers sardonically puts it:

The mythical testing of Australian youth which up until recently was traditionally located by Australian art in the vast outback or at Gallipoli has now been replaced by the hero's confrontation with Asia, in which the hero is required to show nobility of soul in spite of personal failure, and amid the pervasive presence in Asian society of corruption, gargantuan greed, racial hatred, ideological fanaticism and evil.

(Myers 1989: 31)

The ironies are multiple here. For a start, contemporary Australian writers attempting to redefine the coordinates of Australian culture have become aware that they are separated from their Asian 'neighbours' not only by possibly unbridgeable cultural differences, but also by persistent myths and stereotypes that link them back to the West they were self-consciously trying to leave behind. All of a sudden, the 'turn to Asia' begins to look suspiciously like a return to Europe. This suspicion is confirmed by the tendency to see Asia as a loose conglomerate of non-European cultures, situated 'out there', which white Australians must reach out to discover, thereby overlooking the significant impact that several generations of Asian immigration have had on the national culture 'back home'. A valuable imaginative resource, Asia also serves as an effective ideological smokescreen; the generic term 'Asia' itself is usefully vague, allowing for 'Asian' religions and philosophies or aspects of 'Asian' aesthetics to be incorporated into fanciful metaphysical quests in which the East is explored as a Western state of mind.

This is, of course, the caricatured sketch of a history of representation that is neither continuous nor consistent. Still, while the critical consensus is that 'the role Asia plays in Australian thought [is becoming] increasingly complex and important' (Tiffin 1984: 479), it is worth speculating whether the new wave of Australian literature that claims to be (re)discovering Asia isn't doing something rather different: using Asia as an imaginative outlet that diverts attention away from everyday social and political problems back home. The litmus test I want to propose for this hypothesis is Brian Castro's brilliant first novel *Birds of Passage* (1983), still probably the best-known single work by an Asian Australian writer (Castro is of Chinese and Portuguese extraction) to date.

Birds of Passage weaves together the life-stories of a contemporary Australian-born Chinese, Seamus O'Young [*sic*], and his (spiritual) ancestor, the migrant worker Lo Yun Shan, who arrives in Australia in the mid nineteenth century with one of the first waves of mainland Chinese lured over by the Gold Rush. The two stories counteract rather than complement one another, providing subtle variations on Castro's main theme: the multiple guises and dissimulations of ethnic identity. Charting O'Young's ambivalent status as an 'ethnic' Australian through a succession of historical discontinuities and geographical displacements, *Birds of Passage* explores the irony that 'one only becomes ethnic through the eyes of another; the labelling is never one's own' (Brydon 1987: 94). O'Young's attempt to decipher the runic manuscript bequeathed to him by Shan leads him to conjure up a past which then proceeds to haunt him—a past he must piece together if he is to understand his own origins, but whose scattered fragments do not belong to him. O'Young initially seeks to learn about himself through Shan, but eventually comes to realize that his survival in an intolerant and potentially hostile society depends as much on a process of *un*learning, on the voluntary contraction of a kind of strategic amnesia that allows him to reinvent his own origins rather than become a prisoner to another's past.

At one level, *Birds of Passage* aligns itself with other early 1980s' revisionist interpretations of Australian history, like David Foster's *Moonlite* (1981) or Rodney Hall's *Just Relations* (1982), in which the Gold Rush features as a discursive site for the uncovering of self-glorifying cultural myths. A less likely but equally important interlocutor is the French semiotician Roland Barthes, who makes a cameo appearance in the middle of the novel. (He stumbles into the train compartment into which O'Young is sitting, introduces himself, then abruptly excuses himself and leaves—it seems he is in the wrong compartment.) What are we to make of this odd, seemingly gratuitous intrusion? More than meets the eye; for Castro's novel—which, like all his work, is nothing if not theoretically informed—plays cleverly on Barthes' (inter)cultural semiotics and, in particular, on his analysis of another Asian country, Japan, in his short but characteristically incisive travel study, *Empire of Signs* (1971).

Empire of Signs documents the guided tour of a fictive 'Japan' which resembles, but is not reducible to, the 'real' country. In fact, Barthes professes not to be interested in Japan at all, but rather in the possibility of interrogating Western ways of seeing and thinking about 'other' cultures; to adopt his own simile, 'Japan' is like 'the slender thread of light' which searches out 'not other symbols but the very fissure of the symbolic', and which allows him to 'entertain the idea of an unheard-of symbolic system, one altogether detached from our own' (Barthes 1982 [1971]: 3–4). The 'fissure of the symbolic' provides a moment of ideological rupture in which the Western observer is forced to recognize the limitations of his/her own knowledge of the Orient, and to confront the partiality of the various European-dominated languages through which that knowledge is mediated and controlled. In Roger Hurcombe's gloss, 'the otherness of things Japanese [in the text thus] serves to mark the specificity, and [to] contradict any idea of the universality, of the things of the West' (Hurcombe 1990: 109).

What does all of this have to do with Castro's novel? In fact, a great deal; for the interwoven narratives of *Birds of Passage* themselves constitute a kind of empire of ephemeral signs, a kaleidoscope of shifting fragments which refuses to set into any single pattern or to conform to any one shape or design. Take gold, for instance, one of the central motifs in the novel. Most obviously, gold signifies wealth, or perhaps the illusory promise of it. But there are any numbers of signifieds for the one signifier. Gold, after all, may promise one thing, but deliver quite another. Consider O'Young's devious employer, Abraham Feingold. Consider the Gold Rush. Consider gold as burnished yellow: the colour of the Yellow Peril, of Shan's journal, of his skin.

By playing on the multiple connotations of gold—by fossicking in the semantic goldfield—Castro is doing more than just indulging in the pleasures of the text; he is also emphasizing the susceptibility of signs and symbolic systems to ideological manipulation. The informing metaphor here, as the novel's title suggests, is that of *migration*. *Birds of Passage* is clearly a novel, at one level, about the hardships of migration and the embattled position of the migrant in a racially stratified society. But at another, it is also a novel about the ways in which meanings and established systems of meaning 'migrate'.

O'Young's survival in late twentieth-century Australia, like his predecessor's a century before him, depends to some extent on his capacity to elude definition, to displace the dominant ideologies of White Australia that seek to impose their ground rules, their naturalized ways of seeing and thinking, on him. O'Young's official status is that of an Australian-born Chinese. ABC: the arbitrary alphabetic designation seems to come straight out of Barthes. 'So you're one of those bloody Chinese-born Australians', gibes a British customs official during one of O'Young's numerous border-crossings (Castro 1983: 8). Like Barthes, the customs official gets the wrong compartment; but which is the right one? While O'Young's hybridity—his uncertain status as an orphan, a refugee, a 'displaced person'—is one of the sources of his subordinate position in Australian society, it also allows him to disrupt conventional categories of national and racial identity. Defying the categories that the white authorities impose on him, O'Young seeks instead to define himself through the medium of his ancestor's journal. But the journal is fractured, the medium self-defeating, and O'Young soon finds himself reproducing the hysterical tendencies of his earlier shadow self. Only when he learns to relocate himself in the interstices of Shan's writing, in the 'symbolic fissure' that separates Shan's history from his own, is he able to negotiate a space for himself between other people's imprisoning definitions of him. This space is necessarily provisional and contestatory; for O'Young's cross-cultural translations, mirroring the attempts of the white authorities to 'translate' him, are shot through—like all translations—with uneven relations of power (Bassnett and Trivedi 1999).

Birds of Passage is a seminal work of Asian–Australian cultural relations, situated at the faultline between Orientalist inscription and Western institutional power (Huggan 1992; Said 1978).[3] The novel complicates the 'turn to Asia' thesis in at least three ways: (1) by suggesting that Asia continues to act as a projection screen for Western fantasy, e.g. through the self-privileging manoeuvres of exoticism; (2) by questioning the functionalization of Asia as a 'limit text' (Bhabha 1994) to Western modes of authority and self-understanding; and (3) by insisting that Asia is an integral component of modern Australian culture, but not necessarily in the ways that white Australians might imagine it to be (psychic reterritorialization, philosophical immersion, political rapprochement).

However, what the text certainly does *not* suggest is the special status of the Asian Australian writer as 'excluding insider' (Said 1986: 229). Nor does it allege the heightened vision of the culturally hyphenated migrant; after all, O'Young hardly qualifies as a visionary, and his halting attempts to discern his place within the larger history of Asian migration to Australia are, at best, a limited success. If anything, the novel interrogates the powerfully deceptive myth of migrant 'double vision', as well as uncovering the metonymic fallacy by which migrant writing, in encapsulating migrant lives and livelihoods, dissolves individual experience within the national whole.

4.3.2 Double visions

Two very different takes on 'double vision' are those of the novelist C. J. Koch and the playwright John Romeril, among white Australia's foremost literary commentators on Asia. Koch's and Romeril's best-known works, *The Year of Living Dangerously* (1978) and *The Floating World* (1975), both provide not one but a dizzying proliferation of dualities. *The Year of Living Dangerously* presents, in Koch's own words, a 'double hero' combining the 'tormented' Chinese–Australian photographer Billy Kwan and the 'cool' English–Australian correspondent Guy Hamilton, these being seen as linked aspects of the same dual personality: 'mystic and simple soul, thinker and man of action; both of them products of a dying colonial world' (Koch 1987: 23). Alter egos abound as the two set off in different pursuits of the 'demi-god' Sukarno, self-styled liberator of his own 'second-hand' colonial country (Koch 1983 [1978]: 97). Kwan, in particular, cuts a grotesquely semi-mythic figure poised between contending alter egos—Hamilton/Sukarno, Sukarno/Vishnu—and between the hallucinatory temptations these alternative identities offer: world-ly mystic, poet-prophet, multiply reincarnated god (Koch 1983: 13, 98, 132).

The Kwan-Hamilton dyad features the giant knight (Hamilton) and his dwarf-squire (Kwan), inseparable descendants of numerous Indo-European mythologies (Koch 1983: 117); while the Kwan-Sukarno pairing reveals the former to be the latter's fiercest advocate-cum-adversary, as well as his cartoonish shadow self. The Indonesian *wayang* (puppet theatre) provides a further source of relentlessly duplicated and/or duplicitous representations, reflecting on Indonesia itself as theatrical site of political turmoil and mythic fantasy: the land of seemingly perpetual *Konfrontasi*; the land of 'enormous hopelessness [and] queer jauntiness', forever displaying a bewildering 'double face' (Koch 1983: 59).

The text thus repeatedly reduces cultural, political, and historical complexities to a melodramatic interplay of opposing mythic forces, presided over by the pathological figure of Kwan in his alternate (double) guises as louche photographer-voyeur, compulsive classifier-manipulator, exhibitionist point-man and surreptitious 'Peeping Tom on other people's souls' (Koch 1983: 7, 108). Under Billy's gaze, people are turned, *wayang*-style, into puppets and back again into people, while the ideological contorsions of recent Indonesian history are transformed into the predetermined, endlessly self-repeating antics of the country's ever-popular shadow plays (Koch 1983: 282).

Labouring under the weight of these self-replicating caricatures and stereotypes, Koch's novel still manages to create a vivid pastiche of modern Indonesian history—one in which the twinned Australian journalists Kwan and Hamilton end up being sacrificed on the altar of cultural-nationalist expediency, and Australia is left to confront its own ambivalent position as an emergent South Pacific nation still embedded within an ancient Indo-European world. Indonesia, Koch suggests in his 1987 essay 'The Lost Hemisphere', is 'where Asia begins'; it shares 'a political and cultural destiny' (Koch 1987: 104–5) with Australia in which the two countries will come increasingly to understand each other's beliefs and thought-systems, and to retrace the lineage of those systems to the powerful Indo-European civilizations located 'to the north of [them] both' (Koch 1987: 25).

If this is pure cultural journalese, Koch's work is frequently disabused of its own journalistic inclinations. *The Year of Living Dangerously*, for example, pokes fun at its correspondent-protagonists' exoticist fantasies and production-line generalities; at their tenuous grasp of current social and political realities; and at their tendency to cocoon themselves from the very people and places they imagine themselves to confront. The novel therefore inhabits a highly constructed, imaginatively febrile and artificially self-sustaining universe: a precarious life-world which, when put under severe pressure, is always likely to implode.

Here, it acknowledges its place within a geneaology of self-ironizing Australian 'journalist novels'—by Robert Drewe, Ian Moffitt, Margaret Jones, and several others—that play critically on the prospect of generating instant knowledge about the foreign culture, in this case 'Asia', for their audience back home (Broinoskwi 1992; Tiffin 1984). These novels take issue with the view of journalists as colourless functionaries of the factual, dedicated to the uncovering of actuality; instead they show just how far journalism can produce powerful mystifications of its own (Bennett 1989). Journalism is revealed in the process to be a medium of obfuscation, a means of charting the limits of knowledge and testing the claims of information; or as a vehicle for the recycling of exotic stereotypes about the inscrutable cultural other; or as the pretext for an exploration of duplicitous cultural politics and a fraught exposure of the need to withhold sources; or, quite often, as an ironic demonstration of all of these at once. The search for news collapses into a tautology of difference as, dogged by the impossibility of accurate documentation, the journalist-protagonists of these novels find themselves precipitated back into reconfirming the strangeness of the culture(s) they imaginatively confront.

Irony is their punishment; as Alison Broinowski observes, the type they conform to is, by and large, a combination of the inexpert and the pragmatic, 'conscientiously free of the racial prejudice and imperialism of earlier generations, but [still] mostly disinclined to get caught up in contentious local issues' (Broinowski 1992: 178–9). Sometimes, however, they *do* get caught up, and the punishment may be more than they deserve. Enlightenment, if it is found at all, is usually discovered to carry a heavy penalty; and it is no surprise to learn that the price Hamilton pays for his complacency in a novel that eventually collapses under the accumulated weight of its dualities is, precisely, the loss of sight in one eye.

Romeril's play *The Floating World* also enacts a series of compulsive repeat performances, as a cruise-ship (originally troop convoy) carrying its annual cargo of increasingly addled Australian passengers makes its slow but inexorable way towards the site of previous military nightmares, Japan. The action reads double in several ways: as a reverse invasion (Romeril 1982 [1975]: 6) in which military conflict on foreign soil is replaced by the depredations of modern mass tourism (MacCannell 1976); as a paranoid-nationalist reminder of the Asian takeover of Australian businesses back home; and above all, as a self-defeating opportunity for ex-soldiers to rehearse wartime experiences and atrocities—as Les Harding's hallucinatory alter ego McLeod tells him, 'You will [remember], Les. It all comes back, son, it all comes back' (Romeril 1982: 32).

Repetition compulsion is the structural principle around which the action of the play, otherwise highly impressionistic and episodic, can be seen to operate. At the centre of it all is the gradually disintegrating figure of Les Harding—another in the vintage series of Ocker Aussies—whose bilious resentments eventually expand into full-blown madness, transforming him, like the embattled nation with which he pathologically associates, into a combination of diseased organism and wrecked machine (Romeril 1982: 94). Through the various stages of Les's breakdown, the individual symptoms of postwar traumatic syndrome gradually uncover the traces of a broader ideological systems failure, driven by paranoid fears of alien authority and residual nationalist fantasies of absorption by another 'master race'. These fears and fantasies are manifestly absurd, like the interchangeably Orientalist gibes with which the ship's comic despairingly tries to entertain his audience, or like the manic 'Dippy Bird' toys to which the characters are implicitly likened, whose mechanism runs smoothly if not tampered with, but whose stability is obviously precarious. (As the botched instructions read: 'If the high heat is touched then the pressure of contents are going up'—Romeril 1982: 9.)

Here as elsewhere in the play, comedy becomes an outlet for unsubstantiated rancour, allowing lurking resentments to be brought up to the surface and literally vomited out (Romeril 1982: 6–9). War is the ultimate sick joke, incorporated into the comic's routine as if it were self-evidently hilarious (Romeril 1982: 43). 'You've gotta have a laugh', he says repeatedly, but there is precious little in the play to laugh about: from the surreal exchanges between Les and McLeod, vehicles for tortured memory, to Les and Irene's domestic banter, laced with crude sexist/racist commonplaces, to the comic's own embarrassingly inept stand-up routine.

Nonetheless, as in the tradition of absurdist theatre, the play continually dares its audience to laugh at the preposterousness of its characters' antics, thereby establishing a self-incriminating superiority over them. This superiority is illusory; as Romeril suggests in his author's note to the second edition, the play works towards a collective understanding, not only that no single country has a 'monopoly on atrocity' (Romeril 1982: xxxiii), but also that responsibility for continuing social and cultural divisions within Australia, often projected onto the figure of the sexual/racial adversary, is effectively shared. The last 'double act' of the play, then, is a doubling back on the disoriented spectator, who is confronted with his/her own anxieties and insecurities: anxieties and insecurities he/she is invited to compare with, and challenged to differentiate from, the standard paranoid-nationalist thesis of Australia as a 'British outpost surrounded by hostile Asian hordes' (Ashbolt 1982: viii).

4.3.3   Disorientations

More recently, Yasmine Gooneratne's satirical novel *A Change of Skies* (1991) enacts a similar double repertoire. A young Sri Lankan couple's migration to Australia ironically mimics the journey of their more illustrious nineteenth-century ancestor; both of these journeys are then placed within a genealogy of partly historical, partly imaginary voyages in which 'Asia' and 'Australia' are largely defined by mutual ignorance and by the seemingly irresistible tendency to stereotype both each other and themselves. The cross-cultural dialogue the novel sets up is thus transformed into a comic catalogue of post-Forsterian misapprehensions, products of a reciprocally distorting vision filtered through the reliably unreliable media of Hollywood spectacle and exotic romance (Gooneratne 1991: 13–15; 21–22; 99).

The novel points to the educative advantages of displacement without ever fully accepting the Gandhian dictum that living in another country heightens one's awareness both of the other country and one's own (Gooneratne 1991: 298). Integral to this thesis is the relatively privileged figure of the expatriate, turned throughout the novel into a self-mocking symbol of the very cultural disruption s/he is often most likely to abhor (Gooneratne 1991: 88–90). Gooneratne gives short shrift to the conveniently self-romanticizing view of expatriates as being 'cut off from the mainstream of national life' (Gooneratne 1991: 279), hopelessly out of place and socially marginalized in their new country; but she is equally impatient with the view that transcultural encounters are automatically beneficial, showing a number of instances to the contrary and satirizing the clichéd figure of the migrant-as-chameleon, living proof of the possibilities provided by accelerated global processes of cultural interaction and exchange (Gooneratne 1991: 285).

It seems worth pausing here to unpack the term 'transculturalism', especially since *A Change of Skies* has been cited as an example of the modern 'transcultural novel' (Thieme 1996)—a relatively recent addition, this, to the growing postcolonial lexicon of culturally entangled processes and products, and one sometimes seen as having displaced earlier qualifying adjectives—'multicultural', 'intercultural' or even, in some cases, 'postcolonial'—prematurely considered to be past their sell-by date. 'Transculturalism', in its most evangelical form, involves the almost wilfully naive globalist recognition that since 'everything is within reach... there [can] no longer [be] anything foreign'; and that, as a consequence, 'people can make their own choice with respect to their affiliation' (Welsch 1999: 198). Immodestly offered both as the most complete understanding of culture today and as an antidote to outmoded apprehensions of homogeneous and/or separate cultures, transculturalism assumes a teleology that transcends the binaries of global and local, universalism and particularism, replacing these with a cocktail of negotiated 'mixes and permeations' that are held to be more characteristic of 'cultural conditions today' (Welsch 1999: 197).

While there are obviously more modulated understandings of transculturalism than this (see, for example, Appadurai 1996; Hannerz 1996; Schulze-Engler 2000), the term, like the cultural hybridity with which it is often associated, risks subscribing to a 'closet idealism' that underplays residual, sometimes reintensified, colonial oppression at the global systemic level today (Cheah and Robbins 1998: 302). This allegation can be countered by the claim that transculturalism implies both profitable exchange and persistent inequality: hence the emphasis in most transcultural theory on transnational and/or diasporic socio-political alliances and cultural formations, often global in scope, anti-imperialist in intent, and created or consolidated through the new media and other modern communications systems (Appadurai 1996); but hence also the countervailing acknowledgement of a hierarchy of globalized modernities in the contemporary late-capitalist world order—an order in which obvious questions of unequal access to technology and the conspicuously inequitable distribution and ownership of resources are brought repeatedly to the fore (Schulze-Engler 2000; Huggan 2006).

A Change of Skies can be seen, among other things, as a meditation on the mutually transformative possibilities of transculturalism, envisaged here both in terms of a universality beyond cultural differences (Gooneratne 1991: 117, 167) and a global market of 'contact zones' (Pratt 1992) in which cultural differences are negotiated and exchanged. The latter thesis carries the day, as the novel weaves backwards and forwards between alternative spaces and time-zones, alternative homes and homelands, 'past events and future possibilities' (Gooneratne 1991: 9). Trade is the dominant metaphor for this two-way cultural traffic, with 'authentic' products from different countries circulating on the global market, and 'authenticity' itself operating as a commodity in touristic networks of cultural appreciation and exchange (Gooneratne 1991: 25, 27; see also Huggan 2001). ('I'm reading [*The Tourist's Sri Lanka*] from cover to cover', says one Australian visitor brightly, 's[o] I'll be able to recognise the Real Sri Lanka when I see it' (Gooneratne 1991: 20).)

Here as elsewhere, Gooneratne's novel is ironically aware of its own status as an 'Asian tourist novel' (Broinowski 1992; Huggan 2001; Tiffin 1984)—a readily identifiable subgenre where 'Asia' functions as marketable exotic spectacle, and in which the paraded virtues of 'Asia-literacy' and 'the multicultural sensibility' become further variants on a commodified Orientalism as likely to be peddled by diplomats as by tour-guides, and sometimes by both of these at once:

Harry [the Australian High Commissioner to Sri Lanka] had just returned to Colombo from Tokyo, where he had been discussing meat exports with Japanese businessmen, and next week he would be off to Florida to give a paper on Asian writers in Australia at a conference of the American Association for Australian Literature.

(Gooneratne 1991: 29)

Such meta-Orientalist jokes can easily become just as predictable—and predictably profitable—as the cultural formulae they derisively accumulate. (Significantly, both protagonists cash in: Bharat ('Barry') with a travel journal and a guide for prospective Asian migrants; his wife Navaranjini ('Jean') with a cookbook combining 'Western' and 'Oriental' ingredients—this latter offering further proof that food has recently become *the* iconic medium for current processes of transcultural accommodation and exchange.)

In ironizing its own marketability while also capitalizing on it, Gooneratne's transcultural novel takes us back (via an admittedly circuitous route) to Demidenko's, with whose more obviously reprehensible self-ethnicizing antics this chapter started out. Certainly, both novels are aware of the status of ethnicity as a commodity; while both, if with very different motives and degrees of manipulativeness, ask their readers to consider the mechanisms by which multiculturalism and/or multicultural literature are offered up for public consumption and commercial exchange.

Has multiculturalism, as these novels suggest, turned into something of a liability in Australia? After all, both works highlight the contradictions built into the term—contradictions which only appear to multiply when other terms ('interculturalism', 'transculturalism', etc.) are brought into conflict with it. As previously suggested, these terms are *not* identical to, nor even necessarily contiguous with, one another. To summarize: multiculturalism is a state-sanctioned project involving the celebration and management of cultural diversity. Interculturalism and transculturalism are less immediately bound to state control, but are not as free-floating as some of their apologists would like to think they are. The former involves a critical engagement with the cultural other that is primarily philosophical or epistemological in nature, the latter a more experiential understanding of personal/collective negotiations with 'modernity at large' (Appadurai 1996).

Of the three terms, multiculturalism is most obviously tied into the collective project of the nation. As Barnor Hesse argues, the shift from 'conciliatory' to 'contestatory' understandings of multiculturalism may be seen as a function of the inevitably unsuccessful attempt to 'find a national resolution of the unsettled relation between marked cultural differences' (Hesse 2000: 2). Why unsuccessful? In part, because multicultural nations such as Australia (and, in a different context, Britain) have yet to come to terms with their colonial/imperial history. Multiculturalism, in other words, is both an effect and an extension of the incomplete process of decolonization in a globalized world in which racism—particularly though by no means exclusively *white* racism—remains intact (Hesse 2000).

Multiculturalism, seen this way, registers the transition from Western imperialism to racialized liberal democracy: a transition that Hesse equates with 'the unresolved postcolonial condition'; and one markedly apparent in residually white-dominated settler societies like Australia, where multicultural policies disguise both continuing white privileges and paranoid anxieties about living in a society which is increasingly 'non-white' (Hesse 2000: 13; see also Hage 2003). The problem with Hesse's contestatory view of multiculturalism is that it either becomes virtually ubiquitous, collapsing differences between radically dissimilar societies, or vertiginously plural, collapsing differences between radically dissimilar political projects and effects.

Still, there is much to be said for approaches to multiculturalism that work towards what Stuart Hall has called 'a new multicultural political logic': a logic able to facilitate 'a radical configuration of the particular and the universal, [and] of liberty and equality with difference' (Hall 2000: 236). For Hall and others, this logic presupposes an understanding of multiculturalism that goes beyond the boundaries of the nation. It is worth noting that the implied teleology of transculturalism is rejected here. It is not a question of moving from 'national' multiculturalism via 'transnational' interculturalism to a truly 'global' transculturalism, if such a move were ever possible; rather, the entanglement of prefixes ('multi', 'inter', 'trans') provides further evidence of an unevenly developed world in which there is not one but several possible—possibly incommensurate—modernities, and in which the nation is recognized as only one of several possible—possibly irreconcilable—horizons of cultural identity and juridico-political sites.

AFTERWORD

In viewing the history, particularly the recent history, of Australian literature through the lens of postcolonial and critical race theory, this book supports the claim—made more in theory than in practice—that Australian literary studies has much to gain from going beyond the nation; from adopting a broadly comparative, transnational approach. Such insistence is hardly new; for while the consensus is that Australian literary studies emerged out of (mid) twentieth-century cultural nationalism, regular warnings against disciplinary over-specialization and cultural isolationism have sounded ever since (Dixon 2003).

Not that the warnings have always been heeded by Australian literary scholars; as Gillian Whitlock ruefully remarks in a 1999 essay:

[Australian] literary scholars remain deeply attached to representations of Australia as a nation apart. We are the most well-travelled and internationally well-connected generation of Australian literary scholars. And yet we continue to teach and write in institutional and discursive frameworks which favour the conception of national cultures (our own, and others) as highly integrated.

(Whitlock 1999: 154)

Whitlock's remark is perhaps more ironic than she acknowledges. First, she is appealing to something that has already happened at the level of literary production, since the Australian culture industries have existed for some time now within 'international networks as part of a system of [multidirectional] transnational flows' (Carter 1999: 143). Australian literature, in this context, is both national *and* international; while much the same might be said of other Australian cultural products, obvious examples being television and film.

Second, Whitlock assumes that Australian literary criticism, while needing to expand its own horizons, is still primarily a matter to be debated among *Australians*. This suggests that while it may not be strictly necessary to be Australian to write Australian literature, it certainly helps if one wants to do Australian literary criticism. (This suspicion is hardly allayed by Leigh Dale who, in an essay adjoining Whitlock's, recognizes 'long established links with overseas scholars', only to follow this with the put-down: 'These [international] linkages [are now] a little too well-worn' (Dale 1999: 3).)

To be fair, both Dale and Whitlock practise a sensitive form of Australian literary/cultural criticism that is well attuned to the global dissemination of local cultural debates and issues. One word for this form of criticism is 'postcolonialism'. For Whitlock, postcolonialism's remit includes broad-based approaches to the politics of race, the corrosive influence of which on Australian history, identity, and culture is incontestable, but the comparative transnational study of which 'has only just begun' (Whitlock 1999: 153). She duly calls for 'migratory readings' of race in which 'the nation, nationality and national cultures are primary but not determining or autonomous indices' (Whitlock 1999: 154). These readings might contribute to an Australian-centred postcolonialism capable of generating new ways of thinking about the nation and the national, while also allowing for responses that 'move beyond the boundaries of the nation [to] pursue a comparative approach' (Whitlock 1999: 155).

This type of postcolonialism goes beyond the nation but also, in some cases, beyond the literary, into such disciplinary areas as history, political science, and anthropology, as well as the sociology of literature/culture: publishing and editing, knowledge studies, the history of the book (Dixon 2004). While the interdisciplinarity of postcolonial studies has yet to win over a territory-conscious Western academy (Huggan 2002), postcolonialism has much to offer Australian literary studies, itself showing signs of cross-disciplinary activity despite occasional rearguard calls to 'disentangl[e] [Australian] literature from the embrace of those proximate disciplines [cultural studies, media and communication studies, etc.] which have all but strangled it' (Hassall 2001: 93)—a self-fulfilling doomsday scenario that does Australian literary scholars few favours, and their would-be adversaries none at all.

A rapprochement between literary studies, cultural/media studies, and postcolonialism might well be happening in Australia, even though factional rivalries remain powerful, and the rise of cultural/media studies, in particular, could yet precipitate literary postcolonialism's fall. While it would be unwise to place bets on this emerging configuration of (sub)disciplines, the influence of postcolonialism on Australian literary studies has certainly been significant, if not as epoch-making as some postcolonial practitioners would like to have us think (Dixon 2003).

Less influence has been exerted however by postcolonialism on Australian studies, a relationship largely characterized by mutual suspicion. David Carter's 1996 essay 'Australia/Post: Australian Studies, Literature and Post-Colonialism', is symptomatic here, turning literary postcolonialism into a scapegoat for cultural studies' intellectual triumphalism, on the one hand, and Australian studies' defensive reaction to its own perceived theoretical frailties, on the other. Literary postcolonialism, suggests Carter, has turned oppositionality into an orthodoxy, falsely claiming political purchase for an aesthetic discourse unhistorically applied to the 'subversive' reading of canonical literary texts. This is uncharitable at best, providing another reason why the correspondence between Australian studies and postcolonialism has been so limited, and why 'in practice . . . as teachers, writers and readers, to attempt to 'do' both . . . is to be made aware of occupying different institutional and theoretical sites' (Carter 1996: 103).

Globalization has become the most recent banner under which these wilful misrecognitions and institutional antagonisms, many of them still heavily invested in the nation, are presented and played out. The last ten years have witnessed something of a scramble for globalization, supplementing rather than directly supplanting the scramble for postcolonialism that had occupied the decade before (Slemon 1994). This scramble can be seen in cultural studies' enthusiastic opening up to the transnational, as well as in Australian studies' concerted attempts to develop a more comparative frame of reference (although as Carter notes, just why 'the cry for more comparative studies . . . *keeps* reappearing as a lack is an interesting question too' (Carter 1996: 107; his italics)).

Postcolonialism, too, has become increasingly committed to investigating global cultural and economic processes, in part proceeding from the recognition that 'globalization represents not so much the end of ethnic and colonialist struggles . . . as a force through which these struggles are continually re-articulated and re-placed' (During 1998: 46). These developments can be seen as necessary adjustments to changes, both in (trans)cultural formation and dissemination under the conditions of globalization and in the forms and processes of knowledge production itself (Dixon 2004).

Less salutary is the tendency—hardly unique to Australian academia—for a kind of disciplinary provincialism to operate in the name of 'transnational literacy' (Spivak 1999);[1] for competing rather than collaborating disciplines to claim a greater theoretical, if not necessarily practical, knowledge of the impact of globalization on the (post)modern, late-capitalist world today. Such manufactured rivalries, of course, are deeply counter-intuitive, whether they act in terms of Australian studies' newfound internationalism or postcolonial studies' emergent cosmopolitanism,[2] both of which are in any case acknowledged as being driven by transnational cultural traffic and a variety of global economic flows (Parry 1991: 41; see also Cheah and Robbins 1998). They also deny the productive overlaps that exist between nominally separate fields and disciplines, overlaps already evident for some time now in such apparently homegrown and relatively homogeneous disciplines as Australian literary studies. As Robert Dixon contends,

Australian literary studies is no longer, if in fact it ever was, a separate field whose logic is self-determining. It exists in a series of complex, usually productive relations with numerous neighbouring disciplines and projects. It is both a structured and a structuring field.

(Dixon 2004: 39; see also Carter 1996: 108)

Ghassan Hage has recently suggested another scramble underlying those for postcolonialism and globalization, one particularly evident in contemporary Australia. This is the scramble for *anti-racism*, which Hage sees as being 'part of the lopsided reality of the paranoid nationalist cause of neo-liberal capitalism' (Hage 2003: xii). Symptoms of this scramble are widespread denial—'in Australia today those offended by the term 'racist' almost outnumber those offended by racists' (Hage 2003: x)—and the tendency to imagine threats to the 'core' white identity of Australia, an identity more likely to be couched in terms of cultural than racial homogeneity (Castles 1996; Dixson 1999).

Hage sees Australian postcolonialism as part of the problem, functioning largely as an alibi in the guise of 'confronting' or 'coming to terms' with the nation's violent past. Hage's point is that coming to terms with the past doesn't mean the same thing as changing present attitudes; instead, if offers a kind of temporary 'postcolonial trauma therapy' for white Australians that allows for the perpetuation of colonialist views (Hage 2003: 96). Hage thus rejects the idea of Australia as a postcolonial nation:

> For a long time to come, Australia is destined to become an unfinished Western colonial project as well as a land in a permanent state of decolonisation. A nation inhabited by both the will of the coloniser and the will of the colonised, each with their identity based on their specific understanding, and memory, of the colonial encounter: what was before it and what is after it. Any national project of reconciliation that fails fully to accept the existence of a distinct Indigenous will . . . is destined to be a momentary cover-up of the reality of the forces that made Australia what it is.
>
> (Hage 2003: 94)

Hage is too harsh by half on postcolonialism as the latest of Australia's white redemption narratives, although his critical reading of the booming memory industry rightly points out the continuity between (white) colonial racism and the commodification of (non-white) victim narratives and traumatic historical events. This suggests that postcolonalism needs to be particularly attentive, not just to specific colonial histories, but also to the equally specific historical and material conditions under which such narratives are produced. One way of saying this is: less memory, more history; another way is to insist on more rigorous comparisons between different histories, which can't be treated as if they were somehow the same.

Unreflected comparison is the bugbear of academic postcolonialism. Patrick Wolfe's warning is no less forceful for being entirely recognizable: 'suggestive though recent writing on imperialism can be, much of it is irreducibly heterogeneous with Australian conditions, for the simple reason that, unlike [Homi] Bhabha's India (though like [Edward] Said's Palestine), Australia is a settler colony. For all the homage paid to difference, postcolonial theory . . . has largely failed to accommodate such basic structural distinctions' (Wolfe 1991: 418). I would agree with this, but also take heart that such structural comparisons can be made in the first place. Indeed, they might be made more often for, despite the work of Wolfe and a handful of others, settler colonialism remains seriously undertheorized—and not just in postcolonial studies.

Perhaps the reduction of settler colonialism to vapid statements about 'complicit postcolonialism' or 'ambivalence' isn't so much better in the end than the removal of settler colonies, via such fashionable formulations as Young's 'tricontinentalism' (Young 2003:

16–20), from the postcolonial fray. Similarly, the various literatures to which settler colonialism has given rise deserve a more nuanced and appropriately historicized comparison. A postcolonial approach to Australian literature is more than just a call for a more inclusive nationalism; it also involves a general acknowledgement of the nation's changed relationship to the wider world. *Multiple* acknowledgements, for Australian literary studies today is multi-sited as well as internationally oriented, and needs to be more attentive than it has been to institutional locations other than Australia's own.

In arguing that '[t]he "post-colonializing" of Australian studies and . . . the "Australianising" of post-colonialism remain to be done', David Carter advocates that 'Australian literary studies should find itself engaged on both sides' (Carter 1996: 116). But Australian literary critics would do well to avoid simply renationalizing the postcolonial, adapting its revisionist vocabulary so as to rephrase familiar questions about cultural belonging and identity, undoubtedly important though these questions will continue to be. A more promising move might be to deterritorialize the nation under the sign of the postcolonial, unsettling it from within as well as extending its parameters, and resisting the twin temptations of fetishizing the local or assimilating uncritically to transnational cultural flows. There is no need to abandon the nation, but there is a continuing need for perspectives that move across and beyond it: perspectives that map the changing relations between nationalism and cosmopolitanism, which are not and never have been mutually exclusive options (Brennan 1997; Cheah and Robbins 1998); perspectives that avoid constructing the national literature as a compensatory patrimony for accelerated processes of realignment and fragmentation in the contemporary globalized world.

There is evidence already of these perspectives in Australian literary criticism, as in truth perhaps there always has been; evidence also of a working alliance between postcolonialism, Australian (literary) studies, and transnational cultural studies that is keeping pace with the changes of the day. The alliance is at least two-way, with the former contributing to the deprovincialization of narrow versions of Australian and/or cultural studies, and the latter to a more locally attentive analysis of current global circumstances and conditions, as well as a situated assessment of the shared legacies of the colonial past.

Further gains stand to be made by amalgamating postcolonial and critical race theory. Australian literature, in keeping with other settler literatures, is thoroughly if not always explicitly racialized. A combination of postcolonial and critical race theory seems best equipped to provide the comparative methodological apparatus to account for this, as well as to investigate the historical impact of racialized knowledges and knowledge-systems across different regions of the world today. Critical race theory also has the potential to contribute towards a 'new' postcolonialism that looks much more like the work being done in transnational cultural studies than in Commonwealth literary studies; and that bears similarities, too, with the work currently being done in indigenous studies, with its emphasis on alternative epistemologies and cross-disciplinary intervention into contemporary social/cultural issues and debates (sovereignty and land rights; immigration and multiculturalism). While the 'old' postcolonialism derived much of its momentum from the internationalization of English-language literatures, the 'new' model is much more likely to be invigorated by the globalization of cultures, cultural repertoires, cultural flows. The 'new' postcolonialism is resolutely polyglot and comparatist, counteracting the reintensified parochialisms that are a flip-side of current globalization processes.

Stuart Hall has said that the main task of the twenty-first century will be to learn to live with difference (Hall 1996). Postcolonialism—for all its faults—is more than up to the task, and whether or not Australia is agreed upon to be postcolonial, its increasingly beleaguered universities are among those which stand to gain most from a broadly conceived postcolonial literary/cultural studies, both now and in the years to come.

NOTES

CHAPTER 1

1. See, for example, Docker 1984, ch. 5. Docker associates the thesis with 'an overarching pessimistic view of Australian historical and literary experience' (121), represented at its most extreme in the work of literary critic Harry Heseltine, whose essay 'The Literary Heritage' (1962) is often seen as a classic in the genre. 'Throughout the course of our literary history', says Heseltine in the essay, 'Australian writers have had deeply located in their imagination (either consciously or unconsciously) a sense of the horror of sheer existence' (Heseltine 1962: 45). The gloom thesis is generally seen as a product of its time, as part of what Docker calls the mid-century 'metaphysical orthodoxy' (110; see also ch. 2, fn. 1). It still surfaces, however, from time to time in critical works obsessed by the idea of Australian failure: see, for example, Kane 1998.

2. In 1992, the Australian High Court found for the plaintiff, Eddie Mabo, who had claimed entitlement to his land on Mer, one of the Torres Strait islands. This ruling single-handedly overturned the foundational colonial doctrine of *terra nullius*, the powerful legal fiction that had until then supported 'the longstanding belief that British settlement had extinguished any indigenous property in land' (Macintyre 1999: 263). The Mabo decision has carried enormous weight ever since, being seen by some as an unparalleled opportunity to right the wrongs previously done to Aboriginal people in Australia (Keating, qtd in Attwood 1996), and by others as an effective end to the dominant white-settler view of history, with a radically new appreciation for an 'indigenized' Australia in its place (Attwood 1996; Morton 1996). For these and other views on Mabo and its implications, see the essays in Attwood 1996.

3. Pauline Hanson's crypto-fascist One Nation party, while no longer a feature of the Australian political landscape, staked out important territory within it via a number of virulent mid- to late-1990s populist debates ('the Asian menace', 'the Aboriginal grievance industry', etc.). While hardly striking a light for the Ordinary Australian, the party did at least succeed in illuminating the extraordinary chauvinism of its supporters. One

Nation has probably been credited with more impact than it deserves, although its fleeting presence has arguably managed to cast a long shadow over the Howard years (see, for example, Hage 1998; Hage 2003; Markus 2001).

CHAPTER 2

1. Binary formulations are much beloved of Australian literary historians (see Pierce 1988). Neither the opposition between realism and romance nor that between realism and what John Docker calls 'the metaphysical ascendancy', represented by such writers as Christopher Brennan and Patrick White (Docker 1984: ch. 4), bear closer critical inspection. For more recent, also more nuanced views, see the essays by Dale, Carter, and others in *Southerly* 57, 3 (1997).

2. Radically conflicting views of history have been a feature of recent cultural debate in Australia. Prominent among these is the conservative historian Geoffrey Blainey's notorious 'black armband' view of history—a view which declares that 'the balance sheet of Australian history is overwhelmingly a positive one' (Howard, qtd in Macintyre and Clark 2003: 3), despite considerable evidence to the contrary and numerous, equally well-publicized assertions of the reverse. Perhaps the most acerbic of the exchanges have been those between Henry Reynolds and Keith Windschuttle, the latter of whom has rapidly evolved into an academic hate-figure, and whose controversial views on the 'fabrication of Australian history' have been given a public prominence they scarcely deserve. For an excellent overview of the history wars and their distorting effects, see Macintyre and Clark 2003.

3. In his influential book *The Lonely Voice* (1964), Frank O'Connor—himself both a theorist and a practitioner of the short story—claims that the form is particularly well attuned to the (self-)expression, not only of alienated individuals, but also of marginalized social groups. 'Always in the short story', says O'Connor, 'there is [a] sense of outlawed figures wandering about the fringes of society' (O'Connor 1964: 19). This thesis is eminently contestable, but certainly appropriate for Lawson, whose ironic articulation of life at the fringes of society has not prevented him from being turned into a spokesperson for a wide range of national victim groups.

4. For a good overview of the Bicentenary and its discontents, see Turner 1994, ch. 4. Turner resists seeing the Bicentenary, as several others have seen it, as a crisis in Australian cultural nationalism, preferring to read its 'imputed failure as a national festival [as a sign] that a redefinition of Australian versions of nationalism is on its way' (Turner 1994: 66).

CHAPTER 3

1. The Gramscian dictum that when 'the old is dying and the new cannot yet be born . . . a variety of morbid symptoms appear' (Gramsci 1971: 276) has served a number of not always compatible causes. Whiteness is not dying, of course, but imagined death has always provided an effective means of enlivening oppression (see also Hage 2003).

2. For a classic view of the cultural cringe, see A. A. Phillips's 1958 study *The Australian Tradition*. Phillips distinguishes between two versions of the cringe, the Cringe Direct, which proceeds from 'an assumption that the domestic [i.e. Australian] product will be worse than the imported [i.e. British] article' (89); and the Cringe Inverted, in which cultural chauvinism creates 'the God's-own-country-and-I'm-a-better-man-than-you-are Australian Bore' (90). Phillips sees the cringe as the lingering epiphenomenon of a cultural colonialism that has almost been conquered by Australian writers, even if it still besets Australian readers (94). Colonialism isn't defeated so easily, however, and may resurface in guises far more deadly—and far more enduring—than the cultural cringe.

3. The notion of 'fragment societies' is usually associated with the work of the historian Louis Hartz, who in his influential book *The Founding of New Societies* (1962) suggested that settler societies such as America's, Canada's or Australia's 'are fragments of the larger whole of Europe struck off in the course of the revolution which brought the West into the modern world' (Hartz 1964: 3). Fragment societies, however, are not merely derivative, but spawn nationalist movements that arise 'out of the necessities of fragmentation itself' (5). Postcolonial critics, by and large, have been sceptical toward the 'fragment thesis' while not necessarily disagreeing with Hartz's conclusion: that an alteration of sedimented social and political traditions will provide an 'answer to those who claim that a country cannot outgrow the conditions of its birth' (318).

4. A recent variation on this argument revolves around the similarly contested term 'magic realism'. It makes little sense to see a contemporary writer like, say, Tim Winton or Richard Flanagan as either a 'metaphysical' or a 'realist' since their work—notably their 'magic-realist' novels such as Winton's *Cloudstreet* or Flanagan's *Gould's Book of Fish*—is clearly both.

5. Opinions continue to be divided between those who see reconciliation as a horizon of possibility for both white and black Australians and those who consider it, much more sceptically, as another white redemption narrative in the fraught context of the nation's 'history wars' (see Ch. 2, fn. 2). For alternative views of the reconciliation process, see Dixson 1999 and Hage 2003; for a balanced view, see also Jacobs 1997.

6. On the genealogy of fakery and fraudulence in Australia, see particularly the essays in Nolan and Dawson (2004). See also Dawson (1998), who argues—in a related Canadian context—that imposture is 'a trope through which to interrogate the preoccupation with authenticity in settler cultures' (Dawson 1998: 121). Dawson emphasizes the need to get away from a reductive 'true–false' paradigm of imposture, arguing instead that it represents an attempt to comment on the contingent construction of identity in settler societies, like Canada's or Australia's, in which the question of identity is inextricably linked to the unresolved question of 'who belongs'.

CHAPTER 4

1. Just as this book was going to press, I received an unexpected update. Helen Dale (Demidenko's new name) has now entered the legal world, having completed a law degree at the University of Queensland. In a 2006 article in the journal *The Skeptic*, Dale speaks out against her vilification, and defends the creation of a false authorial persona in her notorious novel. We may have heard the last from Helen Demidenko, but not, it appears, from Helen Dale.

2. In August 2001, an international scandal was created when the Howard government refused to allow the ailing Norwegian container ship, the *Tampa*, to disembark, thereby offloading 433 asylum seekers onto Australian sovereign territory. The asylum seekers were hastily relocated, many of them at Australia's expense (the so-called 'Pacific Solution'). Some weeks later, a second scandal emerged when it was falsely alleged that another group of asylum seekers attempting to enter Australia had deliberately thrown their children into the water in a despairing effort to put pressure on the Australian authorities to take them ashore. These two scandals, particularly the events surrounding the *Tampa*, caused considerable embarrassment while paradoxically allowing the government to ratchet up its anti-immigration rhetoric. For critics like Mares (2001) or Jupp (2002), this confirmed 'the revival of racist and xenophobic populist attitudes' (Jupp 2002: 199) in an increasingly isolationist Australia, which had only succeeded through such gestures in making a mockery of its self-image as one of the most tolerant societies in the world.

3. Edward Said's *Orientalism*, first published in 1978, is often regarded as the founding text of postcolonial criticism. The title term, Said argues, is 'a [Western] style of thought based upon an ontological and epistemological distinction made between "the Orient" and (most of the time) "the Occident"' (Said 1979 [1978]: 21). *Orientalism* is, simultaneously, an ideological and an aesthetic practice aimed at establishing or consolidating Western authority over the Orient (Said 1979: 21). Quite why *Orientalism*

itself has become such an authoritative text is an interesting question; some reasons are given in Prakash (1995).

AFTERWORD

1. Transnational literacy, for Spivak, involves a pluralistic understanding of the roles played by international affairs, development economics, and business administration, as well as cultural politics, in the management of 'globality', defined primarily in terms of the 'financialization of the globe' (Spivak 1999: 376–7, 364). Transnational literacy mediates between the nation and the world in a context of 'capitalist postmodernization' (Spivak 1999: 399); it involves a complex understanding that liberation *here* may yet mean enslavement *there*, and that intellectual humility rather than informational hubris will be the basis for 'a decolonization of the mind' that provides the means 'for an efficient and continuing calculus of . . . justice *everywhere*' (Spivak 1999: 399; her italics).

2. 'Cosmopolitanism' is a much contested term in postcolonial criticism: see, for example, Breckenridge *et al.* 2000; Brennan 1997; Cheah and Robbins 1998. Several recent attempts have been made to rescue cosmopolitanism from its negative association with 'uncommitted bourgeois detachment' (Cheah and Robbins 1998: 31). Such attempts have either centred on the possibility of alternative (non-elite and/or critical) cosmopolitanisms (Brennan 1997); or on the potential for post-national identities (Appadurai 1996); or on the acknowledgement of multiple affiliations and attachments, including the national, towards which cosmopolitanism is not necessarily opposed (Cheah and Robbins 1998). In their critical engagements with globalization, both postcolonial and Australian literary/cultural studies have generally worked toward new understandings of cosmopolitanism which, rather than dismissing the nation, recognize that 'the technologies and institutions that . . . produce national feeling now exist massively and increasingly on a transnational scale' (Cheah and Robbins 1998: 6). Contemporary globality requires an interplay between cosmopolitan and national forms and forces: an interplay, as likely to be conflictual as complementary, which lies behind the renegotiation of Australian national literature in this book.

REFERENCES

Abood, Paula, Barry Gamba, and Michelle Kotevski (eds.) (1999) *Waiting in Space: An Anthology of Australian Writing* (Annandale, NSW: Pluto Press).

Adam, Ian and Helen Tiffin (eds.) (1990) *Past the Last Post: Theorising Post-Colonialism and Post-Modernism* (Calgary, AL: University of Calgary Press).

Ahmad, Aijaz (1995) 'The Politics of Literary Postcoloniality', *Race and Class* 36, 3, 1–20.

Ang, Ien (2001) *On Not Speaking Chinese: Living Between Asia and the West* (London: Routledge).

Anthias, Floya and Nira Yuval-Davis (1992) *Racialized Boundaries: Race, Nation, Gender, Colour, and Class and the Anti-Racist Struggle* (London: Routledge).

Appadurai, Arjun (1996) *Modernity at Large: Cultural Dimensions of Globalization* (Minneapolis: University Of Minnesota Press).

Arthur, Kateryna Olijnk (1988) 'Between Literatures: Canada and Australia', *Ariel* 19, 1, 2–12.

Ashbolt, Allan (1982) 'Nationalist Contradictions', in J. Romeril, *The Floating World* (Sydney: Currency Press), vii–xi.

Ashcroft, Bill, Gareth Griffiths, and Helen Tiffin (1989) *The Empire Writes Back: Theory and Practice in Post-Colonial Literatures* (London: Routledge).

Attwood, Bain, ' "Learning About the Truth": The Stolen Generations Narrative', in B. Attwood and F. Magowan (eds.) (2001) *Telling Stories: Indigenous History and Memory in Australia and New Zealand* (Sydney: Allen and Unwin), 183–212.

Attwood, Bain (ed.) (1996) *In the Age of Mabo: History, Aborigines and Australia* (Sydney: Allen and Unwin).

Back, Les (2002) 'Wagner and Power Chords: Skinheadism, White Power Music, and the Internet', in V. Ware and L. Back, *Out of Whiteness: Color, Politics, and Culture* (Chicago: University of Chicago Press), 94–132.

Back, Les and John Solomos (eds.) (2000) *Theories of Race and Racism: A Reader* (London: Routledge).

Balibar, Étienne, 'Is There a 'Neo-Racism'?' in E. Balibar and I. Wallerstein (eds.) (1991) *Race, Nation, Class: Ambiguous Identities* (London: Verso), 17–28.

Balme, Christopher (1999) *Decolonizing the Stage: Theatrical Syncretism and Post-Colonial Drama* (Oxford: Oxford University Press (Clarendon)).

Barnard, Marjorie (1967) *Miles Franklin* (New York: Twayne).

Barthes, Roland (1982 [1971]) *Empire of Signs*, trans. R. Howard (New York: Hill and Wang).

Bassnett, Susan and Harish Trivedi (eds.) (1999) *Post-Colonial Translation: Theory and Practice* (New York: Routledge).

Bauman, Zygmunt (1989) *Modernity and the Holocaust* (Ithaca, NY: Cornell University Press).

Baynton, Barbara (1983 [1902]) *Bush Studies* (London: Duckworth).

Bennett, Bruce (1989) 'Literature and Journalism: The Fiction of Robert Drewe' *Ariel* 20, 3–16.

Bennett, Bruce and Jennifer Strauss (eds.) (1998) *The Oxford Literary History of Australia* (Melbourne: Oxford University Press).

Bennett, David (ed.) (1998) *Multicultural States: Rethinking Difference and Identity* (London: Routledge).

Bercovitch, Sacvan (1986) *Reconstructing American Literary History* (Cambridge, MA: Harvard University Press).

Beresford, Quentin and Paul Omaji (1998) *Our State of Mind: Racial Planning and the Stolen Generations* (Fremantle, WA: Fremantle Arts Centre Press).

Beston, John (1979) 'David Unaipon: The First Aboriginal Writer (1873–1967)', *Southerly* 39, 3, 334–50.

Bhabha, Homi (1994) *The Location of Culture* (London: Routledge).

—— (ed.) (1990) *Nation and Narration* (London: Routledge).

Bharucha, Rustom (1993) *Theatre and the World: Essays on Performance and Politics of Culture* (Delhi: Manohar Publications).

—— (2000) *The Politics of Cultural Practice: Thinking through Theatre in an Age of Globalization* (London: The Athlone Press).

Birch, Tony, ' "The First White Man Born": Miscegenation and Identity in Kim Scott's *Benang*', in J. Ryan and C. Wallace-Crabbe (eds.) (2004) *Imagining Australia: Literature and Culture in the New New World* (Cambridge, MA: Harvard University Press), 137–57.

Bird, Delys, 'The "Settling" of English', in B. Bennett and J. Strauss (eds.) (1998) *The Oxford Literary History of Australia* (Melbourne: Oxford University Press), 21–43.

Bird, Delys, Robert Dixon, and Susan Lever (eds.) (1997) *Canonozities: The Making of Literary Representations in Australia*: special issue of *Southerly* 57, 3, 5–15.

Birns, Nicholas, 'May in September: Australian Literature as Anglophone Alternative', in D. Callahan (ed.) (2002) *Contemporary Issues in Australian Literature* (London: Frank Cass), 112–32.

Blainey, Geoffrey (1994) *A Shorter History of Australia* (Port Melbourne, Vic.: Heinemann).

Blake, Ann (1999) *Christina Stead's Politics of Place* (Nedlands, WA: University of Western Australia Press).

Bliss, Carolyn (1986) *Patrick White's Fiction: The Paradox of Fortunate Failure* (Basingstoke: Macmillan).

Boldrewood, Rolf (1961 [1888]) *Robbery Under Arms* (Oxford: Oxford University Press).

Bourdieu, Pierre (1993) *The Field of Literary Production*, ed. R. Johnson (New York: Columbia University Press).

Brah, Avtar and Annie E. Coombes (eds.) (2000) *Hybridity and its Discontents* (London: Routledge).

Breckenridge, Carol A., Sheldon Pollock, Homi K. Bhabha, and Dipesh Chakrabarty (eds.) (2000) 'Cosmopolitanism': special issue of *Public Culture* 12, 3.

Brennan, Timothy (1997) *At Home in the World: Cosmopolitanism Now* (Cambridge, MA: Harvard University Press).

Brewster, Anne (1995) *Literary Formations: Post-Colonialism, Nationalism, Globalism* (Carlton South, Vic.: Melbourne University Press).

Broinowski, Alison (1998) 'Asianization and its Discontents', *Meanjin* 59, 3, 440–52.

—— (1992) *The Yellow Lady: Australian Impressions of Asia* (Melbourne: Oxford University Press).

Brown, Ruth, 'Cyberspace and Oz Lit: Mark Davis, McKenzie Wark, and the Re-Alignment of Australian Literature', in D. Callahan (ed.) (2002) *Contemporary Issues in Australian Literature* (London: Frank Cass), 17–36.

Brydon, Diana (1987) *Christina Stead* (London: Macmillan Educational).

—— 'Discovering "Ethnicity": Joy Kogawa's *Obasan* and Mena Abdullah's *Time of the Peacock*, in R. McDougall and G. Whitlock (eds.) (1987) *Australian/Canadian Literatures: Comparative Perspectives* (North Ryde, NSW: Methuen Australia), 94–110.

Buckridge, Patrick (1995) ' "Greatness" and Australian Literature in the 1930s and 1940s: Novels by Dark and Barnard Eldershaw', *Australian Literary Studies* 17, 1, 29–37.

Bulmer, Martin and John Solomos (eds.) (1999) *Racism* (Oxford: Oxford University Press).

Burke, Peter, 'History as Social Memory', in T. Butler (ed.) (1989) *Memory, History, Culture and the Mind* (Oxford: Blackwell).

Butler, Judith (1990) *Gender Trouble: Feminism and the Subversion of Identity* (New York: Routledge).

Callahan, David (ed.) (2002) *Contemporary Issues in Australian Literature* (London. Frank Cass).

Carey, Peter (1985) *Illywhacker* (London: Faber and Faber).

——— (2003) *My Life as a Fake* (London: Faber and Faber).

——— (1988) *Oscar and Lucinda* (St Lucia, QLD: University of Queensland Press).

——— (1980) *The Fat Man in History* (St Lucia, QLD: University of Queensland Press).

——— (2001) *True History of the Kelly Gang* (London: Faber and Faber).

Carroll, Dennis (1995 [1985]) *Australian Contemporary Drama* (Sydney: Currency Press).

Carter, Paul (1987) *The Road to Botany Bay: An Exploration of Landscape and History* (Chicago: University of Chicago Press).

Carter, David, 'Australia/Post: Australian Studies, Literature and Post-Colonialism', in W. Ommundsen and H. Rowley (eds.) (1996) *From a Distance: Australian Writers and Cultural Displacement* (Geelong, Vic.: Deakin University Press), 103–16.

——— (1999) 'Good Readers and Good Citizens: Literature, Media and the Nation', *Australian Literary Studies* 19, 2, 136–51.

——— (1997) 'Literary Canons and Literary Institutions', *Southerly* 57, 3, 16–37.

Castles, Stephen, 'The Racisms of Globalisation', in E. Vasta and S. Castles (eds.) (1996) *The Teeth Are Smiling: The Persistence of Racism in Multicultural Australia* (St Leonards, Vic.: Allen and Unwin), 17–45.

Castles, S., M. Kalantzis, W. Cope, and M. Morrissey (1988) *Mistaken Identity: Multiculturalism and the Demise of Nationalism in Australia* (Sydney: Pluto Press).

Castro, Brian (1983) *Birds of Passage* (Sydney: Allen and Unwin).

Cheah, Pheng and Bruce Robbins (eds.) (1998) *Cosmopolitics: Thinking and Feeling Beyond the Nation* (Minneapolis: University of Minnesota Press).

Clarke, Marcus (1984 [1882]) *For the Term of His Natural Life* (Sydney: Angus and Robertson).

Coetzee, J. M. (1988) *White Writing: On the Culture of Letters in South Africa* (New Haven: Yale University Press).

Crock, Mary (ed.) (1993) *Protection or Punishment: The Detention of Asylum Seekers in Australia* (Annandale, NSW: The Federation Press).

Culler, Jonathan (1997) *A Very Short Introduction to Literary Theory* (Oxford: Oxford University Press).

Curthoys, Ann, 'Mythologies', in R. Nile (ed.) (2000) *The Australian Legend and its Discontents* (St Lucia, QLD: University of Queensland Press), 11–41.

_____ (1979) 'Race and Ethnicity: A Study of the Response of British Colonists to Aborigines, Chinese and non British Europeans in New South Wales, 1856–81' (PhD thesis, ANU).

Dale, Leigh (1997) 'Canonical Readings: Australian Literature and the Universities', *Southerly* 57, 3, 38–50.

_____ (1999) 'New Directions: Introduction', *Australian Literary Studies* 19, 2, 131–5.

_____ (1992) 'Whose English—Who's English?' *Meanjin* 51, 2, 393–409.

Daniel, Helen (1988) *Liars: Australian New Novelists* (Ringwood, Vic.: Penguin).

Darian-Smith, Kate and Paula Hamilton (eds.) (1994) *Memory and History in Twentieth-Century Australia* (Melbourne: Oxford University Press).

Davies, Will and Andrea Dal Bosco (eds.) (2002) *Tales from a Suitcase: The Afghan Experience* (South Melbourne: Lothian Books).

Davis, Jack (1985) *No Sugar* (Sydney: Currency Press).

Davis, Mark (1997) *Gangland: Cultural Elites and the New Generationalism* (Sydney: Allen and Unwin).

Dawe, Bruce (1969) *Beyond the Subdivisions: Poems* (Melbourne: F.W. Cheshire).

_____ (1995) *Mortal Instruments: Poems 1990–95* (Melbourne: Longman).

Dawson, Carrie (1998) 'Never Cry Fraud: Remembering Grey Owl, Rethinking Imposture', *Essays in Canadian Writing* 65, 101–21.

Deleuze, Gilles and Félix Guattari (1987) *A Thousand Plateaus: Capitalism and Schizophrenia*, trans. B. Massumi (Minneapolis: University of Minnesota Press).

Demidenko, Helen (1994) *The Hand that Signed the Paper* (Sydney: Allen and Unwin).

Derrida, Jacques (2000) *Of Hospitality*, trans. R. Bowlby (Palo Alto, CA: Stanford University Press).

Dirlik, Arif (1994) 'The Postcolonial Aura: Third World Criticism in the Age of Global Capitalism', *Critical Inquiry* 20, 328–56.

Dixon, Robert (2003) 'Australian Literary Studies and Post-Colonialism', *AUMLA* 100, 108–21.

_____ (2004) 'Boundary Work: Australian Literary Studies in the Field of Knowledge Production', *Journal of the Association of Australian Literature* 3, 27–43.

_____ (2001) *Prosthetic Gods: Travel, Representation and Colonial Governance* (St Lucia, QLD: University of Queensland Press).

_____ (1995) *Writing the Colonial Adventure: Gender, Race and Nation in Anglo-Australian Popular Fiction, 1875–1914* (New York: Cambridge University Press).

Dixson, Miriam (1999) *The Imaginary Australian: Anglo-Celts and Identity, 1788 to the Present* (Sydney: University of New South Wales Press).

Docker, John (1984) *In a Critical Condition: Reading Australian Literature* (Ringwood, Vic.: Penguin).

Docker, John and Gerald Fischer (eds.) (2000) *Race, Colour and Identity in Australia and New Zealand* (Sydney: University of New South Wales Press).

D'Souza, Dinesh (1992) *Illiberal Education: The Politics of Race and Sex on Campus* (New York: Vintage).

During, Simon (1996) *Patrick White* (Melbourne: Oxford University Press).

―― (1998) 'Postcolonialism and Globalisation: A Dialectical Relation After All?' *Postcolonial Studies* 1, 1, 31–47.

―― (1992) 'Postcolonialism and Globalization', *Meanjin* 51, 2, 339–53.

Dyer, Richard (1997) *White* (New York: Routledge).

Eagleton, Terry (1999) 'Postcolonialism or "Postcolonialism"?', *Interventions* 1, 1, 24–6.

Eco, Umberto (1990) *The Limits of Interpretation* (Bloomington, IN: Indiana University Press).

Eliades, Patricia (1995) 'Anthologising the Minority', *Hecate* 21, 1, 74–97.

Eliot, T. S., 'Ulysses, Order and Myth', in F. Kermode (ed.) (1975) *Selected Essays* (New York: Farrar, Straus and Giroux), 175–8.

Elliott, Brian (ed.) (1973) *Adam Lindsay Gordon* (Melbourne: Sun Books).

―― 'Introduction', in B. Elliott (ed.) (1979) *The Jindyworobaks* (St Lucia, QLD: University of Queensland Press), xvii–lxvi.

―― (ed.) (1979) *The Jindyworobaks* (St Lucia, QLD: University of Queensland Press).

―― 'Introduction', in M. Clarke (1984) *For the Term of His Natural Life* (Sydney: Angus and Robertson), ix–xlvii.

Essed, Philomena (1991) *Understanding Everyday Racism* (London: Sage).

Fabi, M. Giulia (2001) *Passing and the Rise of the African American Novel* (Urbana; University of Illinois Press).

Featherstone, Mike, 'Localism, Globalism, and Cultural Identity', in R. Wilson and W. Dissanayake (eds.) (1996) *Global/Local: Cultural Production and the Transnational Imaginary* (Durham, NC: Duke University Press), 46–77.

―― (1995) *Undoing Culture: Globalisation, Postmodernism and Identity* (London: Sage).

Fish, Stanley (1997) 'Boutique Multiculturalism, or Why Liberals are Incapable of Thinking about Hate Speech', *Critical Inquiry* 23, 2, 378–95.

Fitzpatrick, Peter (1979) *After 'The Doll': Australian Drama Since 1955* (London: Arnold).

Flannery, Tim (2003) 'Beautiful Lies: Population and Environment in Australia', *Quarterly Essay* 9, 1–73.

Foster, David (1981) *Moonlite* (South Melbourne: Macmillan).

Frankenberg, Ruth (1993) *White Women, Race Matters: The Social Construction of Whiteness* (Minneapolis: University of Minnesota Press).

―――― (ed.) (1997) *Displacing Whiteness: Essays in Social and Cultural Criticism* (Durham, NC: Duke University Press).

Franklin, Miles (1956) *Laughter, Not for a Cage: Notes on Australian Writing* (Sydney: Angus and Robertson).

―――― (1980 [1901]) *My Brilliant Career* (N. Ryde: Angus and Robertson).

Fredrickson, George M. (2002) *Racism: A Short History* (Princeton: Princeton University Press).

Frow, John (1998) 'A Politics of Stolen Time', *Meanjin* 57, 2, 351–67.

―――― 'Postmodernism and Literary History', in D. Perkins (ed.) (1991) *Theoretical Issues in Literary History* (Cambridge, MA: Harvard University Press), 131–42.

Frye, Northrop, 'Conclusion', in C. Klinck (ed.) (1965) *Literary History of Canada: Canadian Literature in English* (Toronto: University of Toronto Press), 821–49.

Gale, Peter, 'Constructing Whiteness in the Australian Media', in J. Docker and G. Fischer (eds.) (2000) *Race, Colour and Identity in Australia and New Zealand* (Sydney: University of New South Wales Press), 256–69.

Gates, Henry Louis (ed.), *'Race', Writing, and Difference* (Chicago: University of Chicago Press).

Gelder, Ken and Jane M. Jacobs (1998) *Uncanny Australia: Sacredness and Identity in a Postcolonial Nation* (Carlton South, Vic.: Melbourne University Press).

Gerster, Robin (1990) 'Gerrymander: The Place of Suburbia in Australian Fiction', *Meanjin* 49, 3, 565–75.

Gibson, Ross (1992) *South of the West: Postcolonialism and the Narrative Construction of Australia* (Bloomington: Indiana University Press).

Giddens, Anthony (1991) *Modernity and Identity: Self and Society in the Late Modern Age* (Cambridge: Polity Press).

Gikandi, Simon (1996) *Maps of Englishness: Writing Identity in the Culture of Colonialism* (New York: Columbia University Press).

Gilbert, Helen (2001) *Sightlines: Race, Gender, and Nation in Contemporary Australian Theatre* (Ann Arbor: University of Michigan Press).

Gilbert, Helen and Joanne Tompkins (1996) *Post-Colonial Drama: Theory, Practice, Politics* (London: Routledge).

Gilroy, Paul (2000) *Against Race: Imagining Political Culture Beyond the Color Line* (Cambridge, MA: Harvard University Press (Belknap)).

―――― (1993) *The Black Atlantic: Modernity and Double Consciousness* (London: Verso).

―――― 'The End of Anti-Racism', in W. Ball and J. Solomos (eds.) (1990) *Race and Local Politics* (Basingstoke: Macmillan).

Ginsberg, Elaine K. (1996) *Passing and the Fictions of Identity* (Durham, NC: Duke University Press).

Goldberg, David Theo, 'Racial Knowledge', in L. Back and J. Solomos (eds.) (2000) *Theories of Race and Racism: A Reader* (London: Routledge), 154–80.

Goldie, Terry (1989) *Fear and Temptation: The Image of the Indigene in Canadian, Australian and New Zealand Literatures* (Kingston, Ont.: McGill-Queen's University Press).

Goodwin, Ken (1986) *A History of Australian Literature* (Basingstoke: Macmillan).

Gooneratne, Yasmine (1991) *A Change of Skies* (Sydney: Pan Macmillan).

Goss, Jasper (1996) 'Postcolonialism: Subverting Whose Empire?' *Third World Quarterly* 17, 2, 239–50.

Graff, Gerald (1992) *Beyond the Culture Wars: How Teaching the Conflicts Can Revitalize American Education* (New York: Norton).

Gramsci, Antonio (1971) *Selections from the Prison Notebooks*, ed. Q. Hoare and G. Nowell Smith (New York: International Publishers).

Grenville, Kate (1988) *Joan Makes History* (St Lucia, QLD: University of Queensland Press).

Guillory, John (1993) *Cultural Capital: The Problem of Literary Canon Formation* (Chicago: University of Chicago Press).

Gunew, Sneja, 'Denaturalizing cultural nationalisms: multicultural readings of "Australia"', in Homi Bhabha (ed.) (1990) *Nation and Narration* (London: Routledge), 99–120.

—— (1994) *Framing Marginality: Multicultural Literary Studies* (Carlton, Vic.: Melbourne University Press).

—— (2004) *Haunted Nations: The Colonial Dimensions of Multiculturalisms* (London: Routledge).

Gunew, Sneja and Jan Mahyuddin (eds.) (1988) *Beyond the Echo: Multicultural Women's Writing* (St Lucia, QLD: University of Queensland Press).

Hage, Ghassan (2003) *Against Paranoid Nationalism: Searching for Hope in a Shrinking Society* (Annandale, NSW: Pluto Press).

—— (1998) *White Nation: Fantasies of White Supremacy in a Multicultural Society* (Sydney: Pluto Press).

Hage, Ghassan and Rowanne Couch (eds.) (1999) *The Future of Australian Multiculturalism: Reflections on the Twentieth Anniversary of Jean Martin's The Migrant Presence* (Sydney: Research Institute for the Humanities and Social Sciences, University of Sydney).

Hall, Rodney (1992) *Unjust Relations* (Ringwood, Vic.: Penguin).

Hall, Stuart, 'Conclusion: The Multi-Cultural Question', in B. Hesse (ed.) (2000a) *Un/settled Multiculturalism: Diasporas, Entanglements, Transruptions* (London: Zed Books), 209–41.

_____ 'Old and New Identities, Old and New Ethnicities', in L. Back and J. Solomos (eds.) (2000b) *Theories of Race and Racism* (London: Routledge), 144–53.

Hall, Stuart, 'When was "the Post-Colonial"? Thinking at the Limit', in I. Chambers and L. Curtis (eds.) (1996) *The Post-Colonial Question: Common Skies, Divided Horizons* (New York, Routledge).

Hamilton, Paula, 'The Knife Edge: Debates about Memory and History', in K. Darian-Smith and P. Hamilton (eds.) (1994) *Memory and History in Twentieth-Century Australia* (Oxford: Oxford University Press), 9–32.

Hannerz, Ulf (1996) *Transnational Connections: Culture, People, Places* (New York: Routledge).

Harris, Max (1974) *Ockers: Essays on the Bad Old Australia* (Adelaide: privately published).

Harrison, Wayne, 'The Text, the Actors and the Audience', in D. Williamson (1995) *Dead White Males* (Sydney: Currency Press), x–xi.

Hart-Smith, William, 'Nullarbor', in B. Elliott (ed.) (1979) *The Jindyworobaks* (St Lucia, QLD: University of Queensland Press), 112–15.

Hartz, Louis (1964) *The Founding of New Societies: Studies in the History of the United States, Latin America, South Africa, Canada, and Australia* (New York: Harcourt, Brace and World).

Hassall, Anthony (2001) 'Australian Literary Criticism: Future Directions', *Australian Literary Studies* 20, 1, 88–93.

Hawthorne, Lesleyanne (ed.) (1982) *Refugee: The Vietnamese Experience* (Melbourne: Oxford University Press).

Haywood, Ian (1987) *Faking It: Art and the Politics of Forgery* (Brighton: Harvester Press).

Healy, Chris (1997) *From the Ruins of Colonialism: History as Social Memory* (Cambridge: Cambridge University Press).

Herbert, Xavier (2002 [1938]) *Capricornia* (Sydney: Angus and Robertson).

Hergenhan, Laurie (1993) *Unnatural Lives: Studies in Australian Convict Fiction* (St Lucia, QLD: University of Queensland Press).

Hergenhan, Laurie *et al.* (eds.) (1988) *The Penguin New Literary History of Australia* (Ringwood, Vic.: Penguin).

Herrnstein Smith, Barbara (1988) *Contingencies of Value: Alternative Perspectives for Critical Theory* (Cambridge, MA: Harvard University Press).

Heseltine, Harry (1962) 'Australia Image: (1) The Literary Heritage', *Meanjin* 21, 1, 35–49.

_____ (ed.) (1972) *The Penguin Book of Australian Verse* (Harmondsworth, Penguin).

Hesse, Barnor (ed.) (2000) *Un/settled Multiculturalisms: Diasporas, Entanglements, Transruptions* (London: Zed Books).

Hesse, Barnor 'Introduction: Un/settled Multiculturalisms', in B. Hesse (ed.) (2000) *Un/settled Multiculturalisms: Diasporas, Entanglements, Transruptions* (London: Zed Books), 1–30.

Hill, Mike (2004) *After Whiteness: Unmaking an American Majority* (New York: New York University Press).

——(ed.) (1997) *Whiteness: A Critical Reader* (New York: New York University Press).

Hodge, Bob and Vijay Mishra (1990) *Dark Side of the Dream: Australian Literature and the Postcolonial Mind* (Sydney: Allen and Unwin).

Hodge, Bob and Vijay Mishra, 'What is Post(-)Colonialism?' in P. Williams and L. Chrisman (eds.) (1994) *Colonial Discourse and Postcolonial Theory: A Reader* (New York: Columbia University Press), 276–90.

Holt, R. F. (ed.) (1991) *Neighbours: Multicultural Writing of the 1980s* (St Lucia, QLD: University of Queensland Press).

Hoogvelt, Ankie (1998) *Globalization and the Postcolonial World: The New Political Economy of Development* (Basingstoke: Macmillan).

hooks, bell (1993) *Black Looks: Race and Representation* (Boston: South End Press).

Hudson, W. Flexmore, 'Song of an Australian', in B. Elliott (ed.) (1979) *The Jindyworobaks* (St Lucia, QLD: University of Queensland Press), 45.

Huggan, Graham (2002) 'Cultural Memory in Postcolonial Fiction: The Uses and Abuses of Ned Kelly', *Australian Literary Studies* 20, 3, 142–54.

——(2006) 'Derailing the "Trans": Postcolonial Studies and the Negative Effects of Speed', in B. Waldschmidt-Nelson, M. Hünemörder, and M. Zwingenberger (eds.) (2006) *Europe and America: Cultures in Translation* (Heidelberg: Winter), 185–92.

——'Looking West to the East: Some Thoughts on the Asianisation of Australian Literature', in W. Senn and G. Capone (eds.) (1992) *The Making of a Pluralist Australia* (Bern: Peter Lang), 219–28.

——(2005) '(Not) Reading *Orientalism*', *Research in African Literatures* 36, 3, 124–36.

——(2002) 'Postcolonial Studies and the Anxiety of Interdisciplinarity', *Postcolonial Studies* 5, 3, 245–75.

——(1994) *Territorial Disputes: Maps and Mapping Strategies in Canadian and Australian Fiction* (Toronto: University of Toronto Press).

——(2001) *The Postcolonial Exotic: Marketing the Margins* (London: Routledge).

——(2006) 'Vampires, again', *Southerly* 66, 3, 192–204.

Hughes, Mary Ann (1998) 'An Issue of Authenticity: Editing Texts by Aboriginal Writers', *Southerly* 58, 2, 48–58.

Hurcombe, Roger (1990) 'Barthes' Empire of Signs', *Arena* 91, 103–13.

Hutcheon, Linda (1984–5) 'Canadian Historiographic Metafiction', *Essays in Canadian Writing* 30, 228–38.

____ 'Circling the Downspout of Empire', in I. Adam and H. Tiffin (eds.) (1990) *Past the Last Post: Theorizing Post-Colonialism and Post-Modernism* (Calgary, AL: University of Calgary Press), 167–89.

Ignatiev, Noel (1995) *How the Irish Became White* (New York: Routledge).

Ingamells, Rex, 'Black Mary'; 'Forgotten People', in B. Elliott (ed.) (1979) *The Jindyworobaks* (St Lucia, QLD: University of Queensland Press), 17; 11.

Ireland, David (1981) *Moonlite* (S. Melbourne: Macmillan).

Jacobs, Jane M., 'Resistance and Reconciliation: The Secret Geographies of (Post)Colonial Australia', in S. Pile and M. Keith (eds.) (1997) *Geographies of Resistance* (London: Routledge), 203–18.

Jacoby, Russell (1995) 'Marginal Returns: The Trouble with Post-Colonial Theory', *Lingua Franca* 30–37.

Jameson, Fredric (1990) 'Modernism and Imperialism', in T. Eagleton, F. Jameson and E. Said *Nationalism, Colonialism, and Literature* (Minneapolis: University of Minnesota Press).

JanMohamed, Abdul (1983) *Manichean Aesthetics: The Politics of Literature in Colonial Africa* (Amherst: University of Massachusetts Press).

Jayasuriya, Laksir, David Walker, and Jan Gothard (eds.) (2003) *Legacies of White Australia* (Nedlands, WA: University of Western Australia Press).

Jillett, Neil (1977) 'Review of Summer of the Seventeenth Doll', *Herald* (Melbourne), 27 January, 23.

Johnson, Colin [Mudrooroo], 'White Forms, Aboriginal Content', in J. Davis and B. Hodge (eds.) (1985) *Aboriginal Writing Today* (Canberra: AIAS), 21–33.

Jupp, James (2002) *From White Australia to Woomera: The Story of Australian Immigration* (Cambridge: Cambridge University Press).

Kane, John, 'From Racialism to Democracy: The Legacy of White Australia', in G. Stokes (ed.) (1997) *The Politics of Identity in Australia* (Cambridge; Cambridge University Press), 117–31.

Kane, Paul (1998) *Australian Poetry: Romanticism and Negativity* (Cambridge: Cambridge University Press).

Kingsley, Henry (1954 [1859]) *The Recollections of Geoffrey Hamlyn* (London: Oxford University Press).

Kincheloe, Joe, Shirley R. Steinberg, Nelson M. Rodriguez and Ronald E. Chennault (1998) *White Reign: Deploying Whiteness in America* (New York: St Martin's Press).

Kirkby, Joan (1998) 'In Pursuit of Oblivion: In Flight from Suburbia', *Australian Literary Studies* 18, 4, 1–19.

Koch, C. J. (1987) *Crossing the Gap: A Novelist's Essays* (London: The Hogarth Press).

____ (1987) 'The Lost Hemisphere', in *Crossing the Gap: A Novelist's Essays* (London: The Hogarth Press), 91–105.

Koch, C. J. (1983 [1978]) *The Year of Living Dangerously* (Ringwood, Vic.: Penguin).

Koundoura, Maria, 'Multiculturalism or Multinationalism?' in D. Bennett (ed.) (1998) *Multicultural States: Rethinking Difference and Identity* (London: Routledge), 69–87.

Kramer, Leonie (ed.) (1981) *The Oxford History of Australian Literature* (Melbourne: Oxford University Press).

Kroetsch, Robert (1973) *Gone Indian* (Toronto: The New Press).

Kuch, Peter (1995) *Bruce Dawe* (Melbourne: Oxford University Press).

Kurtzer, Sonia (1998) '*Wandering Girl*: Who Defines "Authenticity" in Aboriginal Literature?' *Southerly* 58, 2, 20–29.

Langer, Beryl, 'Globalisation and the Myth of Ethnic Community: Salvadoran Refugees in Multicultural States', in D. Bennett (ed.) (1998) *Multicultural States: Rethinking Difference and Identity* (London: Routledge), 163–77.

Larbalestier, Jan, 'What is This Thing Called White? Reflections on "Whiteness" and Multiculturalism', in G. Hage and R. Couch (eds.) (1999) *The Future of Australian Multiculturalism* (Sydney: Research Institute for the Humanities and Social Sciences, University of Sydney), 145–61.

Lawler, Ray (1957) *Summer of the Seventeenth Doll* (London: Angus and Robertson).

Lawson, Alan (1995) 'Postcolonial Theory and the "Settler" Subject', *Essays in Canadian Writing* 56, 20–41.

Lawson, Henry (1976) *Henry Lawson*: selected and edited with an introduction and bibliography by Brian Kiernan (St Lucia, QLD: University of Queensland Press).

Lazarus, Neil (1999) *Nationalism and Cultural Practice in the Postcolonial World* (New York: Cambridge University Press).

Lee, Christopher (1997) 'Fighting Them on the Beaches: The University Versus the People in the Case of Henry Lawson', *Southerly* 57, 3, 152–61.

Lee, Dennis (1974) 'Cadence, country, silence; writing in colonial space', *Boundary 2* 3, 1 151–68.

Lemire, Elise (2002) '*Miscegenation*': *Making Race in America* (Philadelphia: University of Pennsylvania Press).

Lennon, John and Malcolm Foley (2000) *Dark Tourism: The Attraction of Death and Disaster* (London: Continuum).

Lever, Susan (1993) 'Aboriginal Subjectivities and Western Conventions: A Reading of *Coonardoo*', *Australian and New Zealand Studies in Canada* 10, 23–29.

Loomba, Ania (1998) *Colonialism/Postcolonialism* (London: Routledge).

Lopez, Mark (2000) *The Origins of Multiculturalism in Australian Politics 1945–75* (Melbourne: Melbourne University Press).

Lucashenko, Melissa (2000) 'Black on Black', *Meanjin* 59, 3, 112–18.

Lyons, Martyn and John Arnold (eds.) (2001) *A History of the Book in Australia, 1891–1945: A National Culture in a Colonised Market* (St Lucia, QLD: University of Queensland Press).

McAuley, James (1964) *Captain Quiros* (Sydney: Angus and Robertson).

McCann, Andrew (ed.) (1998 [1964]) 'Writing the Everyday: Australian Literature and Suburbia': special issue of *Australian Literary Studies* 18, 4.

—— (1998) 'Introduction: Subtopia, or the Problem of Suburbia', *Australian Literary Studies* 18, 4, vii–x.

McCann, Andrew, Jeff Sparrow and Christen Cornell (2005) 'The Spectres Haunting *Dead Europe*', *Overland*, 181, 26–31.

MacCannell, Dean (1976) *The Tourist: A New Theory of the Leisure Class* (New York: Schocken).

McClintock, Anne (1993) *Imperial Leather: Race, Gender, and Sexuality in the Colonial Conquest* (New York: Routledge).

—— (1992) 'The Angel of Progress: Pitfalls of the Term "Post-Colonial"' *Social Text* 30/32 84–98.

MacCullum, Mungo (2002) 'Girt by Sea: Australia, the Refugees and the Politics of Fear', *Quarterly Essay* 5, 1–72.

McMaster, Don (2002) *Asylum Seekers: Australia's Response to Refugees* (Melbourne: Melbourne University Press).

Macherey, Pierre (1978) *A Theory of Literary Production*, trans. G. Wall (London: Routledge).

Macintyre, Stuart (1999) *A Concise History of Australia* (Cambridge: Cambridge University Press).

Macintyre, Stuart and Anna Clark (2003) *The History Wars* (Carlton, Vic.: Melbourne University Press).

Magarey, Susan, Sue Rowley, and Susan Sheridan (1993) *Debutante Nation: Feminism Contests the 1890s* (North Sydney: Allen and Unwin).

Maley, William (2002) 'Refugees and the Myth of a Borderless World' (Canberra: Department of International Relations, ANU).

Malik, Kenan (1996) *The Meaning of Race: Race, History and Culture in Western Society* (Basingstoke: Macmillan).

Malouf, David (2003) 'Made in England: Australia's British Inheritance', *Quarterly Essay* 12, 1–66.

—— (1993) *Remembering Babylon* (New York: Vintage).

Manne, Robert (2004) 'Sending Them Home: Refugees and the New Politics of Indifference', *Quarterly Essay* 13, 1–95.

Manson, Richard (2004) 'White Men Write Now: Deconstructed and Reconstructed Borders of Identity in Contemporary American Literature by White Men' (PhD thesis, University of Munich).

Mares, Peter (2001) *Borderline* (Sydney: University of New South Wales Press).

Markus, Andrew (2001) *Race: John Howard and the Remaking of Australia* (Sydney: Allen and Unwin).

Marsden, John (1995) *Tomorrow, When the War Began* (Sydney: Macmillan).

Martin, Susan K., 'National Dress or National Trousers?' in B. Bennett and J. Strauss (eds.) (1998) *The Oxford Literary History of Australia* (Melbourne: Oxford), 89–104.

May, Charles E. (ed.) (1976) *New Short Story Theories* (Columbus: Ohio University Press).

Mestrovic, Stjepan (1997) *Postemotional Society* (London: Sage).

Miller, D. A. (1988) *The Novel and the Police* (Berkeley: University of California Press).

Miller, J. Hillis (2002) *On Literature* (New York: Routledge).

Mishra, Vijay (1996) 'Postmodern Racism', *Meanjin* 55, 2, 347–57.

Moreton-Robinson, Aileen, 'Duggaibah, or "place of whiteness": Australian feminists and race', in J. Docker and G. Fischer (eds.) (2000) *Race, Colour and Identity in Australia and New Zealand* (Sydney: University of New South Wales Press), 240–55.

Morgan, Marlo (1994) *Mutant Message Down Under* (New York: Harper-Collins).

Morgan, Sally (1990 [1987]) *My Place* (New York: Arcade Publishing).

Morris, Meaghan, 'White Panic or Mad Max and the Sublime', in K. H. Chen (ed.) (1998) *Trajectories: Inter-Asia Cultural Studies* (London: Routledge).

Morse, Susan (1988) 'Impossible Dreams: Miscegenation and Building Nations' *Southerly* 48, 1, 80–96.

Morton, John, 'Aboriginality, Mabo and the Republic: Indigenising Australia', in B. Attwood (ed.) (1996) *In the Age of Mabo: History, Aborigines and Australia* (St. Leonards, NSW: Allen and Unwin), 117–35.

Mudie, Ian, 'Intruder', in B. Elliott (ed.) (1979) *The Jindyworobaks* (St Lucia, QLD: University of Queensland Press), 95.

Mudimbe, V. Y. (1988) *The Invention of Africa: Gnosis, Philosophy, and the Order of Knowledge* (Bloomington: Indiana University Press).

Mudrooroo (Colin Johnson) (1983) *Doctor Wooreddy's Prescription for Enduring the Ending of the World* (Melbourne: Hyland House).

—— (2002 [1990]) 'Introduction', in X. Herbert, *Capricornia* (Sydney: Angus and Robertson), vii–xiv.

—— (1997) *Milli Milli Wangka: The Indigenous Literature of Australia* (Melbourne: Hyland House).

—— (1990) *Writing from the Fringe: A Study of Modern Aboriginal Literature* (Melbourne: Hyland House).

Muecke, Stephen (1988) 'Aboriginal Literature and the Repressive Hypothesis', *Southerly* 48, 4, 405–18.

Murray, Les (1984) 'The Human Hair Thread', in *Persistence in Folly: Selected Prose Writings* (Melbourne: Sirius), 4–30.

―――― (1998) *Collected Poems* (Manchester: Carcanet).

―――― (1996) *Subhuman Redneck Poems* (Manchester: Carcanet).

Myers, David (1989) 'Oz Lit's Painful Pilgrimage Through Asia and the Pacific', *Social Alternatives* 8, 3, 27–31.

Nettelbeck, Amanda (1997) 'Presenting Aboriginal Women's Life Narratives', *New Literatures Review* 34, 43–56.

Neville, Arthur Octavius (1947) *Australia's Coloured Minority: Its Place in the Community* (Sydney: Currawong Pub. Co.).

New, W. H. (1987) *Dreams of Speech and Violence: The Art of the Short Story in Canada and New Zealand* (Toronto: University of Toronto Press).

Nile, Richard (2002) *The Making of the Australian Literary Imagination* (St Lucia, QLD: University of Queensland Press).

Nile, Richard (ed.) (2000) *The Australian Legend and its Discontents* (St Lucia, QLD: University of Queensland Press).

Nolan, Maggie (1998) 'The Absent Aborigine', *Antipodes* 12, 1, 7–13.

Nolan, Maggie and Carrie Dawson (eds.) (2004) 'Who's Who? Hoaxes, Imposture and Identity Crisis in Australian Literature', special issue of *Australian Literary Studies* 21, 4.

Nowra, Louis (1985) *Displaced Persons*, dir. G. Nottage (ABC TV, unpublished).

O'Connor, Frank (1962) *The Lonely Voice: A Study of the Short Story* (Cleveland, OH: World Publishing Company).

O'Regan, Tom (1996) *Australian National Cinema* (London: Routledge).

Papaellinas, George, 'Christos Mavromatis is a Welder', in R. F. Holt (ed.) (1991 [1984]) *Neighbours: Multicultural Writing of the 1980s* (St Lucia, QLD: University of Queensland Press), 3–7.

Parry, Benita (1987) 'Problems in Current Theories of Colonial Discourse', *Oxford Literary Review* 9, 1–2, 27–58.

―――― (1991) 'The Contradictions of Cultural Studies', *Transition* 53, 37–45.

Pavis, Patrice (ed.) (1996) *The Intercultural Performance Reader* (London: Routledge).

Perera, Suvendrini (1994) 'Unspeakable Bodies' *Meridian* 13, 1, 15–26.

Perkins, David (ed.) (1991) *Theoretical Issues in Literary History* (Cambridge, MA: Harvard University Press).

Perkins, Elizabeth, 'Literary Cultures 1851–1914: Founding a Canon', in B. Bennett and J. Strauss (eds.) (1998) *The Oxford Literary History of Australia* (Melbourne: Oxford University Press), 47–65.

Phillips, A. A. (1962) 'Australia Image: (2) The Literary Heritage Re-assessed', *Meanjin* 21, 2, 172–80.

Phillips, A. A. (1958) *The Australian Tradition: Studies in a Colonial Culture* (Melbourne: F.W. Cheshire).

Phipps, Peter, 'Tourists, Terrorists, Death and Value', in R. Kaur and J. Hutnyk (eds.) (1999) *Travel Worlds: Journeys in Contemporary Politics* (London: Zed Books), 74–93.

Pierce, Peter, 'Forms of Australian Literary History', in L. Hergenhan *et al.* (eds.) (1988) *The Penguin New Literary History of Australia* (Ringwood, Vic.: Penguin), 77–90.

—— (1992) 'Preying on the Past: Contexts of Some Recent Neo-Historical Fiction', *Australian Literary Studies* 15, 4, 304–12.

Praed, Rosa (1988 [1893]) *Outlaw and Lawmaker* (London: Pandora Press).

Prakash, Gyan (ed.) (1995) *After Colonialism: Imperial Histories and Post-colonial Displacements* (Princeton: Princeton University Press).

—— (1995) 'Orientalism Now', *History & Theory* 34, 199–212.

Pratt, Mary Louise (1992) *Imperial Eyes: Travel Writing and Transculturation* (New York: Routledge).

Prichard, Katharine Susannah (2002 [1929]) *Coonardoo* (Sydney: Angus and Robertson).

Puri, Shalini (2004) *The Caribbean Postcolonial: Social Equality, Post-Nationalism and Cultural Hybridity* (New York: Palgrave Macmillan).

Quayson, Ato (2000) *Postcolonialism: Theory, Practice or Process?* (Malden, Mass: Polity Press).

Reid, Ian (1977) *The Short Story* (London: Methuen).

Reynolds, Henry (1996) *Frontier: Aborigines, Settlers, and Land* (St Leonard's, NSW: Allen and Unwin).

Richmond, Anthony (2002) 'Globalization: Implications for Immigrants and Refugees', *Ethnic and Racial Studies* 25, 5, 707–27.

Robinson, Roland, 'Kimberley Drovers', in B. Elliott (ed.) (1979) *The Jindy-worobaks* (St Lucia, QLD: University of Queensland Press), 141.

Roediger, David R. (1994) *Toward the Abolition of Whiteness: Essays on Race, Politics, and Working-Class History* (London: Verso).

Rojek, Chris (1993) *Ways of Escape: Modern Transformations in Leisure and Travel* (Lanham, ML: Rowman and Littlefield).

Romeril, John (1975) *The Floating World* (Sydney, Currency Press).

Rosaldo, Renato (1989) *Culture and Truth: The Remaking of Social Analysis* (Boston: Beacon Books).

Rosello, Mireille (2001) *Postcolonial Hospitality: The Immigrant as Guest* (Palo Alto, CA: Stanford University Press).

Rouse, Roger (1991) 'Mexican Migration and the Social Space of Postmodernism' *Diaspora* 1, 1, 8–23.

Ruthven, Ken (2001) *Faking Literature* (Cambridge: Cambridge University Press).

Said, Edward W. (1975) *Beginnings: Intention and Method* (New York: Basic Books).

—— (1993) *Culture and Imperialism* (New York: Knopf).

—— (1978) *Orientalism* (New York: Vintage).

—— 'Orientalism Reconsidered', in Francis Barker, Peter Hulme and Margaret Iversen (eds.) (1986) *Literature, Politics and Theory* (London: Methuen), 210–29.

Schaffer, Kay (1995) *In the Wake of First Contact: The Eliza Fraser Stories* (Cambridge: Cambridge University Press).

—— (1988) *Women and the Bush: Forces of Desire in the Australian Cultural Tradition* (Cambridge: Cambridge University Press).

Schech, Susanne and Jane Haggis, 'Migrancy, Whiteness and the Settler Self in Contemporary Australia', in J. Docker and G. Fischer (eds.) (2000) *Race, Colour and Identity in Australia and New Zealand* (Sydney: University of New South Wales Press), 231–9.

Schechner, Richard (1985) *Between Theatre and Anthropology* (Philadelphia: University of Pennsylvania Press).

Schulze-Engler, Frank, 'Literature in the Global Ecumene of Modernity in Amitav Ghosh's *The Circle of Reason* and *In an Antique Land*', in H. Antor and K. Stierstorfer (eds.) (2000) *English Literatures in International Contexts* (Heidelberg: C. Winter Verlag), 373–96.

Scott, Kim (1999) *Benang: From the Heart* (Fremantle, WA: Fremantle Arts Centre Press).

Seltzer, Mark (1998) *Serial Killers: Death and Life in America's Wound Culture* (New York: Routledge).

Sheridan, Susan (1995) *Along the Faultlines: Sex, Race and Nation in Australian Women's Writing, 1880s–1930s* (St Leonards, NSW: Allen and Unwin).

Shohat, Ella (1992) 'Notes on the "Post-Colonial"' *Social Text* 31/32, 99–113.

Shoemaker, Adam, 'White on Black/Black on Black', in B. Bennett and J. Strauss (eds.) (1998) *The Oxford Literary History of Australia* (Melbourne: Oxford University Press), 9–20.

Skrzynecki, Peter (ed.) (1985) *Joseph's Coat: An Anthology of Multicultural Writing* (Sydney: Hale and Iremonger).

Slattery, Luke, 'Our Multicultural Cringe', in J. Joost, G. Totaro and C. Tyshing (eds.) (1996) *The Demidenko File* (Ringwood, Vic.: Penguin), 273–5.

Slemon, Stephen, 'The Scramble for Post-Colonialism', in C. Tiffin and A. Lawson (eds.) (1994) *De-scribing Empire: Post-Colonialism and Textuality* (London: Routledge), 15–32.

—— (1991) 'Unsettling the Empire: Resistance Theory for the Second World', *World Literature Written in English* 30, 2, 30–41.

Slessor, Kenneth, 'Five Visions of Captain Cook', in D. Haskell and G. Dutton (eds.) (1994) *Kenneth Slessor: Collected Poems* (Sydney: Angus and Robertson), 87–93.

Smith, Barbara Herrnstein, 'Contingencies of Value', in R. von Hallberg (ed.) (1980) *Canons* (Chicago: University of Chicago Press), 5–40.

Sollors, Werner (1997) *Neither White Nor Black Yet Both: Thematic Explorations of Interracial Literatures* (New York: Oxford University Press).

Sommer, Doris (1991) *Foundational Fictions: The National Romances of Latin America* (Berkeley: University of California Press).

Spence, Catherine Helen (1971 [1854]) *Clara Morison* (London: Rigby).

Spivak, Gayatri Chakrovorty (1999) *A Critique of Post-Colonial Reason: Toward a History of the Vanishing Present* (Cambridge, MA: Harvard University Press).

—— (1987) *In Other Worlds: Essays in Cultural Politics* (New York: Methuen).

—— (1993) *Outside in the Teaching Machine* (New York: Routledge).

Stasiulis, Daiva and Nira Yuval-Davis (eds.) (1995) *Unsettling Settler Societies: Articulations of Gender, Race, Ethnicity, and Class* (London: Sage).

Stead, Christina (1966 [1941]) *The Man Who Loved Children* (London, Secker and Warburg).

Stratton, Jon, 'Multiculturalism and the Whitening Machine, or How Australians Become White', in G. Hage and R. Crouch (eds.) (1999) *The Future of Australian Multiculturalism: Reflections on the Twentieth Anniversary of Jean Martin's The Migrant Presence* (Sydney: Research Institute for Humanities and Social Sciences, University of Sydney), 163–88.

—— (1988) *Race Daze: Australia in Identity Crisis* (Sydney: Pluto Press).

Taylor, Andrew (1987) *Reading Australian Poetry* (St Lucia, QLD: University of Queensland Press).

Tench, Watkin (2004 [1789]) *A Narrative of the Expedition to Botany Bay* (Ivanhoe, Vic: Edition Renard).

Thieme, John (ed.) (1996) *The Arnold Anthology of Post-Colonial Literatures in English* (London: Arnold).

Thomas, Nicholas, 'Collectivity and nationality in the anthropology of art', in Marcus Banks and Howard Morphet (eds.) (1997) *Re-thinking Visual Anthropology* (New Haven: Yale University Press), 256–75.

Tiffin, Chris and Alan Lawson (eds.) (1994) *De-scribing Empire: Post-colonialism and Textuality* (London: Routledge).

Tiffin, Helen (1984) 'Asia and the Contemporary Australian Novel', *Australian Literary Studies* 11, 4, 468–79.

Todorov, Tzvetan (1993) *On Human Diversity: Nationalism, Racism, and Exoticism in French Thought* (Cambridge, MA: Harvard University Press).

_____ ' "Race", Writing and Culture', in H. L. Gates (ed.) (1986) *'Race', Writing, and Difference* (Chicago: University of Chicago Press), 370–80.

Torgovnick, Marianna (1990) *Gone Primitive: Savage Intellects, Modern Lives* (Chicago: University of Chicago Press).

Trivedi, Harish (1999) 'The Postcolonial or the Transcolonial? Location and Language', *Interventions* 1, 2, 269–72.

Tsiolkas, Christos (2005) *Dead Europe* (New York: Random House).

Tucker, James (1953 [1845]) *Ralph Rashleigh* (Sydney: Angus and Robertson).

Turner, Graeme (1994) *Making it National: Nationalism and Popular Culture* (St Leonards, NSW: Allen and Unwin), 1–20.

_____ (1991) *National Fictions: Literature, Film, and the Construction of Australian Narrative* (St Leonards, NSW: Allen and Unwin).

Tyler, Heather (2003) *Asylum: Voices Behind the Razor Wire* (South Melbourne: Lothian Books).

Unaipon, David (1929) *Native Legends* (Adelaide: Hunkin, Ellis and King).

van Toorn, Penny (1996) 'Early Aboriginal Writing', *Meanjin* 55, 4, 754–65.

_____ 'Indigenous Australian Life Writing: Tactics and Transformations', in B. Attwood and F. Magowan (eds.) (2001) *Telling Stories: Indigenous History and Memory in Australia and New Zealand* (Sydney: Allen and Unwin), 1–20.

Vasta, Ellie and Stephen Castles (eds.) (1996) *The Teeth Are Smiling: The Persistence of Racism in Multicultural Australia* (St Leonards, NSW: Allen and Unwin).

Walker, David (1999) *Anxious Nation: Australia and the Rise of Asia 1830–1939* (St Lucia, QLD: University of Queensland Press).

_____ 'Australia as Asia', in W. Hudson and G. Bolton (eds.) (1997) *Creating Australia: Changing Australian History* (St Leonards, Vic.: Allen and Unwin), 131–41.

Walwicz, Ania, 'Australia', in R.F. Holt (ed.) (1991 [1981]) *Neighbours; Multicultural Writing of the 1980s* (St Lucia, QLD: University of Queensland Press), 30–1.

Ward, Russel (1958) *The Australian Legend* (Melbourne: Oxford University Press).

Ware, Vron and Les Back (2002) *Out of Whiteness: Color, Politics, and Culture* (Chicago: University of Chicago Press).

Waring, Wendy (1995) 'Is This Your Book? Wrapping Postcolonial Fiction for the Global Market' *Canadian Review of Comparative Literature* 22, 3/4, 455–65.

Wark, McKenzie (1992) 'After Literature: Culture, Policy, Theory and Beyond' *Meanjin* 51, 4, 677–90.

_____ (1999) *Celebrities, Culture and Cyberspace* (Sydney: Pluto Press).

Webb, Francis (1969) 'Eyre All Alone', in *Collected Poems* (Sydney: Angus and Robertson), 181–92.

Webby, Elizabeth (ed.) (2000) *Cambridge Companion to Australian Literature* (Cambridge: Cambridge University Press).

Webby, Elizabeth (ed.) (1989) *Colonial Voices: Letters, Diaries, Journalism and Other Accounts of Nineteenth-Century Australia* (St Lucia, QLD: University of Queensland Press).

Welsch, Wolfgang, 'Transculturality: The Puzzling Form of Cultures Today', in M. Featherstone and S. Lash (eds.) (1999) *Spaces of Culture: City-Nation-World* (London: Sage), 194–213.

West, Cornel (1994) *Race Matters* (New York: Vintage).

White, Hayden, 'Fictions of Factual Representation', in A. Fletcher (ed.) (1976) *The Literature of Fact* (New York: Columbia University Press), 21–44.

White, Patrick, 'The Prodigal Son', in A. Lawson (ed.) (1994) *Patrick White: Selected Writings* (St. Lucia, QLD: University of Queensland Press), 268–71.

—— (1958 [1957]) *Voss* (London: Eyre and Spottiswoode).

Whitlock, Gillian (1999) 'Australian Literature: Points for Departure' *Australian Literary Studies* 19, 2, 152–62.

—— (2000) *The Intimate Empire: Reading Women's Autobiography* (London: Cassell).

Whitlock, Gillian and David Carter (1992) *Images of Australia: An Introductory Reader in Australian Studies* (St Lucia, QLD: University of Queensland Press).

Wilding, Michael (1975) 'A New Colonialism?' *Southerly* 35, 95–102.

Williamson, David (1995) *Dead White Males* (Sydney: Currency Press).

Willmot, Eric (1991) *Below the Line* (Sydney, NSW: Hutchinson).

Wilson, Rob and Wimal Dissanayake (eds.) (1996) *Global/Local: Cultural Production and the Transnational Imaginary* (Durham, NC: Duke University Press).

Windschuttle, Keith (2002) *The Fabrication of Aboriginal History* (Sydney: Macleay).

Winegarten, Renee (1994) 'The Nobel Prize for Literature', *American Scholar*, Winter 63–75.

Wolfe, Patrick (1991) 'History and Imperialism: A Century of Theory, From Marx to Postcolonialism' *American Historical Review* 102, 2, 388–420.

—— (1994) 'Land, Labor, and Difference: Elementary Structures of Race', *American Historical Review* 106, 3, 866–905.

Wood, Ellen Meiksins (1986) *The Retreat from Class: A New 'True' Socialism* (New York: Verso).

Yarwood, A. T. and M. J. Knowling (1982) *Race Relations in Australia: A History* (North Ryde, NSW: Methuen Australia).

Young, Robert J. C. (1995) *Colonial Desire: Hybridity in Theory, Culture and Race* (London: Routledge).

_____ (2003) *Postcolonialism: A Very Short Introduction* (Oxford: Oxford University Press).

_____ (1990) *White Mythologies: Writing History and the West* (London: Routledge).

INDEX

Abood, Paula 118, 120–1
Aboriginality 96, 103, 106–7
Aborigines xiii, 45, 91–2, 96–8, 103, 106
  identification with 66–9
  literature xii, xiii, 30, 46, 47, 102
    portrayed in 81, 87, 92, 95, 99, 105
  otherness 25
  postcolonialism 27
  racism 19–21, 73–4, 91
  stereotypes 25, 26
  white settlers 18
  writing 7, 70, 115
adventure romance 26, 33
advocacy literature 130
Along the Faultlines (Sheridan) 27, 32
Althusser, Louis 26
Ang, Ien 73, 110, 131, 132
Anglo-Celticism 76, 78, 110–11, 114, 115
Anthias, Floya 14
anthologies:
  multiculturalism 116–19
    integrationist 118;
      interventionist 118, 120, 121
anti-colonial literature 5, 34, 88
  see also colonialism, literature
Appadurai, Arjun 10, 40, 123, 141, 142, 143
Arnold, John 7, 8
Arthur, Kataryna Olijnk 30
artistic license 108–9
Ashbolt, Allan 140
Ashcroft, Bill 28–9, 30
Asians 19, 112, 131, 138, 142
  immigration 133
  as racial stereotypes 25–6, 132

Asylum: Voices Behind the Razor Wire (Tyler) 129
asylum seekers vii, 128–30
Attwood, Bain 97–8, 152n
'Australia' (Walwicz) 119
Australia-Asia relations 131–2, 136
Australian Legend 55–7, 59–61, 77, 83
  feminist revisions 58
Australianness viii, 2, 7, 8, 11, 37, 42, 150

Back, Les 14, 15, 71, 72, 73, 75–6, 77
Balibar, Étienne 14, 16
ballads 1, 51
Balme, Christopher 122, 124, 125–6
Barnard, Marjorie 60
Barthes, Roland 134, 135
Bassnett, Susan 136
bastard complex 91–3
Bauman, Zygmunt 15
Baynton, Barbara 58
Beginnings: Intention and Method (Said) 45
Below the Line (Willmot) 129
Benang (Scott) xiii, 98, 99–101, 102
Bennett, Bruce 37
Bennett, David 113, 114
Bercovitch, Sacvan 36
Beresford, Quentin 96, 97
Beston, John 47
Beyond the Echo: Multicultural Women's Writing (Gunew and Mahyuddin) 118, 119, 120–1
Beyond the Subdivisions (Dawe) 79
Bhabha, Homi 24, 25, 33, 35, 39, 46, 136, 149, 156n
Bharucha, Rustom 122, 123, 124, 126

Birch, Tony 99, 101
Bird, Delys 48, 49, 50–1
Birds of Passage (Castro) 133–6
Birns, Nicholas 3
'Black Mary' (Ingamells) 106
Blainey, Geoffrey 75
Blake, Ann 85
Bliss, Carolyn 84
Boldrewood, Rolf 51, 61
Bourdieu, Pierre 117
Brah, Avtar 90, 96
Breckenridge, Carol A. 156n
Brennan, Christopher 153n
Brennan, Timothy 54, 109, 117, 150, 156n
Brewster, Anne 27, 98
'Brief History, A' (Murray) 81
Bringing Them Home – The Report (Human Rights and Equal Opportunities Commission) 97
Broinowski, Alison 25–6, 131, 132, 138, 142
Brown, Ruth 4, 42, 43, 44
Brydon, Diana 86, 133
Buckridge, Patrick 41, 46
Bulmer, Martin 14
Burke, Peter 62
bush:
    poets 1
    writers, female 58
Bush Studies (Baynton) 58
'Bush Undertaker, The' (Lawson) 57–8
Butler, Judith 105

Callahan, David 7, 43, 44
Capricornia (Herbert) xiii, 92, 93–4, 96, 99
'Captain Quiros' (McAuley) 89
Carey, Peter 2, 62–4, 65, 89, 109
Carroll, Dennis 82
Carter, David x, xii, 9, 13, 40, 41, 42, 145, 147, 148, 150
Carter, Paul 31, 49, 50, 69, 70
Castles, Stephen 16, 22, 81, 110, 112, 113
Castro, Brian 133, 134–6
Chakrabarty, Dipesh 156n

Change of Skies, A (Gooneratne) 140–1, 142
Chapman, Malcolm 16
Cheah, Pheng xii, 141, 148, 150, 156n
Chinese 19, 133
    Australian-born 135, 136–7
'Christos Mavromatis is a Welder' (Papaellinas) 119
Clara Morison (Spence) 52
Clarke, Marcus xiii, 51–4, 61
Coetzee, J. M. 88
colonialism 32, 127, 144
    literature x, 5, 6–7, 34, 46, 47–8, 84–5, 86, 149
    racism 19, 28, 49, 112, 141
    stereotypes 24–5, 33
    writing 51, 60
Comert, Nushet Yilmaz 121
convict novels 52–3
'Contrarieties' (Dawe) 79
Coombes, Annie E. 90, 96
Coonardoo (Prichard) xiii, 92, 93, 94–5, 96
Cope, W. 110, 112
cosmopolitanism xii, 112, 120, 127, 148, 150, 156
critical race theory 145, 150–1
Crock, Mary 128
Culler, Jonathan 8
cultural identity ix, xiv, 24, 103, 104, 105, 144
cultural studies 3, 36, 39–40, 147, 150, 151
culture wars xii, 17–18
    Australian 18, 21, 43
    Shakespeare 82
cultures xiii, 7, 12, 123
    Australian 30, 116
    core 76–8
    diversity 142, 143
    history 36–7
    race onto 16–17
    uniformity 34
Curthoys, Ann x, 19, 34, 56

diary/journal writings 48
Dale, Leigh 5, 41, 46, 146, 153n
Daniel, Helen 103

Darian-Smith, Kate 65
*Dark Side of the Dream: Australian
    Literature and the Postcolonial
    Mind* (Hodge and Mishra) 30,
    31–2
Darville, Helen 108–9
    see also Demidenko, Helen
Davis, Jack 124, 125
Davis, Mark 42–3
Dawe, Bruce 79–80
Dawson, Carrie 103, 110, 155n
Dead Europe (Tsiolkas) vii
Dead White Males
    (Williamson) 82–3
Deleuze, Gilles 91
Demidenko, Helen 103, 108–9, 143
Derrida, Jacques 127
discourse 23–4, 25, 34, 37
    Aboriginalist 49–50
displaced persons 140–1
Displaced Persons (Nowra) 129
Dixon, Robert vi, xi, 26, 32–4, 53, 54,
    145, 146, 147, 148, 154n
Dixson, Miriam x, 10, 40, 44–5, 76,
    77–8
Docker, John 11, 41, 88, 152n, 153n
*Doctor Wooreddy's Prescription for
    Enduring the Ending of the
    World* (Mudrooroo) 68–70
D'Souza, Dinesh 17
During, Simon 10, 85, 86, 87–8, 123,
    147
Dyer, Richard 71, 72, 73, 77, 78, 84, 89

Eco, Umberto 103
egalitarianism v–vi, 55
Eliades, Patricia 117
Eliot, T. S. 85
Elliott, Brian 52, 54, 106, 107
Empire of Signs (Barthes) 134
*Empire Writes Back: Theory and
    Practice in Post-Colonial
    Literatures, The* (1989)
    (Ashcroft, Griffiths, and
    Tiffin) 28
Enlightenment 16, 18, 49
English:
    cultural tastes 6–7

dominance 115
    literature xii, 3, 6
    as world language 6
equal-rights doctrine 20
Essed, Philomena 113
ethnicity v, 16, 72, 74, 77, 100, 103,
    109, 114
    literature 115, 117, 133
Eurocentrism 122, 126
Europe:
    legacy 30, 88
    migration from 73–4
    modernist sensibility 85
    primitivism 81
exploration:
    literature 89
    narratives 48, 50
'Eyre All Alone' (Webb) 89

Fabi, M. Giulia 94, 102, 103
Faiman, Peter 7
Featherstone, Mike 10, 35, 38
fiction 61
    Australian 88
    experimental 85
film 6, 145
Fish, Stanley 120
Fitzpatrick, Peter 83
'Five Visions of Captain Cook'
    (Slessor) 89
Flannery, Tim 34, 49, 103
Floating World, The (Romeril) 136,
    139
Foley, Malcolm 130
For the Term of His Natural Life
    (Clarke) 51–2, 53–4, 61
'Forgotten People' (Ingamells) 106
Fortunes of Richard Mahony, The
    (Richardson) 61
Foster, David 134
Foucault, Michel 23, 33
Framing Marginality (Gunew) 114
Frankenberg, Ruth 71
Franklin, Miles xiii, 58–60
Fredrickson, George M. 14, 15, 16
Frow, John 36, 39, 97, 98
Frye, Northrop 104
Furphy, Joseph 55

Gale, Peter 71
Gamba, Barry 118, 120–1
Gates, Henry Louis 22–3
Gelder, Ken viii, xi, 20–1, 25, 48, 55, 95, 102, 104
Geoffry Hamlyn (Kingsley) 52
Gerster, Robin 79
Gibson, Ross 36
Giddens, Anthony 24
Gilbert, Helen 123, 125
Gilroy, Paul 14, 15, 18, 21
Ginsberg, Elaine K. 102, 103
globalization xii, 10, 11, 13–14, 22, 61, 113–14, 116, 123, 147, 148, 151
gloom thesis 11
going native 103–4
Goldberg, David Theo 14
Goldie, Terry viii, 25, 26, 81, 95, 103, 104
Gone Indian (Kroetsch) 104
Goodwin, Ken 3
Gooneratne, Yasmine 140–1, 142–3
Gordon, Adam Lindsay xiii, 51, 54, 59
Goss, Jasper 32
Gothard, Jan 73
Graff, Gerald 17
Gramsci, Antonio 154n
Grenville, Kate 65–8
Griffiths, Gareth 28–9, 30
Guattari, Félix 91
Guillory, John 42, 117
Gunew, Sneja 36, 37, 109, 114, 116, 118, 119, 120, 121–2, 123–4

Hage, Ghassan xiii, 21, 72, 73, 76, 77, 78, 91, 96, 110, 111, 112, 113, 115, 116, 131, 144, 148, 149, 153n, 154n
Haggis, Jane 75
half-castes 96, 99
Hall, Rodney 134
Hall, Ron 15
Hall, Stuart 144, 151
Hamilton, Paula 65
Hand that Signed the Paper, The (Demidenko/Darville) 108
Hannerz, Ulf 10, 123, 141
Hanson, Pauline 21
Harpur, Charles 51, 54

Harris, Max 82
Harrison, Wayne 82
Hart-Smith, William 106
Hartz, Louis 154n
Hassall, Anthony 146
Haywood, Ian 103
Healy, Chris 46, 61, 65, 97, 103
Herbert, Xavier xiii, 92, 93–4, 95, 96
Hergenhan, Laurie 37, 40, 52
heroic inadequacy 31, 32
Herrnstein Smith, Barbara 42
Heseltine, Harry 1, 152n
Hesse, Barnor 144
Hill, Mike 71, 72
historical novels 45, 61, 72
see also novels
historiography 45, 61, 67
Hodge, Bob viii, 27, 30, 31, 32, 33, 37, 49, 53, 57, 91, 92, 104, 106
Holocaust 108
Holt, R. F. 118, 119, 120
'Homo Suburbiensis' (Dawe) 79
hooks, bell 15
Hope, A. D. 85, 105–6
Howard, John 21
Hudson, W. Flexmore 106
Huggan, Graham xii, xiv, 30, 62, 109, 116, 117, 136, 142, 146
Hughes, Mary Ann 47
Human Rights and Equal Opportunities Commission 97
Hurcombe, Roger 134
Hutcheon, Linda xiv, 30, 61
hybridity 90–2, 95–6, 105, 125, 135, 141

identity, *see* cultural identity
ideologies 26, 36, 40, 61, 77, 92, 131
Ignatiev, Noel 71, 72
Images of Australia (Whitlock and Carter) 40
immigration 111, 112, 113, 116. 127, 129
Immigration Restriction Act 1901 19, 73
imperialism 26, 33, 34, 72, 86, 144, 149
Indo-European world 137–8
Indonesia 137
Ingamells, Rex 106
indigenous peoples 25, 27, 126

indigenous literature viii–ix, xiii,
46, 59
interculturalism xiv, 122–4, 126, 143,
144
internationalization 13–14, 148
Internet 3–4
Intimate Empire, The (Whitlock) 33
'Intruder' (Mudie) 106
Ireland, David 79
Irwin, Steve 7

Jacobs, Jane viii, xi, 20–1, 25, 48, 55,
95, 102, 104
Jacoby, Russell 27
Jameson, Fredric 84
JanMohamed, Abdul 24
Japan 134
Jayasuriya, Laksir 73
Jillett, Neil 83
Jindyworobak movement 105–6
Joan Makes History (Grenville) 65–8
*Joseph's Coat: An Anthology of
Multicultural Writing*
(Skrzynecki) 118
Jupp, James 110, 111–13, 115, 155n
Just Relations (Hall) 134

Kalantzis, M. 110, 112
Kane, John 73
Kane, Paul 54–5, 84, 152n
Kendall, Henry 51, 54, 59
Kiernan, Brian Francis 56
'Kimberley Drovers' (Robinson) 106
Kincheloe, Joe 71
Kingsley, Henry 51, 52
Kirkby, Joan 79
Knowling, M. J. 19, 20
Koch, C. J. 12–13, 132, 136–8
Kotevski, Michelle 118, 120–1
Koundoura, Maria 114
Kramer, Leonie 8, 9, 13, 37
Kroetsch, Robert 104
Kuch, Peter 79, 80
Kurtzer, Sonia 47

Langer, Beryl 116
Larbalestier, Jan 76
Lawler, Ray 83

Lawson, Alan 29
Lawson, Henry xiii, 11, 54, 55–60
Lee, Christopher 56
Lee, Dennis 29
Lemire, Elise 90
Lennon, John 130
Lever, Susan 92
literary criticism xi, 9, 22, 145–6
literary histories xii–xiii, 35–7,
39–40, 44–6, 103, 109
canon xii, 40–4
and geography 38
literary modernity 77–8, 84–5
literary scandals 109
literary studies ix, 3–4, 8, 13, 28, 145,
150
postcolonial 28
racial differences 22–3
literature 46
chronology xviii–xxi
of encounter 48–50
imaginary xi
production of 43–4
see also Aborigines, literature;
colonialism, literature;
indigenous literature;
multiculturalism, literature;
postcolonialism, literature;
settler literature;
transnationalism, literature
Loomba, Ania 24
Lopez, Mark 110
'Lost Hemisphere, The' (Koch) 12,
137
Lucashenko, Melissa 27
Lyons, Martyn 7

McAuley, James 79, 85, 89
McCann, Andrew vii, 79
MacCannell, Dean 139
McClintock, Anne 73, 126
MacCullum, Mungo 127
Macherey, Pierre 26
Macintyre, Stuart 44, 61, 73, 152n,
153n
McMaster, Don 126, 127–8
Magarey, Susan 58
Mahyuddin, Jan 118, 119, 120, 121

Making of the Australian Literary Imagination, The (Nile) 6
Maley, William 127
Malik, Kenan 14, 15, 16, 17, 18, 22
Malley, Ern 103, 109
Malouf, David 76, 104, 105
'Man from Snowy River, The' (Paterson) 1
Man Who Loved Children, The (Stead) 85, 86–7
Manne, Robert 127
Manson, Richard 103, 104
Mares, Peter 128, 155n
Markus, Andrew xii, 19, 20, 21, 22, 78, 110, 115, 153n
Marsden, John 129
Martin, Susan K. 55, 56
May, Charles E. 57
Meaning of Race: Race, History and Culture in Western Society, The (Malik) 14
media-literacy 3, 4, 43
Mestrovic, Stjepan 130
migration 126, 135
    writing 114–15, 117, 136
Miller, D. A. 39
Miller, J. Hillis 4
miscegenation, *see* hybridity
Mishra, Vijay viii, 27, 30, 31, 32, 33, 37, 49, 53, 57, 91, 92, 104, 106, 109
mock-demotic yarns 1, 2
Modernity and the Holocaust (1989) (Bauman) 15
Moonlite (Foster) 134
Moreton-Robinson, Aileen 75, 103
Morgan, Marlo 107
Morgan, Sally xiii, 98, 99, 100, 101
Morris, Meaghan xi, 131
Morrissey, M. 110, 112
Morse, Ruth 92
Mudie, Ian 106
Mudimbe, V. Y. 24
Mudrooroo (Colin Johnson) 47, 68–70, 92, 94, 103
Muecke, Stephen 47
multiculturalism v–vi, xiii–xiv, 20, 39, 44, 75, 82, 96, 107, 108, 109–12, 115, 120, 122, 126, 128, 143–4

literature xiv, 114, 116, 117, 118, 119, 120–1, 131, 143
    and nationalism 111, 113, 121
Murray, Les 80, 81, 82, 105
Mutant Message Down Under (M. Morgan) 107
My Brilliant Career (Franklin) 58, 59, 60
My Place (S. Morgan) xiii, 98, 99–101, 102
Myers, David 132

Narrative of the Expedition to Botany Bay, A (Tench) 49
nation 22, 77
    identity 2, 9, 10, 15, 39
national culture 10, 35, 38, 41, 42
national imaginary 40
national literatures 8, 10, 11, 13, 37–8
    Australia xii, 4–6, 13–14, 28
national narratives 36, 39–40
national unity 111, 119
nationalism 5, 8, 10, 21, 29–30, 31–2, 36, 46, 57, 81, 94, 113, 144, 127, 150
    cultural 78, 145
    radical 55
Native Legends (Unaipon) 47
Neighbours: Multicultural Writing of the 1980s (Holt) 118
neo-colonialism 27, 32
neo-historical fiction xiii, 61, 62, 69
neo-liberalism 10, 148
Nettelbeck, Amanda 98
Neville, A. O. 97, 99
New, W. H. 57
New Age 107
New Penguin Literary History of Australia (Hergenhan) 37–8, 39, 40
new racism 16, 17, 18, 20
    see also racism
Nile, Richard xi, xii, 6, 7, 42, 44, 55, 56
No Sugar (Davis) 124
Nolan, Maggie 103, 110, 119, 155n
novels vii, 59, 65, 67–70, 85, 88–9, 92, 94–6, 101, 104–5, 108, 133, 134–6, 140

convict 52, 53
journalist 138–9
see also historical novels
Nowra, Louis 129
'Nullarbor' (Hart-Smith) 106

O'Connor, Frank 57, 153n
Omaji, Paul 96, 97
O'Regan, Tom 6
Oscar and Lucinda (Carey) 89
other/otherness xiii, 24, 49, 106, 112, 120–1, 131
Outlaw and Lawmaker (Praed) 61
Oxford History of Australian Literature (Kramer) 37, 39

Papaellinas, George 119
Parry, Benita 148
Paterson, A. B. ('Banjo') 1, 2, 54, 55, 59
Pavis, Patrice 123
Perera, Suvendrini 105
performing arts 122
Perkins, David 36, 39, 48
Phillips, A. A. 154n
Phipps, Peter 130
Pierce, Peter xiii, 35, 37, 43, 61, 153
plays 124–5, 129, 139–40
playwrights 81–3, 136
Aboriginal 124
pluralism 36, 39, 73, 77
poetry 54, 79–81, 85, 88, 89, 105–6, 120, 121
romantic 54–5
political correctness 81–2
Politics of Cultural Practice: Thinking Through Theatre in an Age of Globalization, The (Bharucha) 122
Pollock, Sheldon 156n
positive discrimination 120
postcolonialism xiv, 123, 126, 148
Australia vi, viii, 34, 91, 96, 102
criticism x–xi, xii, 26, 32–4
literature ix, x, 27–8, 84–5, 87, 145–147, 149–50
literary histories 39, 46
literary studies 146–7, 151

racism 20–1
theory 32
ties with Britain 27
postmodernism 61, 89, 130
Praed, Rosa 51, 61
Prakash, Gyan 156n
Pratt, Mary Louise 142
Prichard, Katharine Susannah xiii, 60, 92, 93, 95, 96
Prosthetic Gods (Dixon) 33
Puri, Shalini 96

Quayson, Ato vi

race vi, viii, 14–16, 21, 23–5, 72, 74–5, 91
in Australian literature 22–3, 89, 146
'Race', Writing, and Difference (Gates) 22
racial stereotypes 24, 26
racism vi, xi, 14–16, 18, 20, 31, 49, 58, 75, 78, 81, 90, 91, 113, 122, 151
cultural xii, 21
European attitudes 19
radicalism 30–1
Ralph Rashleigh (Tucker) 52
reading 3–4, 43
realist fiction 88
reconciliation narratives 101–2, 105
Refugee (Hawthorne) 129
refugees vii, 126–8, 130, 139
life-narratives 129
literature 130–1
Reid, Ian 57
Remembering Babylon (Malouf) 104
resettlements 111–12
resistance literature 30
revisionism 34, 39, 44, 45, 60, 67, 69, 117, 134, 150
Reynolds, Henry 44
Richardson, Henry Handel 11, 60, 61, 85
Richmond, Anthony 126
Robbery Under Arms (Boldrewood) 61
Robbins, Bruce xii, 141, 148, 150, 156n
Robinson, Roland 106

Roediger, David R. 71, 77
Rojek, Chris 130
romances 60, 61
Romeril, John 136, 139–40
Rosaldo, Renato 26, 106
Rosello, Mireille 127
Rouse, Roger 38–9
Rowley, Sue 58
Ruthven, Ken 110

Said, Edward 33, 45, 49, 84, 136, 149, 155n
'Saltbush Bill' (Paterson) 1
Schaffer, Kay 58, 103
Schech, Susanne 75
Schechner, Richard 122–3
Schulze-Engler, Frank 141, 142
Scott, Kim xiii, 98, 99, 100–1
self-racialization 15
   see also race; racism
Seltzer, Mark 130
settler colonialism vi, 149–50
settler literature viii, 3, 29–30, 32, 103, 151
sexism 23–4, 81, 93
Sheridan, Susan vi, 23, 27, 32, 34, 41, 54, 58, 92
Shoemaker, Adam 45–6, 47
'Sick Stockrider, The' (Gordon) 54
Skrzynecki, Peter 118, 119, 120
Slattery, Luke 108
Slemon, Stephen 29, 30, 147
Slessor, Kenneth 79, 89
Sollors, Werner 90, 94
Solomos, John 14, 15
Sommer, Doris 46
'Song of an Australian' (Hudson) 106
Spence, Catherine Helen 52
Spivak, Gayatri 24, 25, 34, 96, 115, 148, 156n
Stasiulis, Daiva K. xi
Stead, Christina 85, 86, 87
Stephens, A. G. 56–7, 60
Stewart, Douglas 89
Stolen Generations 97, 98, 99, 100, 101, 102, 119
storytelling 1
Stow, Randolph 85

Stratton, Jon 20, 72, 74, 75, 77, 110, 112
Strauss, Jennifer 37, 113
suburbanism 79, 80, 119
Summer of the Seventeenth Doll (Lawler) 83
supremacism 72, 87
   white 89–90, 112
syncretic theatre 124

Tales from a Suitcase (Davies and Dal Bosco) 129
Taylor, Andrew 54, 80, 81
television 145
Tench, Watkin 49, 50
theatrical exoticism 124
Third World 127
'This Land' (Mudie) 106
Tiffin, Helen 28–9, 30, 132, 133, 138, 142
Todorov, Tzvetan 16, 22, 24
Tomorrow, When the War Began (Marsden) 129
Tompkins, Joanne 123, 124
Torgovnik, Marianna 81
transculturalism xiv, 116, 124, 141, 143, 144, 147
transnationalism vi, viii, xiv, 10, 33, 38, 42, 85, 97, 101, 113, 121, 122, 142, 145
   literature 2, 28, 148
Trivedi, Harish 136
True History of The Kelly Gang (Carey) 2, 62–5
Tsiolkas, Christos vii
Tucker, James 52
Turner, Graeme 9, 10, 13, 29, 36, 38, 96, 111, 153n
Tyler, Heather 129–30

Unaipon, David 47
Uncanny Australia (Gelder and Jacobs) 102
USA:
   culture 17–18
   racism v

van Toorn, Penny 47, 98

Vasta, Ellie 81, 112, 113
'Veil, The' (Comert) 121
Voss (White) 85, 86

*Waiting in Space: An Anthology of
    Australian Writing* (Abood,
    Gamba, and Kotevski) 118,
    120–1
Walker, David 73, 101, 131
Walwicz, Ania 119
Ward, Russel 55
Ware, Vron 71, 72, 73, 77
Waring, Wendy 101
Wark, McKenzie 3, 4, 42–3
Webb, Francis 89
Webby, Elizabeth xviii, 48, 49, 50,
    51
Welsch, Wolfgang 141
West, Cornel v
white/Aboriginal co-authorship 47
White Australia x, 26, 30, 73, 77, 92,
    96, 102, 106–7, 112, 113, 128, 131,
    135, 148
  exclusion of Aborigines 32
  policy 19, 73–4, 75, 76
White, Patrick 11, 48, 79, 85, 86,
    87–8, 89, 153n
whiteness xi, xiii, 70, 73, 74, 75–8,
    80, 96, 103–7, 126
  power 71–2, 93–5, 102

history 84–90, 91, 100–1, 105
Whitlock, Gillian vi, x, 33–4, 40, 145,
    146
Wilding, Michael 52
Williamson, David 81–3
Willmot, Eric 129
'Windmill in The West, A' (1980)
    (Carey) 2
Windschuttle, Keith 44
Winegarten, R. 117
Winton, Tim ix
Wolfe, Patrick 91, 149
women's writing 41
  migrants 117
Wongar, B. 103, 119
Wood, Ellen Meiksins 10
workshop theatre 129
World Wars 84
'Worsley Enchanted' (Stewart) 89
Wright, Judith 85
Writing the Colonial Adventure
    (Dixon) 26, 32–3

yarns 51
Yarwood, A. T. 19, 20
Year of Living Dangerously, The
    (Koch) 136, 138
Young, Robert xiii, 85, 90, 96,
    149–50
Yuval-Davis, Nira xi, 14